# Reflections on Grand Strategy

Samir Tata

# Reflections on Grand Strategy

## The Great Powers in the Twenty-first Century

palgrave
macmillan

Samir Tata
Reston, VA, USA

ISBN 978-981-19-3772-9 ISBN 978-981-19-3773-6 (eBook)
https://doi.org/10.1007/978-981-19-3773-6



This Palgrave Macmillan imprint is published by the registered company Springer Nature Singapore Pte Ltd.
The registered company address is: 152 Beach Road, #21-01/04 Gateway East, Singapore 189721, Singapore

# Contents

CHAPTER 1

# The Elements of Grand Strategy

What is Grand Strategy? Grand Strategy is an insurance plan that is designed to ensure that over a foreseeable time period the state's continuing, sustainable existence as a viable entity is safeguarded against likely *external* threats.[1] There are six key elements that frame grand strategy: the articulation of vital national interests; the determination of likely external threats; an evaluation of the degree to which the external threat perceptions of allies and strategic partners converge, overlap, or are congruent with the state's perception of its external threats; an inventory of the likely available resources of military, economic, and diplomatic power; a demonstration that the ends of the plan optimally match the means available; and an assessment of the collective will of the people to support the proposed grand strategy. Grand strategy is process, design, execution, and recalibration in the context of the political world. It is dynamic and not static.

## The Nature of the Political World

The political world is a trinity that reflects its three irreducible and inextricably intertwined aspects: diversity, scarcity, and anarchy. The world, in a political sense, can only be understood if it is viewed through these three fundamental dimensions.



S. Tata, *Reflections on Grand Strategy*,
https://doi.org/10.1007/978-981-19-3773-6_1

Diversity reflects the fact that the political world has a plethora of different units ranging from the smallest—the single individual, to groups of individuals of varying size, to the largest political unit—the state. The state has five defining characteristics: territory, people, identity, sovereignty, and independence. Territory means a geographic area and everything that lies on, underneath, or above it (including air, cyberspace, and electromagnetic spectrums). People means all human beings living permanently within the territory. Identity is the essential bond between the people and their territory, which reflects an intangible, amorphous amalgam of myriad strands including language, custom, traditions, beliefs, ideology, culture, food, dress, symbols, rituals, religion, art, literature, music, dance, philosophy, morals, ethics, history, myths, values, race, and ethnicity. The identity of the state is supreme—it transcends all other identities of the various other political units within the state. The conscious overarching sense of oneness and indivisibility with the state's identity is called nationalism. A motto of the United States, "*E Pluribus Unum* – out of many, one," captures this profound sentiment perfectly.[2] Accordingly, all other political units within the state, both individually and collectively, pledge eternal and unlimited fidelity, devotion, and allegiance to the state. Sovereignty is the condition that there exists no entity superior to the state, and as such the citizens and residents of the state accept its decisions and commands as final and beyond appeal and which they must obey. This submission to the state's ultimate authority is absolute and unconditional.[3] Independence means that the state has the capacity to use its free will to exercise its authority, and is subject to no external influence, pressure, duress, coercion, or control. At present, and for the foreseeable future, the state in its pentagonal incarnation represents the highest stage of evolution of the political world. There are currently 195 states.[4]

Scarcity reflects the unchangeable reality of the world we live in—limited resources. Land, water, coal, oil, natural gas, minerals, chemicals, salt, food, and the other variety of goods and services that symbolize modern life are ultimately finite. Moreover, the distribution of these scarce resources is not uniform, and this varying, asymmetric pattern of resource endowment contributes significantly to the shaping of the diversity of political units, including states. The fact of limited resources places an unavoidable practical constraint on the activities of the various political units, most importantly, states.[5] Since autarky or complete self-sufficiency is an impossibility, interdependence is an existential necessity.

Therefore, states are mutually dependent on each other, albeit to varying degrees, to ensure that their resource requirements (or more accurately, the resource requirements of their constituents) are met. Resource imbalances are mediated through trade, which in turn, depends on connectivity via land, sea, air, or cyberspace. Thus, interdependence is the corollary of scarcity, and connectivity is the corollary of interdependence. In the absence of trade, access to external scarce resources may have to be secured by coercion, which, in extremis, could lead to war.

Anarchy reflects the fundamental condition that there is no single supreme authority which *all* constituent units of the political world, whether jointly or severally, ultimately must obey.[6] At its apex, the political world reflects systemic order and stability through dynamic equilibrium rather than rigid hierarchy. The state, the highest and largest political unit that exists in the world, neither recognizes nor is accountable to any higher authority.[7] Consequently, states must resolve differences among themselves by themselves either through persuasion or coercion within an environment of dynamic equilibrium—a framework of bespoke and self-created checks and balances. In such an environment, the ultimate form of coercion is the use of overwhelming military force—war.

The only constraint on war is if the opposing sides have the capability of annihilating each other and, perhaps as an unintended consequence, the rest of the world. When the atom bomb was first successfully exploded, J. Robert Oppenheimer, who directed the project to develop the weapon, claimed that two verses of the ancient Indian religious text, the *Bhagavad Gita*, flashed through his mind about the enormity of the awesome power that had been unleashed: "'If the radiance of a thousand suns were to burst into the sky, that would be like the splendor of the Mighty One.' and 'I am become Death, the shatterer of worlds.'"[8] Such a capability for mutual assured destruction exists if the opposing sides possess and exercise ultimate control over strategic nuclear weapons that can be delivered via land, sea, air, or space-based systems.[9] In a conflict between two nuclear weapons states, the war would be limited to the use of conventional weapons—weapons other than those that could result in mutual annihilation. Crossing this line surely would mean a return to conditions prevailing before the beginning of creation of life on earth. Sri Aurobindo, a renowned Indian revolutionary politician, poet, and philosopher, in his epic poem *Savitri* provides a haunting image of the world's original primordial condition: "Athwart the vain enormous trance of Space, /Its formless stupor without mind or life, /A shadow spinning through a soulless Void, /Thrown back once more into unthinking dreams, /Earth wheeled abandoned in the hollow gulfs /Forgetful of her spirit and her fate."[10] If survival is the paramount objective of the state, then it will not choose extinction—if it is behaving rationally. If both sides possess weapons capable of mutual assured destruction, will they ever use them against each other?[11]

The corollary of the trinity of diversity, scarcity, and anarchy is power, since power is necessary for survival and preservation of the state. In the pre-nuclear weapons era, conventional power was both a necessary and sufficient condition for survival of the state. Since the apple of knowledge of nuclear power has been eaten and the nuclear weapons production threshold has been crossed, power remains necessary but is no longer sufficient for survival of the state.[12] For what is also needed for the preservation of the state in a nuclear age (because of the enduring reality of the trinity of diversity, scarcity, and anarchy) are political ecosystems consisting of allies and strategic partners within the framework of symbiotic mutual interdependence to counterbalance adversarial political ecosystems. Forging a modus vivendi to ensure mutual assured survival is ultimately the only alternative to mutual assured destruction, and as such, is an existential necessity. Chaos, the complete absence of order, is a nightmare which mankind left behind at the beginning of history, while the ideal of human unity embodied in a universal supranational state as the pinnacle of world order is a dream at the end of history.[13]

## A Trio of Assumptions

The constituent units of this political world, of which the state is the most important, are *assumed* to function according to three intertwined operating characteristics: rationality, uncertainty, and sense of time. The unique singularity of human beings is the ability to think—to create or identify a thought, nurture it into an idea, and develop and articulate the idea into a fully born concept. And decision-makers are assumed to think rationally—to have the ability to identify information; process information in a logical, consistent, and coherent manner; reach conclusions from the available information; and make decisions based on such information. Uncertainty is the recognition that human beings are not omniscient and, therefore, the universe of available information is only a subset of the universe of information.[14] Thus, there may be information which is known or believed to exist but which is not available and the nature of which may be known or unknown. Also, there may be information that we do not know or believe exists. Accordingly, the information that is processed and from which conclusions are drawn and decisions made may be incomplete and of varying degrees of reliability. Also, human beings are assumed to have some sense of time: of the past, present, and future.

While rationality and uncertainty are conditions that can be addressed and are assumed to be taken into account by decision-makers, time is not so much a condition as it is a separate dimension. Accordingly, *ceteris paribus*—all other things being the same—decision-makers with fundamentally different time perspectives are likely to formulate very different grand strategies. A sense of time bounded by a single period—the present—will likely produce a grand strategy that focuses on immediate gratification; a sense of time that values the future is more amenable to accommodating strategic patience and deferred gratification; and a sense of time that is obsessed with the past, will most likely reflect strategic impatience and a nostalgia for restoring an imagined prior existence.[15]

There is a discipline and skill to "thinking in time"—just as there is to developing an ability to think logically and make decisions under uncertainty.[16] The eminent historian, E. H. Carr, has astutely pointed out that time is a continuum and "the present has no more than a notional existence as an imaginary dividing line between the past and the future."[17] The present focuses on what is happening, the past on why something happened, and the future on where one might be headed. Henry Kissinger, the erstwhile Secretary of State and perhaps America's foremost strategic thinker, has cautioned that American exceptionalism—the confident sense of uniqueness and optimism—must be bounded by rationality, a respect for uncertainty, and a balanced time perspective. He particularly makes a plea to understand rather than ignore history.[18]

The lifetime of a state transcends the lifetime of its decision-makers and stretches far into the future beyond that which can be foreseen or imagined. A state's decision-makers are presumed to have not only a historical perspective but also the ability to think clearly about the present and have a credible and realistic grasp of the foreseeable future. A generation is reasonably far out in the future and yet within the time frame of most forecasting models in business and government. Twenty years is the time horizon used in this essay.

## What Is Power?

Power, in the context of the political world, is the *perceived* or *expected* capability of a state to (1) persuade, compel, or coerce another state or states to accept, acquiesce, or refrain from challenging the first state's claims with respect to its own vital national interests; and (2) deny another state or states the realization of claims with respect to the vital national interests of such other state or states. Power has four different dimensions: hard power, economic power, soft power, and will power.

Hard power is quintessentially military power which currently has as its upper limit the capacity of mutual assured destruction via strategic nuclear weapons. Conventional military power—the capacity to apply lethal, violent force other than strategic nuclear weapons—has three prongs: regular armed groups under the direct authority of the state (such as the US Army, China's People's Liberation Army); irregular armed militias, both overt and covert, under the indirect authority of the state (such as Sunni Iraqi tribes of Anbar province paid by the United States to fight along with regular US and Iraqi military forces, Pakistani jihadi groups under the patronage of the Pakistani Army targeting the Indian Army); and covert armed groups under the direct or indirect authority of the state (such as CIA or Israeli Mossad undercover assassination teams, and coup efforts to effect regime change).[19]

Military power reflects the confluence of four interrelated forces: economy, demography, geography, and technology. The size of the economy, typically measured by Gross Domestic Product (GDP) on a purchasing power parity basis, is the fundamental indicator of *latent* military power because it quantifies the upper limit of the amount of resources potentially available for defense.[20] The amount of defense spending as a percentage of GDP, which reflects a political decision with respect to the tradeoff between "guns and butter," is an indicator of *actual* military power.[21] Demography has four characteristics reflecting the population's size, age distribution, sex ratio, and expected net growth rate (the combined impact of birth and mortality rates). The potential size of the armed forces, another measure of latent military power, is indicated typically by the size of the population in the 18–50 age bracket. Crudely put, it is an indicator of the potential available amount of "cannon fodder." The amount of active military personnel is another important indicator of actual military power. Geography often endows a state with unique natural physical features that have strategic military potential: land chokepoints (the Khyber Pass is the traditional land route connecting Afghanistan and Pakistan); maritime choke points (Iran overlooks the Strait of Hormuz through which most Persian Gulf oil exports flow); mountainous terrain that favors defenders and presents formidable obstacles to invaders (Afghanistan, Nepal, Switzerland); seas and oceans serving as natural moats protecting against external invasion (the Atlantic and Pacific Oceans have long served this function in the case of the United States); the enormous size of a country (Russia's vast size provides it with strategic depth against foreign invading armies, such as Napoleon's *Grand Armée* and Hitler's *Wehrmacht*, whose supply lines were stretched to the breaking point); and the nature of extreme weather (Russia's bitter cold, snow and ice, dubbed "General Winter," have helped defeat foreign invaders such as France and Germany). Technology has four facets: knowledge, education, innovation, and efficiency.[22] Technology provides a qualitive edge that can be decisive. For example, in the case of the United States, guns versus bows and arrows decimated American Indians and using the atom bomb vanquished Japan. The advanced state of technology is a significant indicator of latent military power. The possession of strategic nuclear weapons is a crucial indicator of actual military power.

Economic power is the capacity of a state to (1) control access of another state or states to the first state's markets and resources through targeted trade barriers such as tariffs, quotas, boycotts, embargoes, divestment, and other punitive restrictions and sanctions; (2) transfer a portion of the state's own resources to another state or states through targeted preferences, subsidies, investments, and foreign aid; and (3) sabotage and disrupt the normal functioning of the target state's economy, particularly manufacturing, commercial and service sectors, through covert cyber operations and other covert actions designed to disable computer networks that control critical communications, logistics, financial, and energy infrastructure and systems.[23] Economic power can wreak enormous damage and wield enormous influence despite its non-kinetic nature, and for this reason has been viewed as an attractive alternative to the use of military force to ensure that the target state (a) does not pursue policies or activities that would adversely impact the first state's vital national interests, or (b) supports, accepts, or refrains from challenging the first state's pursuit of its claimed vital national interests.

Wielding economic power to further vital national interests has very deep roots. For example, while the United States was still in its infancy, it used embargoes to safeguard its neutrality and freedom of navigation. President Thomas Jefferson resorted to measures he called "peaceable coercion" to ensure that Great Britain and France, which were locked in conflict with each other, did not interfere with US transatlantic trade, and signed the Embargo Act of 1807 banning all US trade with Europe, and its successor, the Non-Intercourse Act of 1809, banning all US trade with Great Britain and France.[24] In the run-up to World War II, President Franklin D. Roosevelt, in an effort to tilt American neutrality in favor of Great Britain and against Japan, issued a series of executive orders beginning July 1940 banning US exports of oil, gasoline, aviation fuel, steel, iron, and metal scrap—products that were vital to sustain Japan's military machine.[25] In conjunction with American withdrawal from the Iran nuclear deal in 2018, President Donald Trump, via a series of executive orders imposed a sweeping and comprehensive array of economic sanctions designed to bring about the collapse of the Iranian economy and precipitate regime change.[26] Besides using economic sticks, the United States has also opened up its purse to further its vital national interests. Following the end of the Second World War, the United States launched the "Marshall Plan," a massive foreign aid program amounting to about $13 billion over four years, to help reconstruct and revive Western Europe and ensure that countries of the region were able to resist Soviet subversion and remained allied to America.[27]

Soft power is the capacity of the state to (1) apply intellectual (including international law and customary practice), ideological, religious, moral, or emotional suasion to convince a target state that (a) it is in the target state's self-interest to accept, acquiesce, or refrain from challenging the first state's claims of vital national interests, or (b) the target state should not attempt to realize its own vital national interests as they are in conflict with the first state's vital national interests, or would generate unintended consequences that could adversely impact the target state's vital national interests; (2) communicate and explain its own vital national interests to other states (including decision-makers, opinion-makers, and the general public); and (3) understand the vital national interests and assess the capabilities of other states. Soft power has three facets: diplomacy; covert influence and intelligence operations; and non-governmental organizations closely linked to the state.[28]

Sir Harold Nicholson, courtesy of the Oxford English Dictionary, provides a classic definition of diplomacy, which is the enduring manifestation of soft power: "Diplomacy is the management of international relations by means of negotiations; the method by which these relations are adjusted and arranged by ambassadors and envoys the business or art of the diplomat."[29] Simply put, diplomacy is communicating and negotiating between and among states through accredited representatives. Since it constitutes the official line of communication between states, diplomacy represents the default option when states need to resolve disagreements among themselves. The nearly two-year-long negotiations between Iran and the United States (along with the United Kingdom, France, Germany, and the European Union as well as Russia and China) over Iran's nuclear energy program culminating in the Joint Comprehensive Plan of Action (JCPOA) is an example of diplomacy in action.[30] Communicating clearly a state's position with respect to sensitive issues to avoid any misunderstanding is an essential part of diplomacy. For example, immediately after the United Nations, with strong backing from the United States, voted for the partition of Palestine and the establishment of a separate Jewish state and a separate Arab state, the Saudi King Ibn Saud met with the American ambassador J. Rives Childs in Riyadh on 2 December 1947 to assure him that Palestine was not a matter of vital national interest and would not jeopardize the relationship between the two countries: "Although we differ enormously on the question of Palestine … still we have our own mutual interests and friendship to safeguard … I do not anticipate that a situation will arise whereby I shall be drawn into conflict with friendly western powers over this question."[31] As Indian intervention in the civil war between East and West Pakistan tilted the conflict decisively in favor of East Pakistan, National Security Advisor Henry Kissinger met with the Chinese Ambassador to the UN in New York on 10 December 1971 to assure him that the United States would not object to any actions that China might take along the disputed Sino-Indian border in order to signal support for West Pakistan: "[T]he President wants you to know that … if the People's Republic were to consider the situation on the Indian subcontinent a threat to its security, and if it took measures to protect its security, the US would oppose efforts of others to interfere."[32]

And, at its best, diplomacy, since it involves close and substantive interaction with counterparts and decision-makers of another state, is a superb means of gaining an understanding of the motivations and intentions of the other state. A classic example is George F. Kennan's "long telegram," which he sent to the State Department on 22 February 1946 while he was a diplomat stationed in Moscow, explaining the rationale and basis of Soviet conduct of its foreign policy—a missive that helped shape US policy toward the Soviet Union during the Cold War.[33] A pivotal set of diplomatic meetings that enhanced mutual understanding and repositioned the course of US–China relations from confrontation to cooperation was the series of meetings of National Security Advisor Henry Kissinger and President Richard M. Nixon with Chinese leaders Mao Tse-tung and Chou En-lai in China during 1971 and 1972.[34]

Certainly, when issues involving claimed vital national interests are involved, at least in theory, diplomacy is considered the preferred first option and war the option of last resort. As Hans Morgenthau has observed, "[A] diplomacy that ends in war has failed its primary objective: the promotion of the national interest by peaceful means."[35] In practice, the reality is far more muddled with the conflict resolution arc far too often progressing from war to diplomacy. For example, on 24 June 1950 North Korea launched a massive invasion suddenly and unexpectedly crossing the 38th parallel dividing it from South Korea in a bid to unify forcibly the two parts of Korea.[36] Similarly, on 29 October 1956 the United Kingdom, France, and Israel launched a sudden invasion of Egypt to seize the Sinai Peninsula and Suez Canal zone.[37]

Will power, despite its nebulous and intangible character, is the most crucial dimension of state power because it embodies the people's collective, conscious acceptance of not only the continued use of hard power, economic power, and soft power, but also the scope and duration of the use of such power to safeguard or further claimed vital national interests. The centrality of will to the exercise of power has been acknowledged since the beginning of recorded history. In the ancient Indian religious text, the *Bhagavad Gita*, Prince Arjuna's poignant lament expresses his loss of will to fight at the very moment the epic battle of Kurukshetra is to take place between the armies of the virtuous Pandavas and their evil cousins, the Kauravas: "What do I want with / Victory, empire, / Or their enjoyment? / … Evil they may be, / … Yet if we kill them / Our sin is greater. / … Am I indeed / So greedy for greatness? / … I shall not struggle, / I shall not strike them."[38] The inability to stem and reverse the loss of the American public's will to continue fighting in Vietnam was the pivotal turning point in the US decision to end the war.[39]

## The Determination of Vital National Interests

The supreme vital national interest of the state is to ensure its continued, sustainable existence as a viable political entity preserving its five defining features: territory, people, identity, sovereignty, and independence. Continuity, sustainability, and viability are the three interlinked dimensions within which the pentagonal features of the state must be safeguarded. Accordingly, there are eight elements that must be considered in the formulation of a state's vital national interests. A threat to any of these eight elements constitutes an existential threat, and failure to counter such a threat will mean that the state will cease to exist. It is useful to consider each of these critical elements.

The term "continued existence" implies at a minimum a time span covering the foreseeable future. External pressures can constrict the time available to a state to pursue its current path. The Soviet Union's life span as a single state was about 74 years, after which it voluntarily dissolved into 15 separate states. The Soviet Union could not sustain the economic burden of continuing the Cold War against the United States, and internal political fissures aggravated by the drain of resources meant that continued centralized control by the Communist Party within a single state structure was no longer possible. Pakistan's life span as a single state was a mere 24 years and, as a result of a civil war in which Indian military intervention favored one side decisively, split into two separate states—a recognition that Pakistan could not continue as a unitary state. Currently, as a result of foreign involvement in domestic quarrels, Ukraine and Syria are in intensive care while Libya and Yemen are on life support with respect to their continued existence as states. For how long can the State of Israel continue to exist as a Jewish state while maintaining control over the Land of Israel?

Sustainability highlights the fact that the state must possess or have access to scarce resources to ensure the people's physical, economic, and mental well-being (e.g., food, clothing, shelter, health, sanitation, education, and technology), as well as physical safety and security. Clearly, external pressures such as blockades and drone attacks could cause devastating humanitarian crises.[40] South Africa's policy of apartheid, designed to maintain the state's white (European) identity, could not be sustained and after 45 years eventually collapsed under the pressure of external economic boycotts and divestments organized by foreign private groups and non-governmental organizations, and governmental sanctions imposed by other states that were enacted through the efforts of foreign anti-apartheid groups. Yemen, reflecting the impact of policies that invited or encouraged foreign meddling, is a prime example of a state whose current condition is unsustainable.[41] Determining what is a sustainable level of defense spending relative to the size of the economy is an important factor in the formulation of the scope of a state's vital national interests. The fate of the now extinct Soviet Union is a cautionary tale.

Viability, closely linked with continuity and sustainability, represents the third dimension with respect to the determination of vital national interests. For example, a state with borders that are not considered defensible, may not be viable. At its establishment in 1947, the State of Pakistan was born with two wings separated by about 1700 km of Indian territory. Ultimately, such a state could not demonstrate its viability and was torn asunder in 1971 by civil war abetted and skewed by Indian military intervention. Israel considers the borders it was endowed with under the 1947 UN resolution accepting the partition of Palestine as well as the expanded de facto borders reflecting the 1949 armistice lines as a result of Israel's War of Independence, as not defensible and therefore not viable. Israel views its current de facto borders acquired as a result of the June 1967 Arab–Israeli War to be defensible as it provides the state with greater geographic depth against external aggression—but the question it is wrestling with is whether maintaining control over such borders is viable as it is accompanied by significant demographic vulnerability since it requires exercising control over a large, potentially hostile non-Jewish population.[42]

The framing and articulation of *specific* vital national interests is anchored in the five definitional aspects of the state.

Territorial integrity and inviolability loom large in specifying a state's vital national interests. The concept of territory, while intuitively simple, is fraught with complexity and can be strategically challenging, which can tempt decision-makers to prefer opacity and ambiguity rather than specificity and clarity. India shows on all its official maps Kashmiri territories over which it claims sovereignty but over which another state exercises administrative control (Azad Kashmir and Gilgit-Baltistan areas of Kashmir which are under the administrative control of Pakistan, and the Aksai Chin area of Kashmir which is under Chinese administration). Do these disputed territories constitute a vital national interest of India for which it is prepared to go to war to recover?[43] The gap between Indian rhetoric and action is enormous on this matter. The People's Republic of

China (PRC) claims sovereignty over Taiwan although it has never exercised administrative control over the area. Does the PRC consider it a vital national interest to gain control over the territory and is it willing to go to war to ensure that Taiwan is unified with China? China's right to exercise its sovereignty claim over Taiwan through military force is not recognized by the United States. Similarly, China claims sovereignty over India's northeastern state of Arunachal Pradesh which it calls Southern Tibet and Japan's Senkaku Islands in the East China Sea which it calls Diaoyu Islands. Are these disputed territories a vital national interest for which China is prepared to go to war to recover? Is India willing to go to war to protect Arunachal Pradesh and is Japan willing to go to war to retain the Senkaku Islands? Also, China has asserted a maritime boundary claim in the South China Sea, the so-called "Nine Dash Line," that is disputed by other regional states and is not recognized by the United States. Is this claimed maritime boundary a Chinese vital national interest? Kaliningrad is a Russian exclave surrounded by Poland and Lithuania. Is the defense of Kaliningrad, which as Konigsberg was part of Germany but became a part of the Soviet Union at the end of World War II, a vital national interest of Russia? Likewise, is Crimea and its naval base of Sevastopol, formerly a part of Ukraine until its annexation by Russia in 2014, a vital national interest of Russia? Since its founding in 1948, the State of Israel has consistently avoided specifying its borders.[44] Clearly articulating a state's vital national interest with respect to its territory is an enormously challenging task.

Safeguarding a state's people is another vital national interest that is considered "self-evident." In 1998, the then president of Iran, Mohammad Khatami, declared: "Defending oneself and deterring others from committing aggression is the most important right of any country."[45] President George W. Bush in September 2002 asserted: "Defending our Nation against its enemies is the first and foremost commitment of the Federal Government."[46] Yet who is included in the state's conception of people very often can pose difficult challenges both for the state as well as other neighboring states.

President Donald Trump argued that illegal migrants transiting through as well as from Mexico across the southern US border constituted a threat to the safety and security of America's citizens and legal residents, and this flood of illegal migrants could only be contained by the construction of a border wall the cost of which ultimately should be borne by Mexico.[47] Following America's entry into World War II,

Japanese-Americans were considered to be a potentially subversive "fifth column" working on behalf of the Japanese Empire, and were quarantined in internment camps for the duration of the war.[48] During the 1971 civil war between West and East Pakistan, the West Pakistani Army in an effort to quell the rebellious eastern province, unleashed a brutal reign of terror resulting in a tsunami of nearly 10 million East Pakistani refugees streaming across the border to India's neighboring state of West Bengal.[49] According to India, this massive influx threatened to destabilize and overwhelm the state. To stem the exodus, India intervened militarily in support of East Pakistan, and succeeded in ending the civil war and facilitating the establishment of Bangladesh as a separate, independent state.

At the end of World War II, the expulsion of an estimated 12 million ethnic Germans from parts of Eastern Europe and the Soviet Union reflected concerns that the German minorities were obstacles to national integration and potential security risks.[50] The 1947 partition of British India into two separate independent states—Pakistan and India—was accompanied by a two-way mass population transfer of nearly 15 million people and the brutal killing of 1–2 million people and innumerable rapes of women.[51] This trauma has poisoned the relations between the two countries ever since. The State of Israel, which has extended to Jews living outside the state the right to immigrate to Israel in perpetuity, has steadfastly refused to recognize the right of return of Palestinian refugees and their descendants who fled or were expelled at the time of the Jewish State's establishment in 1948.[52] The burden of dealing with these refugees has been borne by the neighboring states—Jordan, Lebanon, and Syria.[53] It is a challenge yet to be resolved.

The ultimate perversion of considering a group of people to be an existential threat to the state is the perpetration of mass genocide in a bid to eliminate such a group. In the throes of World War I, the Ottoman Empire virtually wiped out its Armenian population through a terror campaign of mass killings and forced deportations that resulted in the deaths of 1.5 million out of an estimated population of 2 million.[54] The Holocaust that was systematically planned and executed by Nazi Germany resulted in the extermination of 6 million European Jews.[55]

The vital national interest in safeguarding a state's people is closely linked to preserving the state's identity. For example, ensuring that the national identity of the Vietnamese people, which was bifurcated in two separate states following the Second World War, was restored and embodied in a single, unified state (as it was prior to the war) was the supreme national interest driving Communist North Vietnam's effort to force unification on the various non-Communist governments of South Vietnam (which were viewed as clients and dependents of the United States). As such, the Vietnam war far from being a war between communism versus capitalism or totalitarianism versus democracy was a war of nationalism.[56] The central question hanging over the Korean Peninsula is whether, after nearly 74 years of separation, the sense of nationalism embracing a unified Korean state remains sufficiently strong and resilient to transcend the enormous economic, political, and military differences that have grown over time between North and South Korea? The People's Republic of China has waited for 73 years hoping Taiwan will unite with China. Does this signal that unification of Taiwan with the PRC is not a vital national interest and is not an essential part of Chinese national identity? Or is China simply biding its time until it feels it is strong enough to force the issue?

The apartheid government of South Africa believed that preservation of the exclusively white (European) identity of the state was an existential necessity and succeeded in its effort for almost 45 years. Indeed, around 1980 South Africa became a nuclear weapons state to underscore its determination to safeguard its continued existence. By 1992, however, the combination of external economic pressure and international delegitimization of the state's white identity persuaded a majority of South Africa's white electorate that apartheid was no longer sustainable—and this changed sentiment and loss of willpower was reflected in a national referendum.[57] So even in the absence of any external military coercion or the threat of such coercion, a state's identity can change quite dramatically if such a change is perceived to be an existential necessity. Today, South Africa's identity more fully reflects the diversity of its people.

Since its founding in 1948, the State of Israel has insisted that preservation of its exclusive Jewish identity is an existential necessity. This imperative is reflected in its dual policy of promising Jews living outside the state an eternal right to immigrate to Israel and denying the right of return to Palestinian refugees (and their descendants) who fled or were expelled during the 1948 war of independence.[58] The State of Israel controls the Land of Israel, which includes a Jewish and Arab population of nearly equal size. Is the State of Israel's exclusively Jewish identity central to its existence? Can the State of Israel change its identity to reflect the demographic reality of the Land of Israel? Can the evolving Palestinian identity accommodate and include a Jewish identity? How accurate and reliable are the state's population statistics and projections? What is the likelihood of significant numbers of Jews in the diaspora exercising their right to immigrate to Israel? Equally, what is the likelihood of significant numbers of Palestinian refugees exercising a right of return if such a right were ever conceded? Can the State of Israel renounce the Jewish People's claims to and control over a significant portion of the Land of Israel? Is the willpower to preserve the state's exclusive Jewish identity strong enough to resist successfully external economic pressure and international delegitimization? Clearly, no grand strategy for Israel can ignore the state's identity as a vital national interest.

Sovereignty of the state is perhaps the most jealously guarded vital national interest, and yet it is undoubtedly the most difficult vital national interest to articulate with any degree of precision. To ward off perceived external threats to the state's supremacy, the English Parliament in its Act of Supremacy of 1559 attempted to articulate and formalize its conception of English sovereignty: "[N]o foreign prince, person, prelate, state or potentate hath or ought to have any jurisdiction, power, superiority, preeminence or authority ecclesiastical or spiritual within this realm."[59] The US Constitution in article I, section 8, paragraph 10 empowers Congress "To define and punish Piracies and Felonies committed on the high Seas, and Offenses against the Law of Nations" and in article VI, paragraph 2 explicitly includes as part of US law, international treaties which the United States is party to: "This constitution, and the Laws of the United States which shall be made in Pursuance thereof; and all Treaties made, or which shall be made, under the Authority of the United States, shall be the supreme law of the Land."[60] These provisions suggest that the framers of the Constitution acknowledged that sovereignty may co-exist with and be circumscribed by the Law of Nations, albeit in a rather tenuous and vague sense, which the US Supreme Court would presumably interpret.[61]

To complicate matters further, the alleged inability or unwillingness of a state to exercise its sovereignty also can be invoked by another state as contrary to its own vital national interest. For example, President Richard Nixon justified his decision to send US troops into Cambodia to go after North Vietnamese troops using sanctuaries in that country on the basis that Cambodia did not have the ability to prevent North Vietnamese troops from entering their country.[62] In 1982, Israel invaded Lebanon and occupied the southern portion of the state on the grounds that the government of Lebanon was unwilling or unable to exercise control over Palestinian terrorists who were launching attacks against Israel from bases within Lebanese territory.[63] India conducted a preemptive airstrike against an alleged jihadi terror base in Pakistan on 26 February 2019 claiming that the Government of Pakistan was unwilling to dismantle the anti-India terror infrastructure within Pakistan.[64]

A state engaged in peaceful activities pursuant to its perception of vital national interests may nevertheless find itself being challenged by another state or states who consider such activities to be potentially threatening to their own vital national interests. Iran's nuclear energy program illustrates the problem. Iran, which is endowed with significant oil and gas reserves, believes that the foreign exchange earned through energy exports will fund the country's economic development and growth. To maximize the amount of oil and gas available for export, it must minimize the amount of oil and gas it consumes for domestic purposes such as the production of electricity. Also, it fears that if it does not curb domestic consumption of non-renewable fossil fuels, it will essentially cease being an energy exporter and would become an energy importer within a generation. Rather than use oil and gas to fuel the production of electricity, Iran has tried to turn to nuclear powered plants to generate electricity. In this connection, it has mastered the technology required to enrich uranium so that Iran can manufacture nuclear fuel rods required to operate nuclear powered plants. The United States, Israel, and Saudi Arabia have asserted that Iran's nuclear program will enable it to become a nuclear weapons state, which they consider to be a potential threat to their security. Iran's dream of energy and economic security is viewed as a national security nightmare by its adversaries and the issue—pitting different conceptions of sovereignty—remains unresolved.

A state cannot take its sovereignty for granted, which is why it is an enduring vital national interest. The decision of the United States (together with NATO) to intervene in the brutal civil war between Serbia and its breakaway province of Kosovo in 1999 is an example of a state asserting its vital national interest as justification for not respecting the sovereignty of another state. In a speech explaining the launching of airstrikes against Serbia, President Bill Clinton claimed that given the geographic propinquity of the Balkans to southern Europe, the Balkan conflict, if not quickly ended, would result in a flood of refugees from Kosovo, mostly Muslim, that could destabilize neighboring NATO allies such as Greece and Italy, and consequently shake the foundations of the alliance that maintained peace in Europe.[65] In the case of Iraq under

Saddam Hussein, after the September 11, 2001 attacks by al Qaeda on the World Trade Center and the Pentagon, the mere suspicion that his regime had links to the terrorist organization together with the misimpression that there existed a covert Iraqi nuclear weapons program, was sufficient for the United States, invoking vital national interests, to ignore Iraq's sovereignty and in 2003 invade and occupy the country.[66]

Independence as a vital national interest is intimately tied to sovereignty because the focus is on ensuring that no external factors adversely impact the ability of the state to exercise its free will in conducting its own domestic and foreign policies. The alleged Russian meddling in favor Donald Trump (and against Hilary Clinton) in the US presidential elections of 2016 raised concerns with respect to potential Russian influence in shaping US foreign policy with respect to Russia. Was American foreign policy under President Donald Trump truly independent or did it reflect Kremlin's hidden hand? Given the heavy dependence of the Israeli military on American military equipment, is Israeli foreign policy truly independent or is it constrained by US policy preferences? Israeli leaders have been at pains to underscore their independence from the United States. For example, Yitzhak Rabin, in his first statement in the Israeli Knesset as Prime Minister, acknowledged US support that helped Israel prevail over Egypt and Syria in the Yom Kippur War of 1973 and then insisted: "The friendly relations between us and the U.S. … have not prevented us in the past, nor will they prevent us in the future, from meticulous insistence on positions vital to Israel's survival and development, even if our positions are not acceptable to the United States."[67]

A key issue with respect to independence is the reality that the asymmetric endowment of scarce resources could make a state without such resources dependent upon (a) another state that has such resources or (b) another state that can control access to such resources. For example, both India and China are heavily dependent on imported oil and gas for their energy requirements. In the case of India, does its reliance on significant oil imports from Saudi Arabia make it vulnerable to Saudi pressure to accommodate Saudi foreign policy preferences? Could India be threatened with a Saudi oil cut-off in the event of an Indo-Pak war as the United States was in 1973 as a result of the Yom Kippur War (Arab–Israeli war) of that year?[68] In the case of China, oil and gas imports from Saudi Arabia and Iran rely on sea lines of communication connecting the Persian Gulf to the South China Sea that are controlled by the US Navy. Does such dependence on maritime trade routes make China vulnerable to US pressure to accommodate American foreign policy preferences? Freedom of navigation has been a vital national interest of the United States since its birth, as it is separated from Europe by the Atlantic Ocean and Asia by the Pacific Ocean. Sans freedom of navigation—the quintessence of connectivity—those seas would imprison and isolate the United States, with the ability to trade with other states dependent upon those who controlled the sea lines of communication. To safeguard freedom of navigation so essential to its independence, the United States was willing to go to war with the Barbary States (1801–1805 and 1815–1816), Great Britain (1812), and Germany (1917–1918).[69]

While the framework for the determination of vital *national* interests is provided by the foregoing eight elements—continuity, sustainability, viability, territory, people, identity, sovereignty, and independence—vital *domestic* interests can have a significant but *temporary* impact in shaping perceptions of a state's vital national interests. Ultimately, however, vital national interests trump vital domestic interests. The entry of the United States in both the First and Second World wars was delayed because of the strong isolationist sentiment of the American electorate that was determined to keep out of foreign wars, reflecting the widespread conviction that involvement in such wars was not in the country's vital national interest. The Japanese attack on Pearl Harbor and Nazi Germany's declaration of war on the United States silenced the isolationist chorus in the case of WW II, relieving President Franklin D. Roosevelt from the burden of having to convince the country about the vital national interests that actually were at risk. What finally swayed public opinion in favor of entry in WW I was the publication of the Zimmerman telegram, suggesting a covert German plan, in the event of a US decision to enter the war on the side of the allies, to help Mexico regain territories previously lost to the United States—it was the burning match that lit the fuse represented by the mounting anger over the continuing loss of American lives in the sinking of passenger and merchant ships crossing the Atlantic by German submarines.[70]

On the other hand, decision-makers—at least in democracies—will often embrace foreign policy positions favored by the public at large or by domestic special interest groups (in effect branding such policies for domestic political purposes as vital national interests—albeit virtual rather than real), even if such policies do not help what decision-makers believe to be the real vital national interests of the state, provided such decision-makers are convinced that these popular foreign policy positions will not adversely affect the country's real vital national interests. Hence, sometimes it is difficult to discern the actual vital national interests of a state when domestic groups have an intense emotional interest in a particular foreign policy issue. However, if decision-makers are convinced that adopting such popular foreign policy positions will adversely impact the real vital national interests of the state, they will resist pressure to adopt such policies or try to work around such popular but misguided policies.

For example, US support for Israel, routinely claimed to be absolute and unconditional, reflects the influence of strong domestic public sentiment as well as powerful domestic interest groups in favor of a special relationship with the Jewish State. Thus, President Harry S. Truman could support the establishment of Israel, which was domestically popular, because he was fully aware that such support would not adversely affect America's critical relationship with Saudi Arabia.[71] Yet, at the time of the Suez Crisis, President Dwight D. Eisenhower did not hesitate to force the United Kingdom, France, and Israel to withdraw their armies from the Suez Canal Zone and Sinai Peninsula, because their invasion of Egypt was seen as damaging to American vital national interests.[72] Similarly, with respect to the 2015 nuclear deal with Iran, President Barack Obama was convinced that the deal was in the vital national interest of the United States and therefore he was willing to face down intense Israeli opposition as well as furious domestic lobbying efforts (including by some important pro-Israel groups) against the deal.[73]

## Assessing Likely External Threats

The strategic calculus involved in accurately assessing external threats is crucial. Sun-tzu, ancient China's most renowned strategist (about 544–496 B.C.), has provided timeless advice: "'[K]now the enemy, know yourself/And victory is never in doubt, not in a hundred battles.'/ He who knows self but not the enemy/Will suffer one defeat for every victory/He who knows neither self nor enemy/Will fail in every battle."—[74] Assessing likely external threats to a state's specific vital national intereststerritory, people, identity, sovereignty, and independence—in their three dimensions—continuity, sustainability, and viability—proceeds along two prongs: intentions and capabilities of another state.[75] The greater the gap between intentions and capabilities, the lower is the likelihood of the threats materializing; while smaller the gap, the higher is the likelihood of the threats being realized.

The key to understanding another state's intentions is to understand its vital national interests. Intentions are a function of vital national interests, and a change in intentions reflects a change in perceived vital national interests.[76] Assessing intentions requires piercing the veil of political rhetoric and clearly focusing on the eight elements that constitute the framework for the determination of vital national interests. Determining capabilities of another state requires an accurate evaluation of its military, economic, and diplomatic power as well as its will power. By calculating the other state's power, a state can determine the level of confidence the other state has in pursuing its vital national interests. A state must then compare its own vital interests to those which it believes to be of the other state and determine which of its own vital interests are in conflict with those of the other state. It is the existence of conflicting vital national interests that constitute potential existential threats.

A state must also compare the four aspects of its power—hard power, economic power, soft power, and will power—with those of the other state, to determine the relative power balance (or imbalance). It is the existence of an asymmetric balance of power that will determine the likelihood of the potential existential threat growing into an actual existential threat.

If a state finds itself in a situation that it is currently and/or likely in the foreseeable future to have an adverse asymmetrical balance of power relative to another state with which there exists conflicting vital national interests, it must consider a strategic alliance with a third state that (a) also has conflicting vital national interests of a comparable degree of importance with the second state, and (b) has sufficient power, which when combined with the first state's power, will be greater than or equal to the power of the adversary state. The target alliance state's power may be greater than, equal to or less than the first state's—the greater the symmetry and congruence in vital national interests and power between the first and third state, the more robust the alliance is likely to be. To be strategically useful, such an alliance must incorporate a clear commitment of the parties to fight alongside each other against the common adversary under carefully defined circumstances. Clarity is essential to ensure that the alliance focuses on congruent vital national interests and does not make the parties hostage to other vital national interests that are not mutually shared. Ambiguity, while it may appear to be politically expedient, will be counterproductive and lead to misunderstanding and miscalculation.

Crafting such an alliance is an enormous challenge since it in effect involves shaping a mutually interdependent, symbiotic ecosystem. Inevitably this effort to address a shared threat entails difficult compromises with respect to sharing certain aspects of sovereignty and independence. It is for this reason that a state almost invariably will seek to optimize its own power to support its vital national interests before (or at least contemporaneously with) structuring a strategic alliance.

What if the first state fails to structure such a robust alliance? The prospect of major war beckons. According to Dale C. Copeland, a political scientist who has thought deeply about the causes of war, certain adverse asymmetric power relationships, whether actual or expected, increase the likelihood of war:

> A state ...that is superior in military power but *inferior* in economic and especially potential power is more likely to believe that, once its military power begins to wane, further decline will be inevitable and deep. This is especially so if the trends of relative economic and potential power are downward as well .... Under these circumstances, a dominant military power is likely to be pessimistic about the future and more inclined to initiate major war as a 'now-or-never' attempt to shore up its waning security.[77]

Of course, if the opposing sides both have nuclear weapons, the consequences could be catastrophic if they do not step off the escalatory ladder, edge away from the brink, recalibrate their vital national interests, and craft a modus vivendi.

## The Architecture of National Security

In order to safeguard its vital national interests against external threats, a state traditionally has had to envision designing a security envelope with 7 different layers, of which only the first one is common to every state by definition while the other 6 may or may not be available either by choice or as a function of its current position in the hierarchy of power relative to other states.[78]

The first layer is the physical core of the state, which is represented by the bulk of its territory with significant population concentrations and areas (regardless of population) that are strategically important (for example oil fields, a key mountain pass or maritime chokepoint). Loss of the state's core means that the state ceases to exist in the political sense. A state can be expected to resist such a loss. If it is a nuclear-armed state, the likelihood that it would threaten to invoke the nuclear option is extremely high. For example, Pakistan might threaten to use tactical nuclear weapons if faced with the prospect of losing Lahore, the capital of Punjab province, to invading Indian troops.

The second layer, in effect the second fold of the first layer, represents "peripheral" areas of the state. These may be (a) remote border territories that are sparsely populated and with little or no strategic value, or (b) territories that are controlled by the state but that are subject to competing sovereignty claims of another state. A state will resist the loss of such peripheral areas by conventional military means (weapons other than nuclear weapons). If the state is a nuclear weapons state, it is unlikely to threaten the use of such weapons with respect to (a) but there is a risk with respect to (b), particularly if those territories are populated and well-integrated with the rest of the state, that an escalatory spiral can spin out of control and bring the contestants to the nuclear brink. For example, in 1962 India and China fought a border war, which resulted in India losing the Aksai Chin area of the Ladakh region of Kashmir. Aksai Chin is sparsely populated and has no strategic value for India (although it has great strategic value to China because the road linking Tibet to Xinjiang runs through Aksai Chin). Since then, India has evinced no revanchist desire to recover the lost territory. On the other hand, India and Pakistan have fought three wars over the Indian-controlled portion of Kashmir (1948, 1965, and 1999). In the last conflict, the specter of nuclear war briefly hovered overhead, but both countries edged away from the nuclear abyss. The status quo prevailing after the first Indo-Pak war continues to hold.

The next three layers reflect different folds of a state's sphere of influence. The innermost fold represents a *cordon sanitaire*—a band or ring of weaker states (or bodies of water) bordering the more powerful state. The purpose of the cordon sanitaire is to provide a physical buffer zone, under the control of the dominant state, to shield it from any military attack. Ultimately, the states that are part of this security belt have no choice in deciding to play such a role, and their sovereignty and independence depends on the sufferance of the dominant state. A state within the cordon sanitaire may try to defect and seek the protection of another powerful state that is the rival of the dominant state, but its sovereignty and independence will simply be subordinated to the will of the rival state. Of course, such a defection will be opposed by the dominant state. The stage will then be set for a possible conflict between the dominant state and the rival state. To protect its cordon sanitaire, the dominant state will be prepared to wage a war with conventional weapons. If the dominant state has nuclear weapons, it may threaten the use of tactical nuclear weapons in the event it appears likely to lose a conventional war. The tension between Russia and the United States over Ukraine's attempt to join NATO is an example of this dynamic. On 24 February 2022 (23 February in the United States) Russia launched an invasion of Ukraine to preempt any possibility of a NATO penumbra enabling the country to slip out of Russia's sphere of influence.[79] The United States has explicitly ruled out military intervention on behalf of Ukraine.[80]

The next fold of a state's sphere of influence consists of one or more junior partners in a mutual security partnership (often, but not always, in the form of a formal bilateral or multilateral alliance) of which the dominant state, reflecting its status as the predominant power, is the sole general or managing partner. The junior partners are less powerful states that have shared vital national interests with the senior, more powerful state and the arrangement reflects the mutual security interdependence of the parties. The junior partners voluntarily agree to a limited subordination of their sovereignty and independence (limited to matters directly related to the rival state against which the alliance is directed) in deference to the senior partner in return for a security guarantee underwritten by the senior partner. The dominant state is willing to underwrite such a security guarantee because the alliance strengthens its position with respect to the rival state which the alliance seeks to counterbalance and deter. The dominant state and its junior partners, to safeguard shared vital national interests, are prepared to wage war using conventional weapons against the target rival state. And the nuclear option, certainly with respect to tactical nuclear weapons, is implicitly on the table, particularly if nuclear weapons of the senior partner are stationed in one or more junior member states. NATO is an example of such a formal alliance, while the US–Israel "special relationship" based on declaratory statements arguably is an example of an informal strategic partnership.

The last fold of a state's sphere of influence is represented by an opaque security penumbra projected over one or more client states voluntarily seeking the protection of a powerful patron state. Usually, the client state is militarily weak and does not make a significant difference in the military power balance. However, the client state may have other assets of value to the patron state such as a strategic location or scarce natural resources (oil and gas). Pakistan offers China a land corridor to the energy rich Persian Gulf and port facilities on the Arabian Sea. Saudi Arabia offers the United States control over access to its oil and gas resources. Clients subordinate their sovereignty, independence, and vital national interests in deference to the patron. The patron–client relationship is consensual and contingent—either party may withdraw from the relationship at any time—and, not surprisingly, fickleness is inherent in such an arrangement of convenience. Egypt, which controls the Suez Canal, is an example of a client state which first sought the Soviet Union as a patron, and subsequently (after its humiliating defeat in the June 1967 War with Israel) turned to the United States as a patron. It is unlikely that a patron state will embark on a major conventional war with a rival state to protect a client; instead, it is more likely to settle for a localized, proxy war to ensure that the military action is contained and does not lead to an escalatory spiral. On the other hand, there is a risk that the patron state may be sucked in a quagmire. The decade-long Vietnam War (1963–1973) is an example of the United States being drawn into a long proxy war on behalf of its client.

Beyond the sphere of influence is a layer representing a zone of neutrality separating rival spheres of influence. The neutral zone is important because within this zone some states may tilt toward the powerful state or the rival state, while other states may strive to be strictly neutral. During the Cold War, India, albeit at different times, was an example of all three. Until 1962, India tried to be strictly neutral between the US and Soviet Union. Then, after the Sino-Indian War of 1962, India tilted toward the United States and by 1971, in the run-up to the Indo-Pak War of that year, tilted toward the Soviet Union. It is unlikely that a powerful state will go to war on behalf of a weak state in a neutral zone.

The final layer of the security envelope is represented by the global commons—the open seas and waterways and the open skies—that are available to all states as a means of connectivity. Given the voluntary nature of customary international law, this connectivity, most familiarly known as freedom of navigation—cannot be taken for granted. Hence, powerful states almost always will be willing to enforce their freedom of navigation rights by military means if necessary. Indeed, a state's connectivity can be viewed as the security thread that ties its security envelope tightly together.

## Notes

1. Of course, if there are no likely external threats to the state's continuing existence as a viable entity, grand strategy then may morph from an insurance plan into a growth plan to seize opportunities to enhance and expand the sustainable scope of the state (such as annexing additional territory) or sphere of influence (such as additional client states). Opting for expansion beyond the existing borders or sphere of influence of the state assumes that the domestic situation (a) is satisfactory but can be materially improved by such expansion, or (b) is perilous (for example, indefensible borders or lack of access to critical natural resources such as oil or water) and can only be made reasonably secure by such expansion. Arguably, Israel following its spectacular victory in the June 1967 War, and the United States after its comprehensive victory in the Cold War resulting in the 1991 demise of the Soviet Union, pivoted from insurance to growth in designing their respective grand strategies.
2. About 113 years ago, Aurobindo Ackroyd Ghose (later known as Sri Aurobindo), one of the fathers of Indian nationalism, wrote an illuminating article explaining the nature of nationalism as the indissoluble bond between the state and its people. See Sri Aurobindo, "The Country and Nationalism," in *On Nationalism: Selected Writings and Speeches* (Pondicherry, India: Sri Aurobindo Ashram Press, 1996), 488–490, and http://surasa.net/aurobindo/on_nation/country.htm. For an interesting discussion of the continuing challenge of the United States to forge a unique, unifying identity that transcends all other identities of all other political units see Jill Lapore, "A New Americanism: Why a Nation Needs a National Story," *Foreign Affairs*, 5 February 2019, https://www.foreignaffairs.com/articles/united-states/2019-02-05/new-americanism-nationalism-jill-lepore. Israel's current Basic Law on the nation-state, passed on 19 July 2018, attempts to codify the claims that (a) the identity of (i) the Jewish People everywhere is vested exclusively in and bound to the territory, sovereignty and independence of the State of Israel; and (ii) the State of Israel is bound exclusively to the Land of Israel and the Jewish People in the Land of Israel; and (b) the State of Israel's sovereignty and independence is exercised exclusively on behalf of the Jewish People in the Land of Israel, who exclusively hold the rights to the State of Israel's territorial integrity, sovereignty and independence. For the text of the law, see "Basic Law: Israel—The Nation State of the Jewish People," https://knesset.gov.il/laws/special/eng/BasicLawNationState.pdf. For some of the issues raised by this formulation of nationalism, see David M. Halbfinger and Isabel Kershner, "Israeli Law Declares the Country 'the Nation-State of the Jewish People'," *New York*

*Times*, 19 July 2018, https://www.nytimes.com/2018/07/19/world/middleeast/israel-law-jews-arabic.html.

3. The state's apex governing institutions are the custodians of this sovereignty on behalf of the people. Accordingly, in extremis, the people may decide to withdraw their consent to the trusteeship of existing governing institutions and establish new governing institutions to act as the successor custodians of the sovereignty of the state.
4. US Department of State, Bureau of Intelligence and Research, "Fact Sheet: Independent States in the World, February 15, 2019," https://www.state.gov/s/inr/rls/4250.htm.
5. A state ignores this reality of limited resources at its peril. Philip II of Spain trusted that God would provide what Spain lacked in order to further God's plans (which was the same as Spain's grand strategy): "I trust that, because he has removed other worse obstacles, He will remove this one too and give me the means to sustain my kingdoms, so they will not be lost." Quoted in Geoffrey Parker, "The Making of Strategy in Habsburg Spain: Philip II's 'Bid for Mastery,' 1556–1598," in Williamson Murray, MacGregor Knox and Alvin Bernstein (editors), *The Making of Grand Strategy: Rulers, States, and War* (Cambridge: Cambridge University Press, 1994), 129.
6. Thomas Hobbes in his magnum opus, *Leviathan*, which was published in 1651, first articulated the conception of anarchy in the political world: "[I]n all times kings and persons of sovereign authority, *because of their independency* [emphasis added], are in continual jealousies, and in the state and posture of gladiators, having their weapons pointing, and their eyes fixed on one another; that is, their forts, garrisons, and guns upon the frontiers of their kingdoms, and continual spies upon their neighbours, which is a posture of war." See Thomas Hobbes, *Leviathan* (University of Adelaide, ebook edition 2016), https://ebooks.adelaide.edu.au/h/hobbes/thomas/h68l/chapter13.html. Anarchy is also the necessary and sufficient condition of the political world in the theoretical framework of leading realist international relations scholars such as Hans Morgenthau, *Politics Among Nations: The Struggle for Power and Peace, Fifth Edition* (New York: Alfred A. Knopf, 1973), 27–33; Kenneth N. Waltz, *Theory of International Politics* (New York: McGraw-Hill, 1979), 79–106; and John J. Mearsheimer, *The Tragedy of Great Power Politics* (New York: W. W. Norton, 2001), 29–54.
7. Thus, anarchy arguably is a condition of the political world that reflects the conscious choice of states. Unlike diversity and scarcity, which are natural conditions which states cannot change, anarchy reflects the deliberate and considered decision of states not to subordinate their individual sovereignty to a higher political unit such as a single supranational state.

8. See "Obituary: J. Robert Oppenheimer, Atom Bomb Pioneer, Dies," *New York Times*, 18 February 1967, https://archive.nytimes.com/www.nytimes.com/learning/general/onthisday/bday/0422.html.
9. Currently 9 states have such nuclear weapons of mass destruction: the United States, Russia, China, the United Kingdom, France, Israel, India, Pakistan, and North Korea. Of these, only Israel has refused to officially declare or acknowledge its nuclear weapons status. South Africa previously had nuclear weapons but made the political decision to destroy them in conjunction with the transfer of power from the minority white apartheid government to the majority black government. Japan and Germany have accumulated significant amounts of nuclear fissile material to make nuclear weapons very quickly but have not made the political decision to do so. Iran has the capability to accumulate nuclear fissile material to make nuclear weapons but has agreed under the terms of the JCPOA to pursue a supervised, time-bound restricted nuclear energy program for civilian purposes only. See Hans M. Christensen and Robert S. Norris, "Status of World Nuclear Forces, November 2018," Federation of American Scientists, https://fas.org/issues/nuclear-weapons/status-world-nuclear-forces/. For a discussion of the unique case of South Africa, see Joseph Cirincione et al., *Deadly Arsenals: Tracking Weapons of Mass Destruction* (Washington, DC: Carnegie Endowment for International Peace, 2002), 359–367, and Uri Friedman, "Why One President Gave Up His Country's Nukes," *Atlantic*, 9 September 2017, https://www.theatlantic.com/international/archive/2017/09/north-korea-south-africa/539265/. For Japan and Germany nuclear fissile material stocks see International Panel on Fissile Materials, "2017 Civilian Plutonium Declarations Submitted to IAEA, 19 September 2018," http://fissilematerials.org/blog/2018/09/civilian_plutonium_infcir.html. For a summary of the Joint Comprehensive Plan of Action (JCPOA), see The White House, "Key Excerpts of the Joint Comprehensive Plan of Action (JCPOA), July 14, 2015," https://obamawhitehouse.archives.gov/the-press-office/2015/07/14/key-excerpts-joint-comprehensive-plan-action-jcpoa.
10. See Sri Aurobindo, *Savitri*, 1999 electronic edition, Book I, Canto I, lines 23–28, http://savitrithepoem.com/b1c1.html.
11. Twice in the twentieth century, nuclear armed adversaries came perilously close to having to make the decision to use nuclear weapons—the Cuban missile crisis of 1962 between the United States and Soviet Union, and the 1999 mini-war between India and Pakistan over Kargil in the Indian-administered area of Kashmir. In both cases the adversaries stepped back from the nuclear precipice. For the turning point of the Cuban missile crisis see Ernest R. May and Philip D. Zelikow (editors), *The Kennedy Tapes: Inside the White House During the Cuban Missile Crisis, the Concise*

*Edition* (New York: W. W. Norton, 2002), 297–314. For a discussion of the Kargil episode see Scott D. Sagan and Kenneth N. Waltz, *The Spread of Nuclear Weapons: A Debate Renewed* (New York: W. W. Norton, 2003), 88–124.

12. The Treaty on the Non-Proliferation of Nuclear Weapons (NPT), signed on 1 July 1968, reflects the attempt to restrain the spread of nuclear weapons. For the text of the treaty see United Nations, Office of Disarmament Affairs, "Treaty on the Non-Proliferation of Nuclear Weapons," https://www.un.org/disarmament/wmd/nuclear/npt/text.

    According to the American interpretation of the treaty, what is not explicitly prohibited is implicitly permitted and, therefore, a non-nuclear weapons state may develop a nuclear weapons capability under international safeguards but could not produce, acquire or control nuclear weapons. If a non-nuclear weapons state that had developed the capability to produce nuclear weapons were to make a decision to produce such weapons, it would have to withdraw from the treaty prior to commencing production. See United States Senate Committee on Foreign Relations, *Nonproliferation Treaty: Hearings Before the Committee on Foreign Relations, United States Senate, Ninetieth Congress, Second Session* (Washington, DC: US Government Printing Office, 1968), 3–13, 27–29, 38–39, 43–45, and 64–66, https://babel.hathitrust.org/cgi/pt?id=uc1.$b643615;view=1up;seq=5. The International Court of Justice, the Hague, at the request of the UN General Assembly, issued an advisory opinion on 8 July 1996 affirming the legality of the use of nuclear weapons in connection with a state's inherent right of self-defense. See International Court of Justice, *Legality of the Threat or Use of Nuclear Weapons, Advisory Opinion of 8 July 1996, I.C.J. Reports, 1996, p. 226*, https://www.icj-cij.org/files/case-related/95/095-19960708-ADV-01-00-EN.pdf.
13. For two radically different visions of the path to an imagined world-state see Hans Morgenthau, *Politics Among Nations*, 479–515, and Sri Aurobindo, "The Ideal of Human Unity," in *The Human Cycle, The Ideal of Human Unity, and War and Self-Determination, Volume 25* (Pondicherry: Sri Aurobindo Ashram, 1997), 279–579, https://www.sriaurobindoashram.org/sriaurobindo/writings.php.
14. William Shakespeare in his play *Hamlet*, written and presented about 1599, conveys this sense of man's limited knowledge: "There Are More Things in Heaven and Earth …/ Than Are Dreamt of in Your Philosophy." See William Shakespeare, *The Tragedy of Hamlet, Prince of Denmark* (New York: Washington Square Press, 1992), Act I, Scene V, lines 187–188. The concept of uncertainty stretches as far back as approximately 1500 B.C. in ancient Indian hymns of the *Rig Veda* which imagine the possibility that not even god is omniscient: "The creation, whence it came to be, whether it was made or not – he who is its overseer in the

highest heaven, he surely knows. Or if he does not know ...?" See Ainslie T. Embree (editor), *Sources of Indian Tradition, Second Edition, Volume One: From the Beginning to 1800* (New York: Columbia University Press, 1988), 21.

15. An example of strategic myopia resulting from an intense focus on the present is the headlong rush of the George W. Bush administration to launch an invasion and occupation of Iraq to ensure immediate and permanent regime change. See Bob Woodward, *Plan of Attack* (New York: Simon & Shuster, 2004). An example of strategic patience that flows from a long-term perspective is the willingness of the People's Republic of China under the leadership of Mao Tse-tung to defer the realization of the unification of Taiwan with mainland China. See Henry Kissinger, *On China* (New York: Penguin Press, 2011). The Government of Israel's desire immediately following Israel's victory in the June 1967 War to annex Jerusalem and establish settlements throughout the Land of Israel (Eretz Israel) to restore its control over the area considered the Jewish State's historical, biblical patrimony reflects its fixation on resurrecting and recreating a Jewish empire that last existed about 2500 years ago. See Gershom Gorenberg, *The Accidental Empire: Israel and the Birth of the Settlements, 1967–1977* (New York: Henry Holt, 2006).
16. For a thoughtful primer on developing a historical perspective, see Richard E. Neustadt and Ernest R. May, *Thinking in Time: The Uses of History for Decision-Makers* (New York: Simon & Shuster, 1986).
17. Edward Hallett Carr, *What Is History?* (New York: Random House, 1961), 142.
18. Henry Kissinger, *Diplomacy* (New York: Simon & Shuster, 1994), 832–835.
19. See John A. McCary, "The Anbar Awakening: An Alliance of Incentives," *The Washington Quarterly*, vol. 32, no. 1, January 2009, 43–59, https://csis-prod.s3.amazonaws.com/s3fs-public/legacy_files/files/publication/twq09januarymccary.pdf. Also see TNN et al., "Uri Terror Attack: 17 Killed, 19 Injured in Strike on Army Camp," *Times of India*, 30 September 2016, https://timesofindia.indiatimes.com/india/Uri-terror-attack-Indian-Army-camp-attacked-in-Jammu-and-Kashmir-17-killed-19-injured/articleshow/54389451.cms, and Vivek Chadha, Rumel Dahiya et al., "Issue Briefs: Uri, Surgical Strikes and International Reactions, 4 October 2016," Institute for Defence Studies and Analyses (IDSA), https://idsa.in/issuebrief/uri-surgical-strikes-and-international-reactions_041016. For state use of covert assassination teams, see Serge Schmemann, "Israelis Criticize Netanyahu Over Assassination Attempt," *New York Times*, 6 October 1997, https://archive.nytimes.com/www.nytimes.com/library/world/100697israel-hamas.html, and Paul McGeough, *Kill Khalid: The Failed Mossad Assassination of Khalid Mishal and the Rise*

*of Hamas* (New York: New Press, 2009). On the killing of Osama bin Laden see The White House, "Remarks by the President on Osama Bin Laden, May 2, 2011," https://obamawhitehouse.archives.gov/blog/2011/05/02/osama-bin-laden-dead. For efforts to overthrow hostile regimes such as the CIA organized coups in Iran in 1953 and Guatemala in 1954, see Stephen Kinzer, *All the Shah's Men: An American Coup and the Roots of Middle East Terror* (Hoboken, NJ: John Wiley, 2003), and Nick Cullather, *Secret History: The CIA's Classified Account of It's Operations in Guatemala, 1952–1954* (Stanford, CA: Stanford University Press, 1999). For the key underlying official documents on US orchestration of the Iran coup, see US Department of State, Office of the Historian, *Foreign Relations of the United States [FRUS], 1952–1954, Iran, 1951–1954, Planning and Implementation of Operation TPAJAX, March–August 1953*, (Documents no. 169–308), https://history.state.gov/historicaldocuments/frus1951-54Iran/ch3. For the official CIA history of the Iran coup, see Daniel Siegel and Malcolm Byrne (editors), "CIA Declassifies More of 'Zendabad Shah!'—Internal Study of 1953 Iran Coup," (Briefing Book no. 618), 12 February 2018, National Security Archives at The George Washington University, https://nsarchive.gwu.edu/briefing-book/iran/2018-02-12/cia-declassifies-more-zendebad-shah-internal-study-1953-iran-coup.

20. For the ranking of countries by GDP calculated on the basis of purchasing power parity (which adjusts nominal GDP for exchange rate and cost of living in US dollar terms) see Central Intelligence Agency (CIA), *World Factbook*, https://www.cia.gov/the-world-factbook/. An alternative metric—GDP per capita—indicates that the United States with a GDP per capita of $62,530 (2019) outranks China ($16,117) by a wide margin. However, as an indicator of relative latent power such a metric is useless as it yields nonsensical results. For example, in 2019, on a GDP per capita basis, the United States was outranked by such countries as: Qatar, Luxembourg, Singapore, Ireland, Norway, United Arab Emirates, and Switzerland. See CIA, *World Factbook*.
21. In a speech on 16 April 1953 before the American Society of Newspaper Editors, President Dwight D. Eisenhower highlights the cruel dilemma faced by decision-makers with regard to the proper balance between spending on defense and addressing pressing domestic economic needs: "Every gun that is made, every warship launched, every rocket fired signifies, in the final sense, a theft from those who hunger and are not fed, those who are cold and are not clothed." See "April 16, 1953: Chance for Peace" in "Presidential Speeches: Dwight D. Eisenhower Presidency," Miller Center at University of Virginia, https://millercenter.org/the-presidency/presidential-speeches/april-16-1953-chance-peace.

22. Knowledge is that which is known; education is the diffusion of knowledge among the people; innovation is the expansion of the body of knowledge and its applications; and efficiency is the optimal use of scarce resources for clearly defined purposes. Of course, these four facets of technology are embedded to varying degrees in all forms of power, not just military power.
23. For an assessment of the damage that covert cyber operations could inflict on the US economy, see the Council of Economic Advisors, *The Cost of Malicious Activity to the U.S. Economy, February 2018*, https://www.whitehouse.gov/wp-content/uploads/2018/02/The-Cost-of-Malicious-Cyber-Activity-to-the-U.S.-Economy.pdf.
24. See Howard Jones, *Crucible of Power: A History of American Foreign Relations to 1913* (Wilmington, DE: S R Books, 2002), 63–68.
25. See Patrick J. Hearden, *Roosevelt Confronts Hitler: America's Entry into World War II* (DeKalb, IL: Northern Illinois University, 1987), 174–182. See also, US State Department, Office of the Historian, "Economic Measures by the United States Affecting Trade with Japan," in *Papers Relating to the Foreign Relations of the United States, Japan, 1931–1941, Volume II*, https://history.state.gov/historicaldocuments/frus1931-41v02/comp4.
26. The White House, "Statement from the President on the Reimposition of United States Sanctions with Respect to Iran, August 6, 2018," https://www.whitehouse.gov/briefings-statements/statement-president-reimposition-united-states-sanctions-respect-iran/; and "Executive Order Reimposing Certain Sanctions Related to Iran, August 6, 2018," https://www.whitehouse.gov/presidential-actions/executive-order-reimposing-certain-sanctions-respect-iran/.
27. The Marshall Plan is the rubric used to refer to the foreign aid program for Europe proposed by Secretary of State George C. Marshall in his speech at Harvard on 5 June 1947. See "Speech by George C. Marshall, 'European Initiative Essential to Economic Recovery', June 5, 1947," in "Truman the Marshall Plan Research File" at the Harry S. Truman Presidential Library and Museum, https://www.trumanlibrary.org/whistlestop/study_collections/marshall/large/documents/index.php?documentid=8-7&pagenumber=1. For further background on this seminal speech, see "The Marshall Plan Speech," George C. Marshall Foundation, https://www.marshallfoundation.org/marshall/the-marshall-plan/marshall-plan-speech/.
28. See Kevin A. O'Brien, "Interfering with Civil Society: CIA and KGB Covert Action During the Cold War," in Loch K. Johnson and James J. Wirtz (editors), *Intelligence and National Security: The Secret World of Spies, An Anthology, Second Edition* (New York and Oxford: Oxford University Press, 2008), 267–280. Covert influence

operations designed to sway public opinion and elections in a target state have a long history. For example, the CIA played a major role in the 1948 Italian elections to defeat Communists and promote the Christian Democratic Party, and similarly Russia is alleged to have made a major effort to swing the 2016 presidential election against the Democratic Party candidate Hillary Clinton and tilt it in favor of the Republican candidate, Donald J. Trump. See Peter Kihss, "C.I.A. Funding in Europe Said to Go Back 3 Decades," *New York Times*, 7 January 1976, https://www.nytimes.com/1976/01/07/archives/cia-funding-in-europe-said-to-go-back-3-decades.html, and Jane Meyer, "How Russia Helped Swing the Election for Trump," *New Yorker*, 1 October 2018, https://www.newyorker.com/magazine/2018/10/01/how-russia-helped-to-swing-the-election-for-trump. For a detailed discussion of the controversial 2016 Presidential election tampering allegations, see Greg Miller, *The Apprentice: Trump, Russia and the Subversion of American Democracy* (New York: Harper Collins, 2018). State funded media non-governmental organizations such as Radio Free Europe/Radio Liberty (US), RT (Russia), BBC (UK), and Al-Jazeera (Qatar) reflect overt yet subtle and sophisticated efforts to shape public opinion in target states.

29. Sir Harold Nicholson, *Diplomacy, Third Edition* (Oxford: Oxford University Press, 1969), 3–4.
30. For President Barack Obama's acknowledgment of the critical role of diplomacy in dealing with the Iran nuclear issue, see The White House, "Statement by the President on Iran, July 14, 2015," https://obamawhitehouse.archives.gov/the-press-office/2015/07/14/statement-president-iran. For a detailed examination of President Obama's diplomacy on the Iran nuclear issue see Trita Parsi, *Losing an Enemy: Obama, Iran, and the Triumph of Diplomacy* (New Haven: Yale University Press, 2017) and *A Single Roll of the Dice: Obama's Diplomacy with Iran* (New Haven: Yale University Press, 2012).
31. See telegram "The Minister in Saudi Arabia (Childs) to the Secretary of State, 4 December 1947" (Document no. 932) in US Department of State, Office of the Historian, *Foreign Relations of the United States [FRUS], 1947, The Near East and Africa, Volume V*, https://history.state.gov/historicaldocuments/frus1947v05/d932.
32. See "Memorandum of Conversation, December 10, 1971" (Document no. 274) in *FRUS, 1969–1976, Volume XI, South Asia Crisis, 1971*, https://history.state.gov/historicaldocuments/frus1969-76v11/d274.
33. See "Telegram, George Kennan to George Marshall [Long Telegram], February 22, 1946," in "Harry S. Truman Administration File, Elsey Papers," Truman Library, https://www.trumanlibrary.org/whistlestop/study_collections/coldwar/documents/pdf/6-6.pdf.

34. See *FRUS, 1969–1976, Volume XVII, China, 1969–1972, China, October 1971–February 1972* (Document no. 161–204), https://history.state.gov/historicaldocuments/frus1969-76v17/ch4?start=1.
35. Hans Morgenthau, *Politics of Nations*, 519.
36. See telegram "The Ambassador in Korea (Muccio) to the Secretary of State, 24 June 1950" (Document no. 59) and "Intelligence Estimate Prepared by the Estimates Group, Office of Intelligence Research, Department of State, June 25, 1950" (Document no. 82) in *FRUS, 1950, Korea, Volume VII*, https://history.state.gov/historicaldocuments/frus1950v07/d59 and https://history.state.gov/historicaldocuments/frus1950v07/d82. See also speech of Secretary of State Dean Acheson to the National Press Club on 12 January 1950 that omitted South Korea from US defense perimeter in Asia, "Crisis in Asia—An Examination of U.S. Policy, Remarks by Secretary Acheson," in *Department of State Bulletin, 23 January 1950*, 111–118, https://babel.hathitrust.org/cgi/pt?id=umn.31951001228437o;view=1up;seq=109, and "Memorandum by the Assistant Secretary of State for Far Eastern Affairs (Rusk) to the Under Secretary of State (Webb), May 2, 1950" (Document no. 31) *FRUS, 1950, Korea, Volume VII*, https://history.state.gov/historicaldocuments/frus1950v07/d31.
37. See "Memorandum of a Conference with the President, White House, Washington, October 29, 1956" (Document no. 411) and "Message from President Eisenhower to Prime Minister Eden, October 30, 1956" (Document no. 418) in *FRUS, 1955–1957, Suez Crisis, July 26–December 31, 1956, Volume XVI*, https://history.state.gov/historicaldocuments/frus1955-57v16/d411, and https://history.state.gov/historicaldocuments/frus1955-57v16/d418.
38. Swami Prabhavananda and Christopher Isherwood (translators), *Bhagavad-Gita* (New York: Barnes & Noble, 1995), 3–6. What follows is Lord Krishna's eloquently profound response.
39. John Kerry's testimony before the Senate Foreign Relations Committee on 22 April 1971 conveys the profound loss of will to continue to fight in Vietnam: "[H]ow do you ask a man to be the last man to die in Vietnam? How do you ask a man to be the last man to die for a mistake?" See United States Senate Committee on Foreign Relations, *Legislative Proposals Relating to the War in Southeast Asia: Hearings Before the Committee on Foreign Relations, United States Senate, Ninety-second Congress, First Session* (Washington, DC: US Government Printing Office, 1971), 180–210, https://babel.hathitrust.org/cgi/pt?id=umn.31951d03524771l;view=1up;seq=3. Also see President Richard M. Nixon's pivotal speech on his decision to seek an end to American involvement in the war in Vietnam, "January 25, 1972:

Address to the Nation on Plan for Peace in Vietnam," in "Presidential Speeches: Richard Nixon Presidency," Miller Center at University of Virginia, https://millercenter.org/the-presidency/presidential-speeches/january-25-1972-address-nation-plan-peace-vietnam.

40. See for example, "Yemen Conflict: How Bad Is the Humanitarian Crisis?" *BBC News*, 28 March 2017, https://www.bbc.com/news/world-middle-east-34011187; and Amira Haas, "2,279 cal per Person: How Israel Made Sure Gaza Didn't Starve," *Haaretz*, 17 October 2012, https://www.haaretz.com/.premium-israel-s-gaza-quota-2-279-calories-a-day-1.5193157.
41. See International Crisis Group, "Yemen," https://www.crisisgroup.org/middle-east-north-africa/gulf-and-arabian-peninsula/yemen; Associated Press, "Senate Passes Resolution to End US Support for Saudi War in Yemen," *Guardian (UK)*, 13 March 2019, https://www.theguardian.com/us-news/2019/mar/13/senate-vote-war-yemen-saudi-arabia; and Congressional Research Service, "Yemen: Civil War and Regional Intervention, 24 August 2018," https://crsreports.congress.gov/product/pdf/R/R43960.
42. As of December 31, 2018, the Arab population under the control of the State of Israel is estimated to be about 6.6 million, of whom about 1.9 million are citizens of Israel (including about 0.3 million Arabs in East Jerusalem who are permanent residents but who have not applied for citizenship). The Jewish population under the control of Israel is about 6.7 million, all of whom are citizens. See Israel Central Bureau of Statistics, *Monthly Bulletin of Statistics*, February 2019, https://www.cbs.gov.il/he/publications/doclib/2019/yarhon0219/b1.pdf and World Bank, "West Bank and Gaza, Data," https://data.worldbank.org/country/west-bank-and-gaza. The Israel CBS does not include the Arabs of West Bank and Gaza in the population statistics. The Arab population in West Bank and Gaza, about 4.7 million people in 2017 according to the World Bank, are not considered to be citizens of Israel. Since Israel's establishment in 1948 until 1966, Israeli Arabs were subject to martial law under the "state of emergency" regulations carried over from the pre-independence British Mandate of Palestine. See Ofer Aderet, "When the Israeli Right Was the One Fighting for Arabs' Freedom," *Haaretz*, 3 December 2016," https://www.haaretz.com/israel-news/.premium-when-the-israeli-right-was-the-one-fighting-for-arabs-freedom-1.5468898. Since the June 1967 War, the areas that fell under Israeli control as a result of the war are subject to the authority of the Israeli Defense Forces military administration (East Jerusalem, annexed immediately after the war, is under civil administration but East Jerusalem Arabs have not applied for Israeli citizenship). See Coordination of Government

Activities in the Territories (COGAT), http://www.cogat.mod.gov.il/en/about/Pages/default.aspx; and B'Tselem, "Military Courts," https://www.btselem.org/military_courts.

43. In 1962, China and India fought a bitter war over disputed borders, which India lost. As a result, China has retained possession of the Aksai Chin area of the Ladakh region in Kashmir. Pakistan launched three wars against India—in 1948, 1965, and 1999—in failed attempts to acquire all or part of Indian-controlled Kashmir. India claims that Pakistan covertly supports jihadi groups seeking the reversion of Indian held Kashmir to Pakistan's eventual control.
44. The peace treaties signed with Egypt and Jordan respectively implicitly recognize Israel's current boundaries, as both Egypt and Jordan carefully define their borders in such a manner as to exclude and renounce any Egyptian claims to Israeli controlled Gaza and any Jordanian claims to Israeli controlled West Bank and Jerusalem. See Israel Ministry of Foreign Affairs, "Peace Treaty Between Israel and Egypt, March 26, 1979," https://mfa.gov.il/MFA/ForeignPolicy/Peace/Guide/Pages/Israel-Egypt%20Peace%20Treaty.aspx; and "Israel-Jordan Peace Treaty, 26 October 1994," https://mfa.gov.il/mfa/foreignpolicy/peace/guide/pages/israel-jordan%20peace%20treaty.aspx.
45. Quoted in Kori N. Schake and Judith S. Yaphe, *The Strategic Implications of a Nuclear-Armed Iran, McNair Paper no. 64* (Washington, DC: National Defense University, 2001), v, https://apps.dtic.mil/dtic/tr/fulltext/u2/a421941.pdf.
46. The White House, "Introduction," in *The National Security Strategy of the United States of America*, September 2002, https://www.state.gov/documents/organization/63562.pdf.
47. The White House, "Presidential Proclamation on Declaring a National Emergency Concerning the Southern Border of the United States, 15 February 2019," https://www.whitehouse.gov/presidential-actions/presidential-proclamation-declaring-national-emergency-concerning-southern-border-united-states/. See also Caitlin Dickerson, "Border at 'Breaking Point' as More than 76,000 Unauthorized Migrants Cross in a Month," *New York Times*, 5 March 2019, https://www.nytimes.com/2019/03/05/us/border-crossing-increase.html.
48. See The U.S. National Archives and Records Administration, "Japanese Relocation During World War II," https://www.archives.gov/education/lessons/japanese-relocation; and "Transcript of Executive Order 9066: Resulting in Relocation of Japanese (1942)," https://www.ourdocuments.gov/doc.php?flash=false&doc=74&page=transcript. See also US Supreme Court decision in 1944 upholding the constitutionality of Japanese relocation, *Korematsu v. United States*, 323 U.S. 214, https://www.law.cornell.edu/supremecourt/text/323/214.

49. See "Telegram No. 959 From the Consulate General in Dacca to the Department of State, 28 March 1971, 0540Z" (Document no. 125) in *FRUS, 1969–1976, Volumr E-7, Documents on South Asia, 1969–1972*, https://history.state.gov/historicaldocuments/frus1969-76ve07/ch2, and Gary J. Bass, *The Blood Telegram: Nixon, Kissinger and a Forgotten Genocide* (New York: Alfred A. Knopf, 2013).
50. The Allies agreed to the transfer of the German minority populations at the Potsdam Conference in 1945. See "Orderly Transfer of German Populations" in "Protocol of the Proceedings of the Berlin [Potsdam] Conference, August 1, 1945" (Document no. 1383); and "Department of State Minutes, July 21, 1945," in *FRUS: Diplomatic Papers, The Conference of Berlin (The Potsdam Conference), 1945, Volume II*, https://history.state.gov/historicaldocuments/frus1945Berlinv02/d1383, and https://history.state.gov/historicaldocuments/frus1945Berlinv02/d710a-54. Also see R. M. Douglas, *Orderly and Humane: The Expulsion of the Germans After the Second World War* (New Haven: Yale, 2012), and Ian Connor, *Refugees and Expellees in Post-War Germany* (Manchester: University of Manchester Press, 2007).
51. See William Dalrymple, "The Great Divide: The Violent Legacy of Indian Partition," *New Yorker*, 29 June 2015, https://www.newyorker.com/magazine/2015/06/29/the-great-divide-books-dalrymple; and Nisid Hajari, *Midnight's Furies: The Deadly Legacy of India's Partition* (Boston and New York: Houghton Mifflin, 2015). Also see National Archives (UK), "The Road to Partition, 1939–1947," http://www.nationalarchives.gov.uk/education/resources/the-road-to-partition/.
52. In early 1949, Secretary of State George Marshall after meeting with Moshe Sharett, Israel's foreign minister, noted that according to the foreign minister, "In the opinion of the Israeli Government, it was out of the question to consider the possibility of repatriation of any substantial number of the refugees. The most logical solution was resettlement in the Arab countries, where so much land was available." See "Memorandum of Conversation, by the Secretary of State, March 22, 1949" (Document no. 544), in *FRUS, 1949, The Near East, South Asia, and Africa, Volume VI*, https://history.state.gov/historicaldocuments/frus1949v06/d544. In a statement to the Israeli Knesset on 15 June 1949, Moshe Sharett insisted: "A flood of returning Arabs is liable to blow up our State from within … A mass repatriation of refugees without peace with the neighboring countries would thus be an act of suicide on the part of Israel." See Israel Ministry of Foreign Affairs, https://mfa.gov.il/MFA/ForeignPolicy/MFADocuments/Yearbook1/Pages/2%20Statement%20to%20the%20Knesset%20by%20Foreign%20Minister%20Sha.aspx. Also see Benny Morris, *The Birth of the Palestinian Refugee Problem,*

*1947–1949* (Cambridge, UK: Cambridge University Press, 1989) and a subsequent reconsideration, *The Birth of the Palestinian Refugee Problem Revisited* (Cambridge, UK: Cambridge University Press, 2004).

53. The United Nations Relief and Works Agency (UNRWA) estimates (2018) there are about 5 million registered Palestinian refugees distributed as follows: Lebanon (450,000), Syria (438,000); West Bank (800,000); Gaza (1.4 million), and Jordan (2 million). Most of the Palestinian refugees in Jordan have been granted Jordanian citizenship. The Palestinian refugees in West Bank and Gaza have been under Israeli control since the end of the June 1967 war. See UNRWA, https://www.unrwa.org/where-we-work. For a contemporaneous US assessment of the Palestinian refugee issue, see "Memorandum by the Coordinator on Palestine Refugee Matters (McGhee) to the Secretary of State, April 22, 1949" (Document no. 608) and "Memorandum by the Coordinator on Palestine Refugee Matters (McGhee) to the Under Secretary of State (Webb), March 15, 1949" (Document no. 533) in *FRUS, 1949, The Near East, South Asia, and Africa, Volume VI*, https://history.state.gov/historicaldocuments/frus1949v06/d608, and https://history.state.gov/historicaldocuments/frus1949v06/d533.
54. See telegrams "The Ambassador in Turkey (Morgenthau) to the Secretary of State, July 10, 1915" (Document no. 1400) and "The Ambassador in Turkey (Morgenthau) to the Secretary of State, August 11, 1915" (Document no. 1406) in US Department of State, Office of the Historian, *Papers Relating to the Foreign Relations of the United States, 1915, Supplement, The World War*, https://history.state.gov/historicaldocuments/frus1915Supp/d1400, and https://history.state.gov/historicaldocuments/frus1915Supp/d1406. Also see Armenian National Institute, "Armenian Genocide," https://www.armenian-genocide.org/genocide.html; Mark Mowzer, "An Archive of Atrocities," *New York Review of Books*, 4 April 2019, https://www.nybooks.com/articles/2019/04/04/talat-pasha-archive-atrocities-armenia/; and John Kifner, "The Armenian Genocide of 1915: An Overview" undated in "Times Topics," *New York Times*, https://archive.nytimes.com/www.nytimes.com/ref/timestopics/topics_armeniangenocide.html.
55. United States Holocaust Memorial Museum, "Documenting Numbers of Victims of the Holocaust and Nazi Persecution," https://encyclopedia.ushmm.org/content/en/article/documenting-numbers-of-victims-of-the-holocaust-and-nazi-persecution; and Yad Vashem (Israel), "Protocols of the Wannsee Conference, January 20, 1942," https://www.yadvashem.org/docs/wannsee-conference-protocol.html.
56. Elisabeth Rosen, "The Vietnam War, as seen by the Victors," *Atlantic*, 16 April 2015, https://www.theatlantic.com/international/archive/2015/04/the-vietnam-war-as-seen-by-the-north-vietnamese/390627/.

57. See Neil Fleming, "South Africa's Reform Referendum Bares Emotions," *United Press International (UPI)*, 17 March 1992, https://www.upi.com/Archives/1992/03/17/South-Africas-reform-referendum-bares-emotions/7068700808400/; and "On this Day, 18 March 1992: South Africa Votes for Change," *BBC News*, 18 March 1992, http://news.bbc.co.uk/onthisday/hi/dates/stories/march/18/newsid_2524000/2524695.stm.
58. With respect to unlimited immigration of diaspora Jews into the State of Israel, see Israel Ministry of Foreign Affairs, "Law of Return 5710–1950, 5 July 1950," https://mfa.gov.il/mfa/mfa-archive/1950-1959/pages/law%20of%20return%205710-1950.aspx. As of year-end 2018, the estimated Jewish population in the United States is 6.9 million, all of whom are eligible to exercise the right of return (immigrate) to Israel. See Jewish Virtual Library, "Jewish Population in the United States by State," https://www.jewishvirtuallibrary.org/jewish-population-in-the-united-states-by-state.
59. Cited by Ferdinand Mount in his article on the British effort to exit the European Union, "Just get us out," *London Review of Books*, 7 March 2019, https://www.lrb.co.uk/2019/02/28/ferdinand-mount/just-get-us-out.
60. See "Constitution of the United States," at the U.S. National Archives and Records Administration, https://www.archives.gov/founding-docs/constitution.
61. For example, in the *Paquette Habana* case, the U.S. Supreme Court in 1900 held that international customary law was implicitly part of US law. See 175 U.S. 677 (1900), https://supreme.justia.com/cases/federal/us/175/677/. In *Hamdan v. Rumsfeld*, the U.S. Supreme Court in 2006 held that the Geneva Conventions, which the United States was a party to, was part of US law. See 548 U.S. 557 (2006), https://supreme.justia.com/cases/federal/us/548/557/. For a discussion of the role of Congress in shaping the nexus of domestic and international law, see Stephen P. Mulligan, "International Law and Agreements: Their Effect upon U.S. Laws, 19 September 2018," Congressional Research Service, https://fas.org/sgp/crs/misc/RL32528.pdf.
62. See "April 30, 1970: Address to the Nation on the Situation in Southeast Asia," in "Presidential Speeches: The Nixon Presidency," Miller Center, https://millercenter.org/the-presidency/presidential-speeches/april-30-1970-address-nation-situation-southeast-asia.

63. See Israel Ministry of Foreign Affairs, "Israel Cabinet Decision, 6 June 1982," https://mfa.gov.il/MFA/ForeignPolicy/MFADocuments/Yearbook6/Pages/3%20Israel%20Cabinet%20Decision-%206%20June%201982.aspx; "Cabinet communique on the entry of I.D.F. into west Beirut, 16 September 1982," https://mfa.gov.il/MFA/ForeignPolicy/MFADocuments/Yearbook6/Pages/77%20Cabinet%20communique%20on%20the%20entry%20of%20the%20IDF%20into.aspx; "Cabinet communique on the massacre at the Sabra and Shatilla camps, 19 September 1982," https://mfa.gov.il/MFA/ForeignPolicy/MFADocuments/Yearbook6/Pages/79%20Cabinet%20communique%20on%20the%20massacre%20at%20the%20Sabra.aspx; and "Report of the Commission of Inquiry into the Events at the Refugee Camps in Beirut, 8 February 1983," https://mfa.gov.il/MFA/ForeignPolicy/MFADocuments/Yearbook6/Pages/104%20Report%20of%20the%20Commission%20of%20Inquiry%20into%20the%20e.aspx. Also see Amir Oren, "With Ariel Sharon Gone, Israel Reveals the Truth About the 1982 Lebanon War," *Haaretz*, 17 September 2017, https://www.haaretz.com/israel-news/with-sharon-gone-israel-reveals-the-truth-about-the-lebanon-war-1.5451086.
64. Amy Kazmin and Farhan Bokhari, "India Carries Out 'Pre-Emptive' Air Strike on Pakistan Terror Camp," *Financial Times*, 26 February 2019, https://www.ft.com/content/7c158bbc-397a-11e9-b72b-2c7f526ca5d0.
65. See "March 24, 1999: Statement on Kosovo" in "Presidential Speeches: Bill Clinton Presidency," Miller Center, https://millercenter.org/the-presidency/presidential-speeches/march-24-1999-statement-kosovo.
66. See President George W. Bush's pair of speeches on the Iraq war decision: "March 17, 2003: Address to the Nation on Iraq" and "March 20, 2003: Address on the Start of War in Iraq" in "Presidential Speeches: George W. Bush Presidency," Miller Center, https://millercenter.org/the-presidency/presidential-speeches/march-17-2003-address-nation-iraq and https://millercenter.org/the-presidency/presidential-speeches/march-20-2003-address-start-iraq-war.
67. See Israel Ministry of Foreign Affairs, "Statement to the Knesset by Prime Minister Rabin, 3 June 1974," https://mfa.gov.il/MFA/ForeignPolicy/MFADocuments/Yearbook1/Pages/31%20Statement%20to%20the%20Knesset%20by%20Prime%20Minister%20Rabi.aspx.
68. See US Department of State, Office of the Historian, "Milestones in the History of U.S. Foreign Relations: Oil Embargo, 1973–1974," https://history.state.gov/milestones/1969-1976/oil-embargo.
69. See US Department of State, Office of the Historian, "Milestones in the History of U.S. Foreign Relations: Barbary Wars, 1801–1805 and 1815–1816," https://history.state.gov/milestones/1801-1829/barbary-wars; Donald R. Hickey, *The War of 1812: A Short History* (Urbana and Chicago: University of Illinois Press), 5–12; and Thomas G. Patterson,

J. Garry Clifford and Kenneth J. Hagan, *American Foreign Relations, A History—Since 1895, Volume II, Fifth Edition* (Boston and New York: Houghton Mifflin, 2000), 68–83.

70. Barbara W. Tuchman, *The Zimmerman Telegram* (New York: Ballantine Books, 1966), 88–106, 116–117 and 137–154. From the perspective of American public opinion, the German plan to entangle the United States in a border war with Mexico appeared plausible since the US Army was winding up a nearly year-long punitive expedition in Mexico against Pancho Villa, the renegade Mexican leader whose forces had mounted a spectacular cross-border raid on the town of Columbus, New Mexico.
71. See "Memorandum from the President's Special Counsel (Clifford) to President Truman, 8 March 1948" (Document no. 79) in *Foreign Relations of the United States, 1948, The Near East, South Asia, and Africa, Volume V, Part 2*, https://history.state.gov/historicaldocuments/frus1948v05p2/d79. Also see telegrams "The Acting Secretary of State to the Legation in Saudi Arabia, 12 December 1947" (Document no. 933) and "The Minister in Saudi Arabia (Childs) to Secretary of State, 15 December 1947" (Document no. 934) in *FRUS 1947, The Near East and Africa, Volume V*, https://history.state.gov/historicaldocuments/frus1947v05/d933; and https://history.state.gov/historicaldocuments/frus1947v05/d934.
72. See Israel Ministry of Foreign Affairs, "Exchange of Letters, Eisenhower-Ben-Gurion, 7–8 November 1956," https://mfa.gov.il/MFA/ForeignPolicy/MFADocuments/Yearbook1/Pages/9%20Exchange%20of%20Letters-%20Eisenhower-%20Ben-Gurion-%207-8.aspx; "Statement to the Knesset by Prime Minister Ben-Gurion, 7 November 1956," https://mfa.gov.il/MFA/ForeignPolicy/MFADocuments/Yearbook1/Pages/8%20Statement%20to%20the%20Knesset%20by%20Prime%20Minister%20Ben-G.aspx; and "Broadcast by President Eisenhower, 20 February 1957," https://mfa.gov.il/mfa/foreignpolicy/mfadocuments/yearbook1/pages/24%20broadcast%20by%20president%20eisenhower-%2020%20february.aspx.
73. The White House, "Remarks by the President on the Iran Nuclear Deal, 5 August 2015," https://obamawhitehouse.archives.gov/the-press-office/2015/08/05/remarks-president-iran-nuclear-deal. Also see, Israel Ministry of Foreign Affairs, "PM Netanyahu's Speech to a Joint Session of the US Congress, 3 March 2015," https://mfa.gov.il/MFA/PressRoom/2015/Pages/PM-Netanyahus-speech-to-Congress-3-March-2015.aspx; and American Israel Public Affairs Committee, "AIPAC Statement on Proposed Iran Nuclear Agreement, 15 July 2015," https://www.aipac.org/learn/resources/aipac-publications/publication?pubpath=PolicyPolitics/Press/AIPAC%20Statements/2015/07/AIPAC%20Statement%20on%20Proposed%20Iran%20Nuclear%20Agreement.

74. Sun-tzu, *The Art of War*, edited and translated by John Minford (New York: Penguin Books, 2003), 19.
75. Non-state actors located in another state are assumed to be under the control of such a state. Accordingly, the host state is held responsible for the actions of such non-state actors.
76. In the six months prior to the outbreak of the Korean War, the United States was publicly signaling that South Korea was not a vital national interest and the country lay outside the US defensive perimeter. The North Korean invasion across the 38th parallel dividing line triggered a dramatic change in America's perception of its vital national interests and led to the US decision to enter the Korean War. NSC 68, the National Security Council policy paper which embraced the domino theory suggesting that a communist threat in one country would inevitably lead to similar threats in nearby countries and therefore a communist threat anywhere was to be resisted, was in the process of being reviewed during this period, and the North Korean attack dispelled any hesitation with respect to the adoption of an expansive Cold War strategy of containment. See "A Report to the National Security Council - NSC 68, April 12, 1950," in "President's Secretary's Files, Truman Papers," Truman Library, https://www.trumanlibrary.org/whistlestop/study_collections/coldwar/documents/pdf/10-1.pdf.
77. Dale C. Copeland, *The Origins of Major War* (Ithaca and London: Cornell University Press, 2000), 20.
78. The concept of a national security envelope was highly developed in ancient India. For example, Kautilya (also known as Chanakya, about 350–275 B.C.), the advisor to King Chandragupta Maurya, wrote a treatise on politics and economics, *Arthashastra*, in which he outlines his idea of a circle of states and a "hub and spoke" security architecture. See "The Circle of States and Interstate Policy," in Ainslie T. Embree (editor), *Sources of Indian Tradition, Second Edition, Volume One: From the Beginning to 1800* (New York: Columbia University Press, 1988), 247–249. For a complete exposition, see Kautilya, *The Arthashastra*, edited and translated by L. N. Rangarajan (New Delhi: Penguin Books, 1992), 505–634.
79. Paul Sonne et al., "Russia Launches Attack on Ukraine, Biden Says," *Washington Post*, 24 February 2022, https://www.washingtonpost.com/world/2022/02/23/russia-ukraine-updates/.
80. The White House, "Remarks by President Biden on Russia's Unprovoked and Unjustified Attack on Ukraine," 24 February 2022, https://www.whitehouse.gov/briefing-room/speeches-remarks/2022/02/24/remarks-by-president-biden-on-russias-unprovoked-and-unjustified-attack-on-ukraine/.

CHAPTER 2

# Whither India's Grand Strategy?

India's grand strategy, a legacy of the British Raj, has shown remarkable continuity and stability, reflecting the immutable realities of geography and the fluctuating ebb and flow of its political, military, economic, and cultural power. The sphere of influence of British India was extensive and elastic: not only was the Indian Ocean considered an "Indian lake" stretching from the shores of East and South Africa to Burma and Siam, but the sphere of influence of British India also extended to the British protectorates in the Persian Gulf in west Asia as well as British India's protectorates of Nepal, Bhutan, and Sikkim, while its northern land frontiers with Tibet and Xinjiang (semi-autonomous provinces of a weak China) were deliberately ambiguous to suit the needs of the British Empire for strategic flexibility.[1] Yet continuity and stability can lead to ossification and rigidity. India's challenge in the twenty-first century, which it has yet to meet, is to reimagine, rethink, and recalibrate its legacy grand strategy in order to address a dramatically changing strategic universe in which it must operate. The Republic of India has six vital national interests with respect to which the Government of India (GOI) must make fundamental decisions: (1) preservation of the state's territorial integrity, (2) reformulation and reaffirmation of Indian national identity, (3) restatement and clarification of the geographic scope of India's sovereignty, (4) safeguarding India's independence while ensuring military and energy security, (5) establishment of India's rights with


S. Tata, *Reflections on Grand Strategy*,
https://doi.org/10.1007/978-981-19-3773-6_2

respect to freedom of navigation and connectivity in the global commons, particularly in the Indian Ocean region, and (6) assertion and acknowledgment of an exclusive sphere of influence. GOI must also clearly identify its principal state adversaries for the foreseeable future, realistically assess India's likely capabilities to counter such adversaries, and determine the appropriateness of other state security partners with converging vital national interests to ensure that the strategic calculus shifts decisively in India's favor.

## Which India?

At the heart of the Republic of India's conception as a state is geography. But the existential question is, which India? The question is critical because there are, in fact, two different geographic conceptions of India: (1) de facto India which encompasses only the territory that is under the ultimate administrative control of GOI, including territory with respect to which there are competing claims of sovereignty, principally Indian-administered union territories of Jammu & Kashmir and Ladakh in the northwest (also claimed by Pakistan as part of the erstwhile princely state of Kashmir) and Arunachal Pradesh in the northeast (also claimed by China as South Tibet); and (2) *aspirational* India which expansively embraces both the preceding de facto India as well as territory over which GOI does not exercise administrative control but with respect to which it nevertheless claims sovereignty, principally the areas of the erstwhile princely state of Kashmir occupied by (a) Pakistan since 1949 (referred to as Azad Kashmir and Gilgit-Baltistan) and (b) China since 1962 (Aksai Chin). New Delhi has been unwilling to decide between the two conceptions, hoping to muddle through. Arguably, *aspirational* India is a political fantasy as GOI lacks both the intention and the capability to strive for the realization of such an expansive claim of sovereignty. With respect to de facto India, it is assumed that GOI has both the intention and capability to enforce its sovereignty over the territory presumed to be under its administrative control. Accordingly, de facto India is assumed to be militarily defensible, and that GOI would strive to ensure both its intention and capability to do so is unchallenged.

Although official GOI maps depict only *aspirational* India, in its actions (but not in its rhetoric) New Delhi endeavors to respect the boundaries of de facto India.[2] As a consequence, the supreme task of the government, the preservation of the territorial integrity of India, is deliberately ambiguous and unintentionally provocative. To insist on maintaining claims of sovereignty over territories that have not been under GOI control (for over 73 years in the case of Azad Kashmir and Gilgit-Baltistan and 60 years in the case of Aksai Chin) arouses suspicions (at least among adversaries) that New Delhi seeks territorial aggrandizement and leaves an opening for irresponsible irredentism and revanchism. Although GOI has been very careful in its actions to respect the reality of Pakistani control over Azad Kashmir and Gilgit-Baltistan, and Chinese control over Aksai Chin, its political leaders are less restrained in their rhetoric that leaves the inadvertent impression that GOI may be willing to use force in support of its claims of sovereignty over these areas. For example, on 6 August 2019, Shri Amit Shah, the Home Minister (second only to the Prime Minister in terms of power), stated in Parliament that he was prepared to die for the recovery of PoK and Aksai Chin.[3] Of course, a similar issue arises in connection with Pakistan's claims with respect to Indian-administered Kashmir and China's claims with respect to Indian-administered Arunachal Pradesh, fostering Indian suspicions with respect to Pakistani and Chinese territorial ambitions.

The boundaries of India must be clearly defined, under the effective administrative control of GOI, and militarily defensible. The development of a viable grand strategy is handicapped by the unwillingness of decision-makers in New Delhi to clarify the territorial boundaries of India. The gap between Indian rhetoric and action is unsustainable as it casts a shadow on the legitimacy of the territorial status quo. Simply put, imaginary borders can promise only illusory upsides but have very real downsides. Accordingly, New Delhi will have to speak truth to the people and (a) acknowledge that GOI has no intention to seek to assert a claim to sovereignty with respect to any portion of the erstwhile princely state of Kashmir currently under the administrative control of Pakistan or China, (b) admit that it is not possible to recover such territories either through persuasion or coercion, and declare that the de facto borders of India are the de jure borders of India.[4] The duty of GOI then becomes crystal clear—the preservation of the territorial integrity of the Republic of India means the defense of the area under GOI administration by virtue of the conversion of the state's de facto borders into its de jure borders.

A unilateral declaration by GOI that the territory of the Republic of India is delineated by the area under its administration does not depend upon an affirmative acknowledgment of India's borders by Pakistan or

China but does require their tacit acquiescence.[5] Ultimately, such acquiescence will be ensured by Indian power sufficient to deter any serious challenge to the country's territorial integrity. GOI must make a determination as to whether India has such capabilities to defend itself by itself. Obviously, any gap between intention and capability to defend the territorial integrity of India would have to be addressed.

## Indian National Identity

The forging of Indian national identity remains a work in progress.[6] While there are several domestic issues, primarily language and religion, that continue to challenge the core tenets of diversity and secularism, it is clear that the inability to find closure on the 1947 partition of British India makes Indian national identity incomplete. The unresolved final status of the erstwhile princely state of Kashmir, British India's largest Muslim majority princely state, is the embodiment of this incompleteness.

The 26 October 1947 decision of the Hindu ruler of Kashmir to have his kingdom, with a Muslim majority and a significant Hindu minority, accede to India was made reluctantly after an invasion by irregular jihadi forces from Pakistan under the covert leadership of regular Pakistani army officers forced his hand (as he preferred not to decide between opting for India or Pakistan in the hope of keeping his kingdom independent).[7] For GOI, under the leadership of Governor General Lord Mountbatten and Prime Minister Jawaharlal Nehru, Kashmir's accession validated and reaffirmed the core tenets of Indian national identity—diversity and secularism. The Government of Pakistan, under the leadership of Governor General Muhammad Ali Jinnah and Prime Minister Liaquat Ali Khan, violently rejected the legitimacy of Kashmir's accession to India as it violated the idea of Pakistan as the home of the Muslim people of the erstwhile British India. The ensuing war between India and Pakistan came to an inconclusive end on 1 January 1949 under the terms of a UN sponsored cease-fire agreement, which left about one-third of Kashmir under Pakistani control and about two-thirds of Kashmir under Indian control.[8] Despite two subsequent Pakistani attempts in 1965 and 1999 to use military force to wrest control of Indian-administered Kashmir, the status quo continues.

India has never made any attempt to recover Pakistani controlled portions of the erstwhile princely state of Kashmir. The reality is that GOI continues to struggle to integrate Indian-administered Kashmir (currently the union territories of Jammu & Kashmir, and Ladakh) with the Republic of India as a significant portion of Kashmir's Muslim population remains skeptical of India's commitment to diversity and secularism, so any irridentist attempt by GOI to expand the area under its control by wresting portions of Pakistani-administered Kashmir would only aggravate existing tensions.[9] Muslims are a minority in India as a whole (constituting an estimated 14.2 percent of the total population as of 2011). India currently has the third largest Muslim population in the world (after Indonesia and Pakistan) and is expected to have the world's largest Muslim population by 2050.[10] The unresolved legacy of Partition cannot become an obstacle in integrating India's Muslim population.[11]

Abandoning diversity and secularism would result in the loss of internal cohesion and risk the territorial integrity of the Republic of India. Although a significant segment of India's Hindus seems willing to be seduced by the siren song of Hindutva—majoritarian Hindu populism, minority demography can be expected to exert a countervailing pressure on nascent Hindu majoritarianism, and ultimately will strengthen diversity and secularism as fundamental aspects of Indian national identity. A majoritarian Hindu India in which disaffected non-Hindu minorities are second-class citizens (whether de facto or de jure) would be a diminished and insecure India. Currently, India has 6 states with non-Hindu majorities: Punjab, Arunachal Pradesh, Nagaland, Mizoram, Manipur, and Meghalaya.[12] In addition, India has 3 union territories—Lakshadweep Islands, Ladakh, and Jammu & Kashmir—with non-Hindu majorities. Islam, Christianity, Sikhism, Buddhism, Jainism, and Zoroastrianism have had a profound impact in the shaping of Indian national identity and cannot be marginalized, wished away, or ignored. India's non-Hindu states and territories are geo-strategically critical as they shield the core of Hindu majority states. Punjab, and Jammu & Kashmir share borders with Pakistan. Ladakh shares borders with Pakistan and China. Arunachal Pradesh shares borders with China, Bhutan, and Burma (also called Myanmar). Nagaland, Mizoram, and Manipur share borders with Burma. Meghalaya shares a border with Bangladesh. Lakshadweep Islands in the Arabian Sea are key to safeguarding western India's sea lines of communications (SLOCs). For India, embracing diversity and secularism as part of its national identity is not a choice but an existential necessity.[13]

## The Limits of Indian Sovereignty

India must finally come to closure on the 1947 partition of British India.[14] The political essence of Partition was that for India, as the successor to British India, sovereignty was bounded by and co-terminus with the area under the administrative control of the GOI. Above all, Partition constituted a *political* divorce, reflecting the demand of the Muslim League under the leadership of Muhammad Ali Jinnah, for a separate Pakistan comprising the Muslim majority provinces of British India.[15] In the process, Punjab and Bengal provinces were divided, with the Muslim majority areas opting to become part of Pakistan and the Hindu majority areas opting to remain as part of India. Kashmir represents the messy unfinished business of Partition as India and Pakistan could not agree on the terms of the division of the princely state (although both agreed that Kashmir, like all other princely states of British India, did not have the option to remain independent). The 1949 cease-fire line, now called the Line of Control, reflects the de facto partition of Kashmir. India gains nothing by denying the reality of Kashmir's division. Indian sovereignty needs to embrace the concept of "no fault" political divorce in the case of Kashmir. West Punjab and East Bengal did not want to remain with India, and their separation was accomplished through a political process. Azad Kashmir and Gilgit-Baltistan constitute the areas of Kashmir that did not want to be part of India and separation was achieved through war.[16] Just as India has accepted the reality of the division of Punjab and Bengal provinces, so too India must accept the reality of the division of the princely state of Kashmir.[17]

In 1962, as a result of its defeat in a border war with China, India lost Aksai Chin, a sparsely populated area of the Ladakh region of Kashmir.[18] In effect, the Chinese occupation and forcible takeover of Aksai Chin represented the second partition of Kashmir. GOI has never demonstrated any serious interest to regain the lost territory, although India continues to claim sovereignty over this Chinese-controlled territory. It is high time that India accepts the unpalatable reality that it has irrevocably lost Azad Kashmir, Gilgit-Baltistan, and Aksai Chin through war. These areas are not vital to India's national security or for safeguarding the territorial integrity of Indian-administered Kashmir.[19] No Indian government has articulated a strategic rationale for their recovery.[20] Accordingly,

India has no intention or will to regain these areas of Kashmir by coercion, including military force. Moreover, given that Pakistan and China are nuclear weapons states, it is unlikely that India would ever have the capability to seize the lost territories.

## Safeguarding India's Independence

Even if sovereignty is effectively anchored in national identity and territory, the Republic of India cannot freely exercise its sovereignty if it is subject to unwanted foreign influence. Safeguarding India's independence is particularly challenging given the overwhelming reliance of the country on imports of (1) military equipment to meet its defense and national security requirements, and (2) oil and gas to meet its energy needs. Such critical import dependency makes New Delhi vulnerable to pressures to (a) support (or at least not oppose) the preferred policy positions of the states of such foreign suppliers, or (b) refrain from pursuing policies consistent with India's vital national interests in deference to the policy preferences of these suppliers. Furthermore, since these foreign suppliers (or more accurately, the home states of such suppliers) do not have a reciprocal dependence on India with respect to any of their vital national interests, New Delhi cannot rely on symmetrical interdependence to counter or neutralize the unwanted influence of these suppliers. Simply put, India needs these foreign suppliers more than they need India. Over the next two decades, GOI can be expected to make an enormous effort to address the threat to India's independence and strategic autonomy posed by such asymmetrical import dependency.[21]

India relies heavily on imports, predominantly from Russia, to meet a substantial majority of its military equipment needs (imports satisfied about 65 percent of military equipment requirements in 2017).[22] In that year, Russia supplied about 48.5 percent (in value) of India's arms imports.[23] Indeed, over the 2011–2020 decade, Russia was India's largest arms supplier, accounting for about 62 percent (in value) of cumulative Indian purchases of foreign military equipment. Over this same period, the United States was the second largest arms supplier to India, accounting for about 12.6 percent of Indian purchases of foreign military equipment.[24] It is obvious that India's overwhelming reliance on Russian military equipment significantly constricts India's strategic autonomy and independence.

Over the next 10–15 years, one of the most important national security imperatives for India will be to drastically reduce the dependency on imports to meet its arms requirements. In order to do so, India will have to follow a two-pronged strategy: import diversification and import substitution. Of course, successful diversification depends upon the availability of comparable military equipment (in terms of quality, quantity, price, and delivery schedules) from other suppliers whose interests are not inimical to those of India. Ultimately, import substitution, which implies a substantial degree of defense autarky, is more within India's control than import diversification.

If India is to ensure its independence and strategic autonomy, GOI will have to jumpstart a domestic defense industry with the objective of meeting 65 percent of its military equipment requirements within a decade (2030) and 85 percent of its arms requirements by 2035.[25] While this target, no doubt, is ambitious and aggressive, it is within India's capabilities.[26] India has a world class information technology industry with global reach (which has been developed by the private sector), and a world class space program (which has been developed by the public sector), so it is reasonable to expect that within 10–15 years India can establish a world class home-grown defense industry. Success, however, does not necessarily mean that India will be able to defend itself by itself against a potential adversary that is significantly larger or more powerful.[27] It does mean that India will be able to optimize its independence within a framework of strategic interdependence in any alliance with another state (with converging vital national interests) that may be formed to counter a larger and more powerful common adversary.

According to the Energy Information Administration (EIA), the statistical arm of the US Department of Energy, in 2019 oil imports of 3.9 million barrels per day (mbpd) met about 80 percent of India's total oil consumption requirements of 4.9 mbpd.[28] By 2039, India is expected to import about 8.4 mbpd to satisfy 91 percent of its total oil consumption requirements of 9.2 mbpd.[29] A similar import dependency prevails with respect to natural gas. In 2019, India relied on natural gas imports of about 1 trillion cubic feet (Tcf) to meet about 48 percent of its total natural gas consumption requirements of 2.1 Tcf.[30] By 2039, India will have to import 3.0 Tcf of gas to satisfy 65 percent of its total gas consumption requirements of 4.6 Tcf.[31]

It is not possible for India to achieve energy independence. As of year-end 2015, India's proved reserves of oil and gas amounted to

5.7 billion barrels and 53 Tcf, respectively.[32] Reflecting these modest reserves, production of oil and gas falls far short of domestic demand. Domestic alternative renewable energy production—nuclear, solar, wind, and water—and conservation efforts, at best, can slow the growth of import dependency but cannot reverse it. Accordingly, India's energy security strategy will have to focus on diversifying (by region and country) its sources of supply to ensure reliable flows of energy imports to meet its current and future requirements. The key to this effort will be to identify a group of foreign suppliers (1) whose home states (a) do not have vital national interests that are in conflict with those of India, and (b) are not subject to the influence of foreign powers whose interests are inimical to the vital national interests of India; and (2) who are expected to have substantial sustainable export capacity over the long term.

India has made significant progress in its energy supplier diversification efforts both with respect to renewable energy as well as fossil fuels. For example, India has long recognized the potential of nuclear power as a major component of its renewable energy portfolio to reduce its dependence on fossil fuels. The US–India nuclear energy deal of 2008 enabled India to significantly enhance its domestic nuclear power capabilities by facilitating the import of uranium and access to critical technologies for civilian purposes.[33] With respect to fossil fuels, India is successfully expanding its sources of supply. In 2019, India's foreign oil suppliers were: Saudi Arabia and its Sunni Persian Gulf allies, United Arab Emirates and Kuwait, collectively 33 percent; Iraq and Iran (Shia Persian Gulf exporters who are strategic rivals of Saudi Arabia), 24 percent; Nigeria, 8 percent; Venezuela, 7 percent; the United States, 5 percent; and other, 23 percent.[34] India's natural gas diversification effort has been constrained by its need to rely on LNG (liquified natural gas) for its imports. Qatar is by far the largest exporter of LNG and is the principal foreign supplier to India. In the future, the United States, Russia, Australia, Canada, Mozambique, Malaysia, Indonesia, and, possibly, Iran are likely to be included in India's gas diversification efforts.[35]

## Freedom of Navigation

Freedom of navigation is vital to India's military, energy, and economic security. Over the next twenty years, India will strive to become the dominant maritime power in the Indian Ocean, particularly with respect to ensuring control over the critical sea lines of communication (SLOCs) linking India to the Persian Gulf, the Arabian Peninsula, east and south Africa, and southeast Asia. By virtue of its geography India stands astride these SLOCs, which is both a blessing as well as a curse.[36] It is a blessing because India, when it was a maritime power in the past, was able to become a major trading partner of the states of southeast Asia, Arabia, and Persian Gulf, and, albeit to varying degrees, exercise considerable influence over them. It is a curse, because a weak India, burdened with defending long coastlines, is vulnerable to attack by sea from both its west and east. The Portuguese, French, and British convincingly demonstrated in the past the importance of sea power to gain control over the Indian subcontinent. India's overwhelming reliance on oil and gas imports, virtually all of which are carried by tankers passing through the Indian Ocean (particularly the chokepoints of the Strait of Hormuz in the Persian Gulf and Gulf of Oman, Bab al-Mandab in the Gulf of Aden, Cape of Good Hope and Mozambique Channel) to Indian ports on the Arabian Sea and Bay of Bengal, means that the country's dependency on maritime transportation for its energy imports is absolute. India has no land-based pipelines connecting it to foreign oil and gas producers, and it is unlikely to have such pipelines in the foreseeable future.[37] The loss of control over access to its energy SLOCs would be catastrophic for India.

From a military defense perspective, India is highly vulnerable to an attack on its eastern coastline (including the strategic offshore Andaman and Nicobar Islands) by sea, particularly from the South China Sea via the Malacca, Sunda, and Lombok Straits to the Bay of Bengal in the Indian Ocean. During World War II, Japan seized the Andaman and Nicobar Islands on 23 March 1942 using naval and expeditionary forces dispatched from Singapore (which earlier fell to Japan on 15 February 1942) and occupied the islands until 7 October 1945.[38] In the future, in the event of a major conflict for example with China, New Delhi could reasonably expect to face such a scenario again. Clearly, freedom of navigation and control of the SLOCs (and chokepoints) of the Indian Ocean (particularly the Arabian Sea and Bay of Bengal) is a vital Indian national interest. If GOI is to successfully safeguard this interest, the Republic of India must have sufficient regional naval power to deter would-be maritime challengers.

## India's Security Envelope

India's security envelope or sphere of influence around its territorial core is more aspirational than real. As discussed above, India has yet to address the challenge of defining its territorial core as the area under its administrative control. Yet, it is around India's de facto core territory that GOI is trying to construct a flimsy security envelope that depends more on the forbearance of potential adversaries and acquiescence in the residual legacy of the British Raj than it does on Indian military and economic power. Over the next two decades, if India is to successfully safeguard its de facto territorial core, it will have to clearly establish the contours of its security envelope. GOI also needs to mobilize the national will and muster the resources to make India's security envelope credible.

India's *cordon sanitaire*, the last remnants of the atrophied legacy of the British Raj, consists of (1) five neighboring countries: Bhutan and Nepal to the north, Bangladesh and Burma (also called Myanmar) to the east, and Sri Lanka (which is separated from India by the Palk Strait in the Indian Ocean) to the south; and (2) a maritime arc in the Indian Ocean from the Strait of Hormuz and Gulf of Oman to the Bab al-Mandab in the Gulf of Aden extending to the Seychelles, Mozambique Channel and Cape of Good Hope and looping back to Mauritius, Maldives and Sri Lanka to the Lombok, Sunda, and Malacca Straits, the Andaman Sea and Bay of Bengal.

Bhutan and Nepal also share borders with China, and, therefore, provide possible pathways for an attack on India. Both countries, although nominally independent, were former protectorates of British India and became protectorates of India at the time of independence in 1947. Since then, the relationship in each case has been diluted from protectorate to an opaque defense relationship, with an implied GOI commitment to safeguard them against the threat of a foreign armed attack.[39] Since India's military defeat by China in the 1962 border war, New Delhi's will, intention, and capability to protect Nepal and Bhutan has become less certain. Nepal has gradually attempted to find a more equidistant relationship between India and China, hoping to reap economic benefits from the attentions of both.[40] With respect to addressing its defense needs, Nepal has relied far more on China than it has on India over the past decade, with China accounting for about 32 percent of purchases of military equipment compared to India (10 percent).[41] Bhutan has remained close to India but could decide to follow the example of Nepal in the future.[42]

Bangladesh shares borders with eastern India on three sides (to the west and north it borders the Indian state of West Bengal, including the strategic Siliguri corridor which serves as the land bridge connecting India's northeastern states to the rest of India; to the east it shares borders with the northeastern Indian states of Assam, Meghalaya, and Tripura as well as Burma); while to the south it overlooks the Bay of Bengal. If a foreign power with interests inimical to those of India were to gain control over Bangladesh, the Siliguri corridor could be sealed and India's sole link between its northeastern states and the rest of India would be cut off.[43] Also, such a hostile power could use Bangladeshi ports on the Bay of Bengal to attack the east coast of India as well as the strategically vital Andaman and Nicobar Islands that overlook the Malacca Strait. Burma borders 4 Indian states (Arunachal Pradesh, Nagaland, Manipur, and Mizoram) and the Bay of Bengal. Burma also shares borders with China and Bangladesh. During the Second World War, the Japanese used Burma as a launching pad for attacks on eastern India. Indeed, the Battle of Imphal and Kohima (which today are the capitals of Manipur and Nagaland, respectively) that was fought in 1944 is considered one of the bloodiest battles of the war.[44] Clearly, if Burma fell under the influence of a hostile foreign power, India could be faced with such an existential threat again.[45] The island state of Sri Lanka, strategically located in the Indian Ocean across the southern tip of India, oversees the SLOCs that provide India maritime connectivity between its west and east coasts. Sri Lanka, under the control of a hostile power, could be used as a base to sever this maritime connectivity and launch armed attacks on southern India.[46]

The maritime portion of India's *cordon sanitaire* has 2 distinct segments: the eastern Indian Ocean and the western Indian Ocean. The focus on the east primarily relates to controlling access to the Malacca, Sunda, and Lombok Straits in order to deter a major naval attack on eastern India launched from the South China Sea through these key maritime chokepoints. India's Andaman and Nicobar Islands, which overlook these straits, represent the lynchpin for controlling such access. The focus on the western portion of the Indian Ocean primarily involves safeguarding India's access to the energy trade SLOCs. The Seychelles, Mauritius, and the Maldives are the three island states that overlook key sections of these SLOCs, and it is a vital national interest of India to ensure that no hostile power gains control over these states.

Over the next two decades, New Delhi will have to make a concerted effort to build a more robust relationship with Nepal, Bhutan, Bangladesh, Burma, Sri Lanka, Seychelles, Mauritius, and Maldives to ensure that these geo-strategically critical countries remain firmly within India's *cordon sanitaire*. From India's perspective, the desired end state would be that the constituent members of the *cordon sanitaire* (1) do not provide transit rights for military purposes or military facilities to foreign powers whose interests are inimical to the vital national interests of India; and (2) do provide India transit rights for military purposes and access to military facilities, if requested in connection with India's need of self-defense in order to (a) deter an imminent threat of an armed attack or (b) respond to an actual armed attack by a hostile foreign power. In return, India would have to ensure the economic and military security of the members of the *cordon sanitaire*.[47]

Although not a part of its security envelope or sphere of interest, but rather as an embellishment to it, over the next twenty years India will attempt to thread together a garland of neutrals around its maritime *cordon sanitaire*. New Delhi's objective, using the soft power of diplomacy and foreign aid, would be to persuade the states making up this garland to remain neutral with respect to any armed conflict between India and another nuclear-armed state.[48] This garland of neutrals is likely to be composed of the following quartet of Indian Ocean states: Indonesia, Oman, Yemen, and South Africa. Indonesia overlooks the Malacca, Sunda, and Lombok Straits; Oman is strategically located near the Strait of Hormuz chokepoint and the Gulf of Oman ports of Chabahar (Iran) and Gwadar (Pakistan); Yemen's ports of Aden and Socotra serve as sentinels of the Bab al-Mandab chokepoint in the Gulf of Aden; and South Africa's Cape of Good Hope is the link from the Atlantic Ocean to the Mozambique Channel. From India's point of view, freedom of navigation would be enhanced by such a garland of neutrals.

## India's Potential Adversaries

India's historic strategic adversaries are Pakistan and China. Since partition and independence in 1947, India and Pakistan have fought four wars (1947–1948, 1965, 1971 and 1999). In addition, India has struggled to contain a steady stream of Pakistani sponsored (or at least tolerated) cross-border terrorism, primarily in Kashmir but also, spectacularly, against Parliament in New Delhi (2001) and the financial capital, Mumbai (2008).[49] India fought and lost a border war with China in 1962. India has longstanding unresolved border disputes with both countries. In addition, a rising China is steadily eroding India's *cordon sanitaire* as Beijing seeks to expand its influence and establish the Middle Kingdom as Asia's hegemon. For the foreseeable future, Pakistan and China (both of whom, like India, are nuclear-armed) will continue to be New Delhi's nemeses. Furthermore, these two states are de facto allies, so India must consider the serious possibility of a two-front war in the event of a major conflict with either Pakistan or China.

Pakistan, by itself, is a strategic threat that India can manage on its own. As of 2019, India's GDP (purchasing power parity basis) of $9.2 trillion was about 9.2 times larger than Pakistan's GDP of $1 trillion, while India's population of 1.3 billion persons was about 5.5 times the size of Pakistan's population of 238.2 million.[50] In terms of defense spending as a percentage of GDP, the 2019 figures for India and Pakistan were 2.4 and 4 percent, respectively.[51] Given the significantly smaller size of the Pakistani economy, however, Pakistani defense expenditures would have to be an impossibly high 22 percent of GDP to achieve parity with India.[52] While the differential in *potential* military power is lopsidedly in India's favor, the relative imbalance in *actual* military power, although significantly smaller, still gives India a decisive edge in any conventional military conflict. As of 2020, India's armed forces numbered 1.4 million active military personnel compared to 0.7 million for Pakistan; India had 4730 tanks compared to 2680 for Pakistan; India had a total of 672 fighter and attack aircraft compared to 447 for Pakistan; and India's submarine fleet amounted to 17 vessels compared to 9 for Pakistan.[53]

In order to offset its comparative disadvantage in conventional military power, Pakistan has resorted to sponsoring and harboring irregular jihadi groups to maintain low-intensity cross-border military pressure on India in connection with the continuing dispute over the erstwhile princely state of Kashmir, while it has developed a significant nuclear weapons capability to deal with the potential of any existential Indian threat. In the past, Islamabad has relied on its strategic partnership with Washington to restrain New Delhi from taking advantage of India's conventional military superiority.[54] Currently, however, China is Pakistan's prime supplier of military equipment, accounting for about 66 percent of Pakistan's cumulative purchases of foreign military equipment over the 2011–2020 decade.[55] Over the next 20 years, Islamabad can be expected to focus on strengthening the strategic partnership with the Middle Kingdom so that India would be deterred from launching a major conventional military attack on Pakistan.[56]

In the event of a major conflict with China, India is unlikely to prevail. In military terms, the 1962 defeat was not an aberration. Quite bluntly, India cannot successfully defend itself by itself against China in any significant conventional conflict. There is no credible strategic calculus that would even suggest that India, single handedly, could fight China to a draw, let alone defeat it. For India, the strategic calculus relative to China is grim for the foreseeable future.

In terms of potential military power, India is a lightweight compared to a heavyweight China. India's 2019 GDP (purchasing power parity basis) of $9.2 trillion was a mere 41 percent of China's GDP of $22.5 trillion.[57] India's population of 1.3 billion persons in 2019 was almost as large as China's population of 1.4 billion people.[58] With respect to defense spending as a percentage of GDP, the 2019 figures for India and China were 2.4 and 1.9 percent, respectively.[59] Reflecting the fact that China's economy is 2.4 times the size of India's, in order to achieve effective parity India would have had to allocate about 4.6 percent of GDP for defense instead of the actual amount of 2.4 percent in 2019. In terms of actual military power, India is decisively outmatched by China on land, air, and sea—a clear reflection of India's relative underspending for defense. In 2020, India's armed forces totaled 1.4 million active military personnel compared to 2.2 million for China; India's tank strength was 4730 vehicles compared to 3205 for China while for armored vehicles India's total was 10,000 compared to 35,000 for China; India had a total of 672 fighter and attack aircraft compared to 1571 for China; and India's submarine fleet amounted to 17 vessels compared to 79 for China.[60]

In the context of a major conventional conflict with China, neither the Himalayan Mountains nor the Indian Ocean will serve as formidable defensive barriers. In 1962, China convincingly demonstrated that it could successfully address the myriad challenges of mountain warfare and rout Indian military forces. China has seven pathways to launch an armed attack on India: (1) from Xinjiang through Aksai Chin; (2) from Tibet across the Sino-Indian border in Himachal Pradesh and Uttarakhand, Sikkim, and Arunachal Pradesh; (3) from Xinjiang through Pakistan (including Gilgit-Baltistan and Azad Kashmir); (4) from Tibet through Nepal; (5) from Tibet through Bhutan; (6) from China through Burma; and (7) from China via the South China Sea through the Malacca, Sunda, and Lombok Straits into the Andaman Sea and Bay of Bengal. The last five options would involve China violating the sovereignty of a neighboring country, although Pakistan, China's de facto ally, may be a willing accomplice. Of course, Beijing gets to choose the time, place, and manner of attack.

India is unlikely to overcome the unfavorable gap in military power with China in the foreseeable future.[61] According to EIA projections, in 2039 India's GDP is projected to be $30 trillion or about 56 percent of China's expected GDP of $53.4 trillion, while India's population is forecasted to be 1.6 billion persons compared to China's population of 1.4 billion.[62] Even though by then India most likely would be the world's second largest economy (ahead of the United States with a projected GDP of $26.5 trillion), New Delhi's prospects or ability to achieve effective parity with China with respect to defense expenditures would not be decisively improved. For example, if Beijing were to increase its level of defense spending as a percentage of GDP from the current 1.9 to 2.5 percent in 2039, India would have to boost defense expenditures as a percentage of GDP to 4.5 percent—a heavy burden which it would find difficult to sustain.[63]

While India could sustain a 4 percent defense spending rate, it would require an extraordinary mobilization of national will to do so. As India spent 4.2 percent of GDP on defense in 1987, it is reasonable to assume that GOI could step up to a 4 percent spending rate on defense over time.[64] It must be recognized, however, that New Delhi continually struggles to balance the very real scourges of malnutrition, disease, and illiteracy that sap the country's vitality with the contingent risk to national security posed by China. As early as 18 November 1950, as Indian decision-makers grappled with the possibility of China emerging as a strategic threat, Prime Minister Jawaharlal Nehru agonized: "If we really feared an attack [by China] and had to make provision for it, this would cast an intolerable burden on us, financial and otherwise ... there are limits beyond which we cannot go at least for some years."[65] This fundamental reality has not changed since then, and the quandary of guns versus butter will bedevil GOI for the foreseeable future.

When China proceeded to reclaim Tibet in 1950, the potential of the Middle Kingdom to morph into a serious threat to India and its sphere of interest had to be assessed. In his letter of 7 November 1950 to Prime Minister Jawaharlal Nehru, Sardar Vallabhbhai Patel, then deputy prime minister and home affairs minister, cautioned "even though we regard ourselves as the friends of China, the Chinese do not regard us as their friends."[66] Sri Aurobindo, an erstwhile freedom fighter and revolutionary politician who had long since withdrawn from the political arena to pursue poetry, philosophy, and yoga, bluntly warned on 11 November 1950: "The basic significance of Mao's Tibetan adventure is to advance China's frontiers right down to India and stand poised there to strike at the right moment and with the right strategy."[67] He recognized India's adverse asymmetry in the balance of power relative to China and, while acknowledging the prospect of making difficult adjustments with respect to sovereignty, presciently suggested a strategic partnership between India and the United States to checkmate China: "[T]ake a firm line with China, denounce openly her nefarious intentions, stand without reservation by the USA and make every possible arrangement consonant with our self-respect to facilitate an American intervention in our favour."[68] Tragically, Prime Minister Nehru dismissed the likelihood of a conflict with China. In his 18 November 1950 note to Patel, Nehru declared: "I think that it is exceedingly unlikely that we may have to face any real military invasion from the Chinese side, whether in peace or in war, in the foreseeable future."[69] Nehru's faith in Chinese restraint, purchased with a decade of conciliatory accommodation, turned out to be a disastrous gamble.

In 1962, India and China fought an undeclared border war involving competing sovereignty claims with respect to the Aksai Chin area of Indian-administered Kashmir and Arunachal Pradesh. India was completely routed. Prime Minister Nehru acknowledged India's peril to President John F. Kennedy in his second letter of 19 November 1962 requesting urgent American aid: "With the advance of the Chinese in massive strength, the entire Brahmaputra Valley is seriously threatened and unless something is done immediately to stem the tide the whole of Assam, Tripura, Manipur and Nagaland would also pass into Chinese hands."[70] China, perhaps to preempt the possibility of a major US military intervention, unilaterally decided to retain Aksai Chin (a strategic priority for Beijing as it provided a vital corridor linking Tibet to Xinjiang) but withdraw completely from Arunachal Pradesh (although it did not relinquish its sovereignty claims over the area).[71]

In 1962, New Delhi failed to understand that the road linking Tibet to Xinjiang through Aksai Chin was a vital national interest for the Middle Kingdom, and that India, which insisted on asserting sovereignty claims over Aksai Chin, posed a potential threat to China's national security. Similarly, the China-Pakistan Economic Corridor (CPEC), particularly the planned energy pipeline linking Pakistan's port of Gwadar to China's Kashgar energy terminus, is a vital national interest for Beijing as it is the lynchpin for China's energy security. India's claims of sovereignty with respect to Pakistani-administered Gilgit-Baltistan province, through which CPEC traverses, pose a potential threat to CPEC and, therefore, China's energy security. China's goal is to achieve energy security and complete its military modernization by 2035.[72] India will be in China's crosshairs for the foreseeable future.

## India's Potential Strategic Partners

An India determined to defend itself by itself faces a strategic dilemma in confronting a significantly larger, and equally determined, adversary such as China. Ultimately, New Delhi cannot afford to pursue a grand strategy that depends on the (1) sufferance or benign neglect of such a powerful adversary, or (2) the altruism of another powerful state that will come to the rescue of India just in time at its moment of peril. The amount of resources India can mobilize for its defense is limited by the size of its economy, and once that limit is reached, New Delhi must accommodate, appease, and accept the hegemony of the more powerful adversary (and the attendant subordination and diminution of India's sovereignty); or seek a military alliance as an equal partner with a powerful state that is in competition with the common foe, which would imply sharing strategic autonomy and sovereignty with the ally with respect to certain national security issues. The purpose of such a military alliance would be to deter the common adversary from using military force to attack a member of the alliance. To be credible and effective the alliance members would have to: (1) collectively possess both potential and actual military power equal to or greater than that of the common adversary; (2) have a shared understanding of the level of threat to their converging vital national interests posed by the common adversary; and (3) commit, jointly and severally, to respond promptly using all appropriate means, including military force, in the event of an armed attack by the common foe on one or more members of the alliance.

Since the fundamental strategic calculus with respect to China is not in New Delhi's favor, there is one, and only one, realistic solution to India's strategic dilemma—a carefully crafted military alliance with the United States. In its essence, such an Indo-American alliance would be strategic and designed to deter China from attacking either party; it would not be merely an opportunistic arrangement struck to deal with the threat of an imminent attack or an actual attack after the fact. Over the next decade, the centerpiece of Indian grand strategy will be the construction of such a robust and enduring Indo-American military alliance in which India and the United States would be equal partners. By 2035, the size of the US and Indian economies would be converging toward parity, so a partnership of equals is a realistic expectation.[73] Such a military alliance will catapult India to the highest rung of world power, and undoubtedly be the most important strategic achievement of the twenty-first century. Success is within GOI's grasp, and it is unlikely that New Delhi will let it slip away.

The strategic calculus of an Indo-American alliance is overwhelming in terms of both potential and actual military power. As of 2019, the combined GDP (calculated on the basis of purchasing power parity) of India ($9.2 trillion) and the United States ($20.5 trillion) amounted to $29.7 trillion, a comfortable 1.3 times China's GDP of $22.5 trillion.[74] The 2019 weighted defense expenditures as a percentage of GDP of such an alliance was 3.1 percent compared to China's figure of 1.9 percent.[75] The 2019 combined alliance population of 1.6 billion (India, 1.3 billion persons and America, 0.3 billion) was also greater than China's population of 1.4 billion persons.[76] In 2039, the combined GDP of the prospective India–US alliance is forecast to be $56.5 trillion (of which India, $30 trillion, and the United States, $26.5 trillion) slightly ahead of China's GDP of $53.4 trillion, while the alliance's combined population is expected to grow to 2 billion persons (India, 1.6 billion and the United States, 0.4) compared to China's population of 1.4 billion persons (reflecting virtually no population growth).[77] If the proposed alliance were to target a defense expenditure rate of 3 percent of GDP for both the United States and India, China will be faced with the fiscal challenge of boosting its defense spending 1.7 times from the current 1.9 percent rate to about 3.2 percent to achieve effective parity.[78]

In terms of actual military power, an Indo-American alliance has a decisive edge (both quantitative and qualitative) over China. As of 2020, the combined active military force of an Indo-American alliance would be

2.8 million servicemembers (India, 1.4 million and the United States, 1.4 million) compared China's standing military force of 2.2 million active duty personnel; the total number of tanks for the alliance amounted to 10,830 (India, 4730 and the United States, 6100) compared to 3205 for China; total number of alliance armored vehicles amounted to 50,000 (India, 10,000 and the United States 40,000) compared to 35,000 for China; total alliance fighter and attack aircraft, 3389 (India, 672 and the United States, 2717) compared to 1571 for China; total alliance submarine fleet, 85 vessels (India, 17 and the United States, 68) compared to 79 for China.[79] There is no reason to doubt that for the foreseeable future an India–US military alliance could serve as an effective deterrent to ensure that China does not resort to military force to challenge the vital national interests of India or America.

While the strategic calculus of an Indo-American alliance is obvious, the strategic logic that would cement the alliance is extraordinarily compelling.

First, such an alliance is the only means of effectively threatening China's energy security by cutting off the country's access to oil and gas imports transported by land-based pipelines or oceangoing tankers. The Middle Kingdom's capacity to sustain a major war effort would be seriously, if not fatally, impaired. Faced with a credible threat to its energy security, China is unlikely to undertake actions that would jeopardize the vital national interests of India or the United States. India's 2659-km northern border with China, which stretches from the Kashmir region in the northwest to the state of Arunachal Pradesh in the northeast provides a unique, albeit geographically challenging, pathway for an air attack and land invasion of China's western Xinjiang province, the terminus for energy pipelines from Central Asia (and planned pipelines from Iran via Pakistan). Indeed, India, by virtue of its long border with China as well as its vast strategic depth, is the only option to use land power to counterattack the Middle Kingdom's weakest military points—Xinjiang and Tibet provinces. With an alliance, Indian and American land and air forces will have the capability, if necessary, to launch an attack from India's northern border to control a crucial swathe of territory in Tibet and Xinjiang and to shut down the terminals in Kashgar and Urumqi, thereby severing China's land-based access to energy imports from Iran and Central Asia. China would lose access to oil imports that would meet about 47 percent of its total oil consumption requirements, and the Middle Kingdom would then be completely dependent upon domestic production together with

Russian oil and gas supplies delivered to the terminal at Daqing.[80] Given its distant location in China's northeast, the most likely threat to the Daqing energy terminal would be intermediate-range ballistic missiles launched from northeastern India that might periodically disrupt the complex, but perhaps not achieve an extended closure. Just as important, India straddles the crucial energy trade's sea lines of communication and maritime chokepoints of the Indian Ocean—from the Strait of Hormuz in the Persian Gulf and the Bab al-Mandab Strait in the Gulf of Aden to the Malacca, Sunda, and Lombok Straits that are the gateways to the South China Sea and the western Pacific Ocean. With an alliance, the Indian and American naval fleets together will have the capability to blockade all five relevant maritime choke points in the Indian Ocean, thereby shutting down China's access to sea-borne oil and gas imports.

Second, in the event of a major military conflict with the Middle Kingdom, a key Indian objective would be to ensure that the Chinese fleet is confined to home ports and territorial waters so that it does not have the ability to roam the Indian Ocean with impunity attacking India's (1) vital sea-borne oil and gas imports, and (2) major cities and critical infrastructure along the east coast. Given that the size of the Chinese submarine fleet is 4.6 times larger than the Indian fleet, New Delhi alone could not achieve this objective. However, the Indian and American navies together could bring to bear the necessary maritime quantitative and qualitative edge to serve as a powerful deterrent to make sure that China's naval forces remain close to home and do not venture into the Indian Ocean to challenge Indian or American vital national interests. The fact that the United States has had a longstanding dominant military presence in the Western Pacific, including the South China Sea, does not mitigate the Chinese naval threat to India as long as Beijing has a credible basis for believing that Washington would not intervene militarily on the side of India in the event of a Sino-Indian conflict. A formal Indo-American alliance would force the Chinese to reassess their strategic calculus and recalibrate their grand strategy.

A mutual defense treaty between India and the United States must be perceived as a partnership of equals and clearly reflect a shared understanding that both are committed to fighting alongside each other to safeguard their vital national interests in a conflict initiated by China. Such a treaty would not cover territories over which India has asserted sovereignty but does not exercise administrative control: Azad Kashmir, Gilgit-Baltistan, and Aksai Chin. Also, the treaty would not cover Indian activities in Nepal and Bhutan, which are the subject of separate bilateral agreements. Likewise, the pact would not cover US activities in Japan, Australia, South Korea, Taiwan, Philippines, and Thailand, which are addressed through separate bilateral security agreements. Reflecting these parameters, the operative part of an Indo-American defense treaty might be formulated as follows:

> In the event of an armed attack by the People's Republic of China against the Republic of India or the United States in (a) any area under Indian or American administration, or (b) international waters or airspace in the Indian or Pacific Ocean regions, such an attack shall be considered an attack against both India and the United States, and consequently both parties agree that, if such an armed attack occurs, each of them in exercise of the right of individual or collective self-defense recognized by Article 51 of the Charter of the United Nations, will assist the party so attacked by taking forthwith, individually and in concert with the other party, such action as it deems necessary, including the use of armed force, to restore peace and security.

The proposed bilateral defense agreement between New Delhi and Washington would be consistent with the existing hub and spoke security architecture for Asia used by both countries. Moreover, the explicit inclusion of the military option would mirror the strong mutual security commitment incorporated in the North Atlantic Treaty Organization agreement.[81]

What would make such an Indo-American defense pact unique and enduring is that it would be based on a symmetrical mutual security interdependence of equal partners: India needs the United States just as much as the United States needs India. Within 15–20 years the size of the Indian and American economies will be near parity. Without the United States, India cannot achieve parity in the balance of power (in terms of both potential and actual power) with respect to China. The same is true for the United States. Sans India, the United States cannot preserve a long-term equilibrium in the balance of power relative to China. Without the United States, India cannot credibly threaten the energy security of China. The same is true for the United States. From India's perspective, only the United States can keep the Chinese Navy bottled in home ports. From the perspective of the United States, only India, by virtue of its unique geostrategic location, can make the use of land power a viable option to counterattack China where it is most vulnerable—the soft southwestern underbelly of Xinjiang and Tibet along the Sino-Indian border. Without such a credible land power option, China's energy security could not be effectively threatened. An Indo-American mutual defense treaty would crystallize the shared understanding of the primacy of the Chinese strategic threat to their respective vital national interests. Jointly, the Indian tiger and the American eagle could contain the threat of the Chinese dragon; severally, neither New Delhi nor Washington can hope to do so.

Arguably, from the time of Prime Minister Nehru's brief encounter with President Kennedy in 1962 to more recent flirtations over the past quarter century of Prime Ministers P. V. Narsimha Rao, Atal Bihari Vajpayee, Manmohan Singh, and Narendra Modi with Presidents Bill Clinton, George W. Bush, and Barack Obama, and the warm embrace of current Prime Minister Modi with President Donald Trump, New Delhi has been signaling its willingness to shed its commitment to nonalignment and strategic autonomy, and albeit gingerly, enter into an arranged mutual security partnership if not marriage.[82] There is no reason the trajectory will not be maintained by Prime Minister Modi and President Biden, the challenge of exiting the 20-year Afghanistan war notwithstanding.[83]

In his pivotal address to a joint session of the US Congress, Prime Minister Narendra Modi confidently declared: "Today, our relationship has overcome the hesitations of history. A strong India-US partnership can anchor peace, prosperity and stability."[84] And in a reassuring sign of strategic continuity, the joint communiqués, issued at the time of Prime Minister Modi's visit with President Obama in June 2016 and his visit a year later with President Trump, were remarkably similar and stressed three key themes: peaceful settlement of territorial and maritime disputes, freedom of navigation, and sharing critical defense technology with India on the same basis as the closest US allies.[85]

Indian public opinion, which must be cultivated and cannot be taken for granted, provides grounds for optimism that an Indo-American alliance would be well received. According to a Pew Research Center survey published on 15 November 2017, 49 percent of Indians have a favorable view of the United States, while only 9 percent have an unfavorable view and 42 percent have no opinion.[86] By contrast, only 26 percent have a favorable view of China, 44 percent have an unfavorable view and 30 percent express no opinion. Furthermore, 56 percent consider China's increasing military power as bad for India, while only 19 percent consider American power to be a negative for India.[87] In an earlier Pew survey issued in September 2016, about 69 percent were worried about the Sino-Indian border dispute.[88]

## An American Perspective

Washington is an ardent and persistent suitor of New Delhi, impelled not by passion but by self-interest. For the United States, the strategic calculus, without India as a partner, is not very attractive: Washington will suffer a continuing decline in its strategic position relative to Beijing. America's longstanding bilateral alliances with Japan and Australia will not materially change this strategic calculus; in fact, it will get worse over the next two decades. In 2019, the combined GDP of the United States, Japan, and Australia totaled $27 trillion slightly ahead of China's GDP of $22.5 trillion, while the combined population of the three allies amounted to 486 million people compared to China's population of 1.4 billion.[89] In terms of actual military power as of 2020, this triple alliance also had a comfortable edge: active military force of the alliance, 1.7 million servicemembers, compared to China, 2.2 million active duty personnel; alliance tank force, 7163 vehicles, compared to China, 3205; alliance armored vehicles, 48,550 compared to China, 35,000; alliance fighter and attack aircraft, 3084, versus China, 1571; alliance submarines, 94, versus China, 79.[90]

However, the triple alliance's advantage is relatively short-lived. The Pentagon anticipates that China will have achieved its military modernization objectives, and effectively closed the quantitative and qualitative military gap with the United States by 2035.[91] Certainly, the Middle Kingdom will have a decisive advantage by 2039. At that time, the combined GDP of the United States, Japan, and Australia is expected to be only $34 trillion or about 64 percent of China's GDP of $53.4 trillion, and the combined population of the trio is expected to be 526 million persons or about 38 percent of China's population of 1.4 billion.[92] Moreover, the US alliances with Japan and Australia are air and sea power-centric and do not provide a geostrategic pathway to use land power to threaten China's long-term energy security via a counterattack on the Middle Kingdom's land-based energy pipeline terminals in Xinjiang (Kashgar and Urumqi) which, when fully operational, Beijing anticipates will circumvent the energy SLOCs controlled by the US Navy. Any Sino-American modus vivendi that might be negotiated, although providing short-term relief, would be inherently unstable, given the underlying asymmetric power differential between the two parties.

From an American viewpoint, an alliance with India is the only credible option to preserve a favorable balance of power with respect to China for the foreseeable future. American foreign policy declarations reflect the strategic calculus and strategic logic that would underpin a prospective Indo-American security partnership. The joint communiqués of 2016 and 2017 emphasize the shared strategic interests of the two countries. In a major foreign policy address in October 2017, then US Secretary of State Rex W. Tillerson highlighted the centrality of the threat posed by China; affirmed the military, geographic, and economic importance of India; recognized New Delhi as an equal partner; conceded India's economy will surpass that of the United States in the foreseeable future; and predicted the strategic partnership between the two countries will endure for a century.[93] Furthermore, the *National Security Strategy of the United States of America* issued by President Donald J. Trump in December 2017, declares China to be a national security threat for the first time: "China seeks to displace the United States in the Indo-Pacific region, expand the reaches of its state-driven economic model, and reorder the region in its favor."[94] Crucially, the strategy embraces India's ambitions to be a leading power and enshrines India as a strategic partner to address China's threat: "We welcome India's emergence as a leading global power and stronger strategic and defense partner." To drive home the central importance of India, the strategy pledges: "We will deepen our strategic partnership with India and support its leadership role in Indian Ocean security and throughout the broader region."[95] American public opinion increasingly reflects the perception of China as a threat to the United States. For example, a 2019 Pew Research Center survey on American attitudes toward China reported that 81 percent of those questioned considered China's growing military power as a bad thing for the United States.[96] Undoubtedly, Washington has come a long way in acknowledging that it needs New Delhi as an equal strategic partner.

## Challenges to an Indo-American Alliance

While a formal Indo-American alliance is likely to be consummated within the next 10 years, it is important to consider possible obstacles: India's legacy commitment to nonalignment and strategic autonomy; possible adverse economic, political, and strategic consequences of provoking

China; and deep-rooted Indian doubts about the reliability of the United States as a strategic partner. None of these potential obstacles are insurmountable.

Since gaining independence from Great Britain in 1947, India has embraced nonalignment as the best way to preserve its sovereignty and to avoid becoming entangled in the bipolar conflicts of the Cold War. As a practical matter, nonalignment and neutrality became synonymous, although rhetoric from New Delhi had a decidedly pro-Soviet tilt. With the end of the Cold War, India adapted its doctrine of nonalignment to reflect a multipolar world and rebranded the updated nonalignment doctrine as "strategic autonomy." One of the architects of this concept, Shyam Saran, a former Secretary of India's Ministry of External Affairs, explained strategic autonomy as follows: "[O]n matters of vital national interest to India, it [the country] should be able to take … *relatively* autonomous decisions. Not take *completely* autonomous decisions because you have to live in a world where you have to interact with so many other powers."[97] Any attempt to sacrifice an Indo American mutual defense pact on the altar of nonalignment and strategic autonomy is likely to fail. Adherents of this legacy doctrine would have to demonstrate that India, absent from the proposed alliance, will have the *capability* to defend itself in a serious non-nuclear kinetic confrontation with China. Given the huge unfavorable asymmetry in potential and actual power relative to China, currently and for the foreseeable future, there is no credible basis for believing New Delhi can independently, or with an alternative security arrangement in which India is the dominant partner with countries other than the United States, close the chasm between India's capability and its intention to defend itself. For example, crafting hub-and-spoke bilateral security cooperation arrangements with smaller Asian states such as Japan, Australia, Vietnam, and Singapore (or a European state such as France which has regional interests in the Indian Ocean) as an alternative to an Indo-American alliance will not materially change India's adverse security calculus relative to China. Such cooperation agreements could usefully supplement and complement an Indo-American mutual defense treaty but could never substitute for it.[98]

In fact, New Delhi has demonstrated that in extremis it is prepared to jettison nonalignment and strategic autonomy to safeguard national security. In 1962, with the Chinese steamroller threatening to overrun northeast India, Nehru proposed what was effectively an Indo-American defense pact that provided for an immediate infusion of US military equipment, the stationing of 12 US Air Force squadrons, and establishing a network of American military radar installations in the country.[99] And, nearly a decade later, anticipating an Indo-Pak war, New Delhi signed a security pact with Moscow on 9 August 1971 that was designed to ensure India retained a continual flow of Soviet military equipment and, crucially, deter a possible Chinese intervention.[100]

While challenging the facts underpinning the decisive advantage of China in terms of capabilities is difficult, some who cling to a policy of nonalignment counter that Beijing's intentions are benign. These proponents believe China is willing to normalize the Sino-Indian border, with possible minor rectifications, and rhetoric notwithstanding, the Middle Kingdom does not have irredentist ambitions toward Arunachal Pradesh—or Southern Tibet in official Chinese terminology—which lies within India's border established by the McMahon Line.[101] The fact that despite sporadic border incidents peace has prevailed over the past 59 years along the LAC representing the de facto Sino-Indian border has lulled India to believe that China was satisfied with the territorial status quo. Yet the May/June 2020 skirmishes along the LAC between Aksai Chin and Eastern Ladakh strongly suggest that Chinese intentions may be more than to prod India to acquiesce to minor border rectifications; rather, the Chinese actions may reflect Beijing's concern that India (by changing the status quo within Indian-administered Jammu & Kashmir and Ladakh in 2019) could be trying to change the strategic calculus vis-a-vis Gilgit-Baltistan through which CPEC runs, and thus threaten Chinese energy security.[102] Consequently, in the view of many Indians who have been convinced of China's benign intentions, an Indo-American security pact would be perceived by Beijing as a threat to the current geostrategic status quo.

It is highly unlikely that fear of arousing the otherwise contented dragon would derail the prospects for an Indo-American alliance. The security pact would cover only the territory under the administrative control of India and would not extend to territory that is under Beijing's or Islamabad's administration but could be claimed by New Delhi. Far from threatening the status quo along the Sino-Indian border, the pact would deter the Middle Kingdom from future attempts to change the de facto border by forcefully reclaiming Arunachal Pradesh or extending westward Aksai Chin's borders with Ladakh. Current intentions do not preclude future Chinese irredentism emboldened by India's continued relative weakness. Even a successful Indian effort to forge a modus vivendi with China, while eminently desirable, would not obviate the need for a mutual security pact with America. Sans an Indo-American alliance, and given the disparity in relative power, India would have to rely on Chinese forbearance. Having gambled once, GOI cannot afford to do so again in the hopes of a more favorable outcome. The devotees of nonalignment and strategic autonomy cannot escape the harsh reality of asymmetric capabilities by invoking wishful symmetrical intentions.

A key driver of New Delhi's nonalignment policy is the desire to avoid conflicts, particularly those between more powerful nations, that do not affect India's vital national interests. An Indo-American alliance, according to some partisans of strategic autonomy, unnecessarily intertwines the Sino-Indian border dispute with the Sino-American dispute over the South China Sea. Certainly, the quid pro quo of such a security pact would be America's willingness to fight beside India to preserve the status quo along the Sino-Indian border in exchange for India's willingness to join arms with America to safeguard freedom of navigation in the South China Sea. This linkage is appropriate because it reflects the convergence of vital national interests and recognizes the security interdependence of both countries. As has been already pointed out, India has a vital national interest in ensuring that the Chinese Navy does not cross the South China Sea and pass through the Malacca, Sunda, and Lombok Straits to attack India's east coast or interdict Indian energy imports. In the event of a Sino-Indian war, New Delhi would also have as a core war objective a blockade of these chokepoints to prevent the flow of Chinese energy imports. India cannot safeguard such vital national interests without the help of the American Navy. Therefore, it is in India's vital national interest that the US Navy operate freely in the international waters of the South China Sea.

Resistance to an alliance between India and the United States could also emerge from those interested in Sino-Indian trade who may raise concerns about the potential adverse economic consequences to India, such as the loss of access to the Chinese market. In terms of two-way trade (merchandise exports and imports), the Middle Kingdom is one of India's most important partners. For the fiscal year ended 31 March 2019, India's two-way trade with China totaled $87 billion (of which exports, $16.7 billion, and imports, $70.3 billion) just slightly behind India's two-way trade with the United States of $88 billion (exports, $52.4

billion, and imports, $35.6 billion).[103] A more sophisticated approach to assessing the strategic importance of trade relations, and to counter misguided concerns, would focus on the relative value of Indian exports, which generate foreign exchange revenues that help fund the country's economic growth. In terms of exports, in FY (fiscal year) 2019 China accounted for only 5 percent of total Indian exports of $330.1 billion while the United States was the destination for 15.9 percent of Indian exports.[104] Clearly, the United States as an export market is far more important than China, so the loss of China as an export market would not be significant in the medium to long term but could cause temporary pain while Indian manufacturers find alternative export markets.[105]

Moreover, both India and the United States have converging vital national interests with respect to a shared urgency in reducing import dependency on China in order to strengthen supply chain resiliency and thereby enhance economic security. According to the CIA, in 2019 China was the single largest source of imports for both India (about 15 percent of India's total imports) as well as the United States (18 percent of US total imports).[106] Obviously, both India and the United States are currently very vulnerable to supply chain disruptions in the event China stopped shipping goods to them. Over the medium to long term, both India and the United States have a shared interest in decoupling their economies from China (effectively reducing bilateral trade with China) and correspondingly increasing US–India trade significantly. For example, rather than relying on Chinese manufacturers to satisfy their merchandise import requirements, US companies could turn to Indian manufacturers instead as alternate suppliers to meet their import requirements—which would be a major boost for the Indian economy. An Indo-American strategic partnership clearly has the potential to grow beyond military security to embrace economic security as well.

Opponents of an Indo-American alliance could also argue that the United States may be an unreliable and fickle partner. They will be sure to point out that Washington placed its interests in forging Sino-American détente to counter the Soviet Union in 1971 over India's national security concerns arising from the civil war between East and West Pakistan. Specifically, the United States assured Beijing that it would not object to intervention in support of West Pakistan, sent a US naval task force into the Bay of Bengal to intimidate India, cut off economic aid to India, and encouraged the transfer of fighter aircraft from Jordan to West Pakistan.[107] The United States is embroiled in a potentially dangerous dispute with North Korea over Pyongyang's nuclear weapons program and is seeking Beijing's help to pressure the Kim regime. Washington could be lured once again by the siren song of a grand bargain with Beijing, which could result in shortchanging India's vital national interests.

This concern regarding American reliability is valid but misplaced. Ultimately, vital national interests will trump commitments to others. This is a truism that applies to all states, including India. The real question, therefore, is whether the vital national interests of the United States and India with respect to China are converging in such a way that a similar threat perception likely will be shared for the foreseeable future. American policy pronouncements, strategic calculus, and strategic logic confirm the strong convergence and congruity of interests. The bogey of a de facto Sino-American condominium that would trifle with India's vital national interests is simply not credible.

## Implications for India

In designing a grand strategy for the remainder of the twenty-first century, New Delhi's decision-makers will have to reaffirm the idea of India articulated by the nation's founding fathers, adopt the realism and pragmatism of Kautilya (ancient India's premier strategic thinker), adapt the flexible strategic framework of Curzon and Panikkar, and abandon the doctrinal orthodoxy of nonalignment.[108] If past is not to be prologue, China must be convinced that it will be unable to achieve local area dominance along India's northern border or in the vital sea lines of communication and maritime chokepoints of the Indian Ocean. Only an Indo-American alliance can effectively counterbalance, deter, and contain an assertive, resurgent Middle Kingdom bent on becoming Asia's hegemon. Entering into a security agreement with the United States will not be easy. Transforming a tentative and hesitant relationship into a formal committed alliance of equals will require strategic patience, persistence, and perseverance.[109] India has the will, intention, and capability within a generation to claim and gain its rightful seat at the head table of world powers. India's chair will not be vacant.

## Notes

1. For a classic statement of the grand strategy of British India see Lord Curzon, *The Place of India in the Empire* (London: John Murray, 1909), 11–14, https://babel.hathitrust.org/cgi/pt?id=umn.319510023281092;view=1up;seq=16. For an incisive and elegant articulation of India's historic maritime strategy see K. M. Panikkar, *India and the Indian Ocean: An Essay on the Influence of Sea Power on Indian History*, 2nd ed. (London: G. Allen & Unwin Ltd., 1951), https://catalog.hathitrust.org/Record/001250787.
2. See Survey of India, "Political Map of India," http://surveyofindia.gov.in/files/POL_MAP_15M_with_watermark.pdf and Maps of India, http://www.mapsofindia.com/maps/. For a map of India showing disputed boundaries, see "Fantasy Frontiers: Indian, Pakistani and Chinese Border Disputes," *Economist*, 8 February 2018, https://www.economist.com/graphic-detail/2012/02/08/fantasy-frontiers.
3. See "PoK, Aksai Chin Integral Part of J&K, Can Die for It: Amit Shah in Lok Sabah," *Times of India*, 6 August 2019, https://timesofindia.indiatimes.com/india/we-will-sacrifice-our-lives-for-kashmir-amit-shah/articleshow/70549004.cms.
4. India is a democracy, and as such, people expect a modicum of truthfulness and transparency from decision-makers.
5. Reciprocal action by Pakistan and China in dropping their respective claims to Indian-administered territory would be desirable but not necessary. India's obligation to preserve its territorial integrity (interpreted as territory under its administrative control) is absolute and unconditional, and independent of any statements by these two states or any other state.
6. See Sunil Khilnani, *The Idea of India* (New York: Farrar, Strauss and Giroux, 1999), and Pew Research Center, "Religion in India: Tolerance and Segregation, 29 June 2021," 123–142, https://www.pewforum.org/2021/06/29/religion-in-india-tolerance-and-segregation/. For an articulate exposition of the roots of Indian national identity by one of the founding fathers of Indian nationalism, see Sri Aurobindo, *On Nationalism* (Pondicherry, India: Sri Aurobindo Ashram, 1996).
7. See V. P. Menon, *Integration of the Indian States* (Hyderabad, India: Orient Longman, 1956), 390–415. For a copy of the actual accession document of Kashmir see Venkatesh Nayak, "The Backstory of Article 370: A True Copy of J&K's Instrument of Accession," *The Wire* (India), 5 August 2019, https://thewire.in/history/public-first-time-jammu-kashmirs-instrument-accession-india.
8. The cease-fire line was formalized in the so-called Karachi Agreement of 1949. See Ministry of External Affairs (India), "Agreement Between

Military Representatives of India and Pakistan Regarding the Establishment of Cease-Fire Line in the State of Jammu and Kashmir, 27 July 1949," https://mea.gov.in/bilateral-documents.htm?dtl/5252/Agreement+relating+to+Ceasefire+Line+in+JampK.

9. For an illustration of GOI's continuing search for a solution to the problem of incorporating Kashmir into the Republic of India, see Rebecca Ratcliffe, "India Set to Withdraw Kashmir's Special Status and Split It in Two," *Guardian* (UK), 5 August 2019, https://www.theguardian.com/world/2019/aug/05/india-revoke-disputed-kashmir-special-status; PTI (Press Trust of India), "Govt Revokes Article 370 from Jammu and Kashmir, Bifurcates State into Two Union Territories," *Times of India*, 5 August 2019, https://timesofindia.indiatimes.com/india/article-370-to-be-scrapped-jk-will-ceases-to-be-a-state-2-union-territories-created/articleshow/70531899.cms; and PTI, "J&K Reorganisation Bill Passage Momentous Occasion: Narendra Modi," *Hindu*, 6 August 2019, https://www.thehindu.com/news/national/jk-reorganisation-bill-passage-momentous-occasion-narendra-modi/article28838574.ece?homepage=true. If the GOI changes to Kashmir's status, which have been approved by Parliament, are upheld by the Supreme Court, then the state of Kashmir (as of 5 August 2019) would be bifurcated into two union territories: Jammu and Kashmir (with a Muslim majority and significant Hindu minority population), and Ladakh (with a sparse Buddhist majority population). It is quite likely that additional steps will have to be taken, including a possible further subdivision of Jammu and Kashmir into two separate union territories of Jammu (with a Hindu majority) and Kashmir (with a Muslim majority), and the subsequent elevation of each to state status. Given its small population, Ladakh most likely would be administered as a union territory for the foreseeable future.
10. See Central Intelligence Agency (CIA), *World Factbook*, https://www.cia.gov/the-world-factbook/; and Conrad Hackett, "By 2050, India to Have World's Largest Populations of Hindus and Muslims," 21 April 2015, Pew Research Center, https://www.pewresearch.org/fact-tank/2015/04/21/by-2050-india-to-have-worlds-largest-populations-of-hindus-and-muslims/.
11. According to a 2021 Pew Research Center survey of religion in India, about 48 percent of India's Muslims believe that Partition has left them worse off. See Pew Research Center, "Religion in India: Tolerance and Segregation, 29 June 2021," 66–67, https://www.pewforum.org/2021/06/29/religion-in-india-tolerance-and-segregation/.
12. Office of the Registrar General and Census Commissioner, India, "2011 Census Data: Religion," http://www.censusindia.gov.in/2011census/Religion_PCA.html. On 5 August 2019, the existing state of Kashmir was restructured and divided into two union territories: Jammu

and Kashmir (with a Muslim majority) and Ladakh (with a Buddhist majority).

13. It also should be noted that there are 4 Hindu majority states in which non-Hindus constitute at least one-third of the population: Sikkim, Assam, Goa, and Kerala. These states are also geo-strategically important, so secularism and diversity are vital to ensuring the integration of their sizable minorities. Sikkim borders China, Nepal, and Bhutan, and overlooks the Siliguri Corridor (the vital land-choke point connecting northeast India to the rest of the country); Assam represents the heart of northeast India and shares borders with Bhutan and Bangladesh; Goa and Kerala on India's west coast are important maritime centers guarding the SLOCs of the Arabian Sea. For population statistics, see Office of the Registrar General and Census Commissioner, India, "2011 Census Data: Religion," http://www.censusindia.gov.in/2011census/Religion_PCA.html.
14. Jawaharlal Nehru's speech of 14 August 1947 to the Indian Constituent Assembly on the eve of independence acknowledged the reality of Partition and the challenge of moving forward. See Jawaharlal Nehru, "A Tryst with Destiny," *Guardian* (UK), 30 April 2007, https://www.theguardian.com/theguardian/2007/may/01/greatspeeches.
15. In sharp contrast, the subsequent 1971 bifurcation of Pakistan into Bangladesh (erstwhile East Pakistan) and Pakistan (formerly West Pakistan) reflected the demand for an ethnically cohesive, linguistically distinct and geographically compact state for the Bengali people who represented the overwhelming majority of East Pakistan. Ultimately, Muslims of the erstwhile British Raj were not a separate people that constituted a singular nation and Islam was not an overarching identity that could hold together the state of Pakistan that emerged from the 1947 Partition.
16. The Government of Pakistan has its own set of challenges in integrating the areas of Kashmir under its administration with Pakistan. The fact that Pakistan refuses to accept the partition of Kashmir should not serve as an excuse for India to do the same.
17. As a result of the 1971 civil war between West and East Pakistan, the erstwhile East Pakistan (the eastern area of Bengal in pre-1947 British India) gained its independence and renamed itself Bangladesh. India's military intervention on the side of East Pakistan was critical in ensuring the crushing defeat of the West Pakistan expeditionary forces sent to quell the rebellion. Despite its overwhelming military victory over the West Pakistani Army, India did not attempt to (1) resurrect pre-partition Bengal through reunification of East Bengal (with its Muslim majority) with West Bengal (with its Hindu majority), or (2) recover any portion of

Pakistani controlled Kashmir. Manifestly, even when it apparently had the capability, India did not have either the intention or the will to reclaim the territorial legacy of British India.

18. See CIA, "The Sino-Indian Border Dispute, Section 3: 1961–1963," 5 May 1964, 62–72, https://www.cia.gov/library/readingroom/docs/polo-09.pdf.
19. From the Government of Pakistan's perspective, Azad Kashmir and Gilgit-Baltistan are strategically important as they provide additional strategic depth to northern Pakistan. Moreover, the Khunjerab Pass, located in Gilgit-Baltistan along the border with China (Xinjiang province), provides Pakistan with its only road link (Karakoram Highway) to China. For the Middle Kingdom, Aksai Chin is strategically vital as it serves as the logistical corridor connecting Tibet and Xinjiang provinces. Over the next 15 years, the nascent China–Pakistan Economic Corridor linking Gwadar (Pakistan) to Kashgar (China), will be critical for the Middle Kingdom's energy security. Since 1962, Pakistan and China have developed increasingly close strategic ties to such an extent that their relationship constitutes a de facto alliance.
20. In sharp contrast, the Government of India (under the leadership of Prime Minister Jawaharlal Nehru) resorted to military force to ensure the accession of the princely states of Junaghad and Hyderabad (both of which had majority Hindu and significant minority Muslim populations under Muslim rulers) in 1948, and the annexation of Goa (a Portuguese colony with majority Hindu and significant Christian minority population) in 1961. From a national security perspective, Junaghad and Goa (both with commanding positions along the Arabian Sea) are geostrategically important for the defense of India's Arabian Sea SLOCs (sea lines of communication) and the western coast of India, while Hyderabad by virtue of its location in the very center of southern India is vital to the defense of South India. Also, it should be noted that the Kingdom of Sikkim (which had a Hindu majority and significant Buddhist minority population, and which was ruled by a Buddhist monarch), was annexed to the Republic of India in 1975. Sikkim, which previously was a protectorate of India (as successor to British India), shares borders with Nepal, Bhutan, China, and West Bengal, and overlooks the strategically vital Siliguri Corridor that connects the rest of northeastern India to India. For two years prior to the annexation, a large Indian Army presence ensured effective GOI control over Sikkim.
21. History has delivered some harsh lessons to India with respect to its reliance on imports for its military and energy security. The Soviet Union suspended the promised delivery of MIG jet fighters to India during the 1962 Sino-India border conflict, while the United States halted deliveries of military supplies to India during the 1971 conflict with Pakistan.

In 1973, Persian Gulf oil producers led by Saudi Arabia imposed an embargo on oil exports to the United States in retaliation for American support of Israel during the Yom Kippur War. In a future conflict with Pakistan, a de facto ally of Saudi Arabia, India could face the threat of a similar oil embargo.

22. Rajat Pandit, "With 12% of Global Imports, India Tops List of Arms Buyers: Report," *Times of India*, 13 March 2018, https://timesofindia.indiatimes.com/india/with-12-of-global-imports-india-tops-list-of-arms-buyers-report/articleshow/63276648.cms.
23. Stockholm International Peace Institute (SIPRI) "Arms Transfers Database," https://www.sipri.org/databases/armstransfers.
24. Ibid.
25. India currently produces 35 percent of its defense equipment. Imports reduce the urgency of self-reliance, so the political will for strategic autonomy is crucial in ensuring the success of a domestic defense industry.
26. For an urgent plea to take on the challenge of developing India's indigenous defense industry, see Arun Prakash, "An 'Atmanirbharta' India Can Look the World in the Eye," *Indian Express*, 21 March 2022, https://indianexpress.com/article/opinion/columns/an-atmanirbhar-india-can-look-the-world-in-the-eye-russia-ukraine-nato-7828628/.
27. Ultimately, India's ability to defend itself by itself is limited by the size of its economy and amount of resources New Delhi can reasonably allocate for military purposes.
28. Energy Information Administration (EIA), *Country Analysis Brief: India*, 30 September 2020, https://www.eia.gov/international/analysis/country/IND. Imports calculated as the excess of consumption over production.
29. See EIA, *International Energy Outlook 2019* (*IEO 2019*) for projections of oil consumption (Table A5), natural gas consumption (Table A6), and oil production (Table G2), https://www.eia.gov/outlooks/archive/ieo19/tables_ref.php. Imports is calculated as the excess of consumption over production.
30. EIA, *Country Analysis Brief: India*, 30 September 2020.
31. See EIA, *International Energy Outlook 2017* (*IEO 2017*) for projections of natural gas imports (Table I4), https://www.eia.gov/outlooks/archive/ieo17/ieo_tables.php. *IEO 2019* did not provide country level data on natural gas production for India although the same was provided in prior IEOs.
32. EIA, *Country Analysis Brief: India* (2016), https://www.eia.gov/international/content/analysis/countries_long/India/archive/pdf/india_2016pdf.

33. See Press Trust of India (PTI), "10 Years of Indo-US Nuclear Deal: What India Gained from the Historic Pact," *Business Standard (India)*, 11 October 2018, https://www.business-standard.com/article/current-affairs/10-years-of-indo-us-nuclear-deal-what-india-gained-from-the-historic-pact-118101001045_1.html; and Suhasini Haidar, "India Gained Exponentially from U.S. Nuclear Deal: Shyam Saran," *Hindu*, 10 October 2018, https://www.thehindu.com/news/national/india-gained-exponentially-from-us-nuclear-deal-shyam-saran/article24646214.ece.
34. EIA, *Country Analysis Brief: India* (2020).
35. ET Bureau, "India Begins Importing LNG from Russia," *Economic Times*, 4 June 2018, https://economictimes.indiatimes.com/industry/energy/oil-gas/india-begins-importing-lng-from-russia/articleshow/64449583.cms. For a future scenario of the natural gas trade see EIA, *IEO 2017*, "Table I4: World Trade in Natural Gas by Region," https://www.eia.gov/outlooks/aeo/data/browser/#/?id=44-IEO2017&cases=Reference.
36. See K. M. Panikkar, *India and the Indian Ocean: An Essay on the Influence of Sea Power on Indian History*, 2nd ed. (London: G. Allen & Unwin Ltd., 1951), https://catalog.hathitrust.org/Record/001250787.
37. Energy imports from Iran and Iraq could flow to India via land-based pipelines transiting through Pakistan, but this will remain purely theoretical as long as India and Pakistan remain strategic rivals. Détente is unlikely for the foreseeable future.
38. Adrija Roychowdhury, "When Japan Ruled Over (a Part) of India," *Indian Express*, 11 August 2017, https://indianexpress.com/article/research/when-japan-ruled-over-a-part-of-india-4786213/.
39. Ministry of External Affairs (India), "Treaty of Peace and Friendship Between the Government of India and the Government of Nepal, 31 July 1950," https://mea.gov.in/bilateral-documents.htm?dtl/6295/Treaty+of+Peace+and+Friendship; and "India-Bhutan Friendship Treaty, 8 February 2007," http://www.mea.gov.in/Images/pdf/india-bhutan-treaty-07.pdf. Article 2 of the respective treaties reflects the implied Indian defense commitment.
40. See Ministry of Foreign Affairs (Nepal), "Nepal-China Relations," https://web.archive.org/web/20171123125935/http://www.nepaldemocracy.org/documents/treaties_agreements/sino-nepal_treaty1969.htm. Also see "Sino-Nepalese Treaty of Peace and Friendship, 25 April 1960," https://web.archive.org/web/20171123125935/http://www.nepaldemocracy.org/documents/treaties_agreements/sino-nepal_treaty1969.htm.

41. See SIPRI, "Arms Transfer Database," https://www.sipri.org/databases/armstransfers.
42. India's decision in 2017 to send an army contingent to Bhutan's Doklam plateau near the trijunction of the Bhutan-China-India border to deter Beijing from extending a strategically located road into territory administered by Bhutan (but claimed also by China) was an important affirmation of New Delhi's commitment to Thimphu. In this case, both China and India agreed to stand down and maintain the status quo. See Michael Safi, "Chinese and Indian Troops Face Off in Bhutan Border Dispute," *Guardian* (UK), 5 July 2017, https://www.theguardian.com/world/2017/jul/06/china-india-bhutan-standoff-disputed-territory; and Ankit Panda, "Disengagement at Doklam: Why and How Did the India-China Standoff End?" *Diplomat*, 29 August 2017, https://thediplomat.com/2017/08/disengagement-at-doklam-why-and-how-did-the-india-china-standoff-end/.
43. Bangladesh, like India, is overwhelmingly dependent on arms imports to meet its defense requirements. Over the 2011–2020 period, China supplied about 74 percent (in value) of Bangladesh's cumulative imports of military equipment. See Stockholm International Peace Institute (SIPRI), "Arms Transfers Database," https://www.sipri.org/databases/armstransfers.
44. See Jasper Copping, "Second World War Clashes Named as 'Greatest British Battle,'" *Telegraph*, 23 April 2013, https://www.telegraph.co.uk/history/10008053/Second-World-War-clashes-named-as-Greatest-British-Battle.html; and National Army Museum (UK), "Battles of Imphal and Kohima," https://www.nam.ac.uk/explore/battle-imphal.
45. Burma (Myanmar), which until 1937 was part of British India, is far more dependent upon China than it is on India. China is Burma's largest trading partner accounting for 24 percent of total exports and 43 percent of total imports. Over the 2011–2020 period, Burma relied on China for 54 percent of its arms imports. See CIA, *World Factbook*, and SIPRI, "Arms Transfers Database." Also, China is building and will operate a major port facility that has dual civilian-military potential at Kyaukpyu on the Bay of Bengal in Burma. See Reuters, "Myanmar Scales Back Chinese-Backed Port Project Over Debt Fears," *Guardian* (UK), 2 August 2018, https://www.theguardian.com/world/2018/aug/02/myanmar-scales-back-chinese-backed-port-project-over-debt-fears; and Gregory B. Polling, "Kyaukpyu: Connecting China to the Indian Ocean," *CSIS Briefs*, 2 August 2018, Center for Strategic and International Studies, https://www.csis.org/analysis/kyaukpyu-connecting-china-indian-ocean.

46. For an example of a possible embryonic threat, China is building and will operate a major port complex with dual civilian-military potential at Hambantota in Sri Lanka. See Kiran Stacey, "China Signs 99-Year Lease on Sri Lanka's Hambantota Port," *Financial Times*, 11 December 2017, https://www.ft.com/content/e150ef0c-de37-11e7-a8a4-0a1e63a52f9c; and Michael Safi and Amantha Perera, "The Biggest Game Changer in 100 Years: Chinese Money Gushes into Sri Lanka," *Guardian* (UK), 25 March 2018, https://www.theguardian.com/world/2018/mar/26/the-biggest-game-changer-in-100-years-chinese-money-gushes-into-sri-lanka.
47. Such a commitment to provide military and economic support would be an additional burden on India's exchequer and would most likely involve expenditures amounting to about 1 percent of India's GDP.
48. As a practical matter, India's likely nuclear-armed adversaries would be Pakistan and China. By narrowing the scope of the neutrality request, New Delhi enhances the prospects of the request's acceptance.
49. See Ian Marlow, "Why India and Pakistan Keep on Clashing," *Bloomberg News*, 4 August 2019, https://www.bloomberg.com/news/articles/2019-08-05/why-india-and-pakistan-keep-on-clashing-quicktake-jyxucquh; Vanessa Gezari, "Indian Suspect Claims Pakistan Aided Parliament Attack," *Chicago Tribune*, 21 December 2001, https://www.chicagotribune.com/news/ct-xpm-2001-12-21-0112210339-story.html; and Gethin Chamberlin, "Mumbai Terror Attacks: Nightmare in the Lap of Luxury," *Guardian* (UK), 29 November 2008, https://www.theguardian.com/world/2008/nov/30/mumbai-terrorism-attacks.
50. CIA, *World Factbook*.
51. World Bank, "Data Base: Military Expenditure (% of GDP)," https://data.worldbank.org/indicator/MS.MIL.XPND.GD.ZS?locations=IN-PK.
52. Given that the Pakistani economy is only 10.9 percent the size of the Indian economy, to achieve effective parity with Indian defense spending of 2.4 percent of GDP, Pakistan's defense expenditures would have to be about 22 percent of GDP.
53. *Global Firepower 2021*, "Comparisons of World Military Strengths: India and Pakistan," https://www.globalfirepower.com/countries-comparison-detail.asp?form=form&country1=india&country2=pakistan&Submit=COMPARE.
54. Although India defeated Pakistan in the Pakistani initiated wars of 1965, 1971, and 1999, New Delhi was unable to convert its victories into a peace settlement that resolved the Kashmir dispute between the two countries. Instead, India had to acquiesce in the continuance of the status quo.
55. SIPRI, "Arms Transfers Database."

56. For example, in the event of an advance of Indian military forces into Pakistan that threatened the geo-strategically important China–Pakistan Economic Corridor (CPEC) linking the port of Gwadar on the Arabian Sea to the Khunjerab Pass in Gilgit-Baltistan, Beijing could intervene to safeguard its vital national interests and ensure at least a return to the *status quo ante*. Islamabad's ultimate objective in its security partnership with Beijing is to persuade the Middle Kingdom that a major Indian attack on Pakistan should be considered as a major attack on China. CPEC is vital to China's energy security as it will connect Iran's oil and gas resources via land-based pipelines transiting through Pakistan to China, outside the military reach of the United States or Russia.
57. CIA, *World Factbook*.
58. Ibid.
59. World Bank, "Data Base: Military expenditure (% of GDP)," https://data.worldbank.org/indicator/MS.MIL.XPND.GD.ZS?locations=IN-CN.
60. *Global Firepower 2021*, "Comparisons of World Military Strengths: India and China," https://www.globalfirepower.com/countries-comparison-detail.asp?form=form&country1=india&country2=china&Submit=COMPARE.
61. The key determinants with respect to forecasts of *latent* military power are: (1) the initial GDP (PPP basis) of each of the two countries, (2) the assumed real rate of growth for each country, and (3) the assumed time period. For example, per the CIA the 2019 GDP (PPP basis) of China was $22.5 trillion while the 2019 GDP of India was $9.2 trillion, so the initial GDP gap in favor of China was $13.3 trillion. For the sake of argument, assuming that over the next 15 years China's GDP growth rate is 5 percent per annum and India's GDP growth rate is 10 percent per annum, then *even though India's assumed rate of growth is twice that of China*, in 2034 China will still have a significantly favorable GDP gap relative to India of about $8.6 trillion. It is not credible to expect that Beijing's forbearance and restraint will last long enough for India to surpass China.
62. EIA, *International Energy Outlook 2019*, "Table A3: World Gross Domestic Product (GDP) Expressed in Purchasing Power Parity by Region," and "Table A14: World Population by Region," https://www.eia.gov/outlooks/archive/ieo19/tables_ref.php.
63. In 2039, per EIA's projections, India's economy will be only 56 percent the size of China's economy (or China's economy will be 1.78 times the size of India's economy). So, in order to achieve defense spending parity with China, India's spending rate will have to be 4.5 percent of GDP or about 1.78 times China's assumed spending rate of 2.5 percent. Historically, independent India's defense spending rate peaked at 4.2 percent in

1987, so it is very doubtful that India could sustain a significantly higher defense burden.

64. According to a 2016 public opinion survey, about 63 percent were in favor of increasing Indian defense expenditures. See Bruce Stokes, "India and Modi: The Honeymoon Continues," Pew Research Center, 19 September 2016, https://www.pewresearch.org/global/2016/09/19/india-and-modi-the-honeymoon-continues/.
65. "The History of Sino-Indian Relations and the Border Dispute Between the Two Nations (5)," *Resurgent India*, 23 March 2015, http://new.resurgentindia.org/the-history-of-sino-indian-relations-and-the-border-dispute-between-the-two-countries-5/.
66. Ibid. See also "Sardar Vallabhbhai Patel's Letter to Jawaharlal Nehru on 7 November 1950," Friends of Tibet, http://www.friendsoftibet.org/main/sardar.html.
67. Quoted in Sudhir Ghosh, *Gandhi's Emissary* (New Delhi: Routledge, 2008), 277.
68. Ibid.
69. "The History of Sino-Indian Relations and the Border Dispute Between the Two Nations (5)," *Resurgent India*, 23 March 2015, http://new.resurgentindia.org/the-history-of-sino-indian-relations-and-the-border-dispute-between-the-two-countries-5/.
70. "Nehru Correspondence, November 1962: 11–19," John F. Kennedy Library Archives, https://www.jfklibrary.org/Asset-Viewer/Archives/JFKNSF-111-016.aspx.
71. For a lucid discussion of the factors shaping China's decision to end the war, see Bruce Riedel, *JFK's Forgotten Crisis: Tibet, the CIA, and Sino-Indian War* (Washington, DC: Brookings Institution Press, 2015), 140–146.
72. US Department of Defense, Office of the Secretary of Defense, *Annual Report to Congress: Military and Security Developments Involving the People's Republic of China 2020*, https://media.defense.gov/2020/Sep/01/2002488689/-1/-1/1/2020-DOD-CHINA-MILITARY-POWER-REPORT-FINAL.PDF.
73. EIA, *International Energy Outlook 2019*, "Table A3: World Gross Domestic Product (GDP) Expressed in Purchasing Power Parity by Region," https://www.eia.gov/outlooks/archive/ieo19/tables_ref.php.
74. CIA, *World Factbook*.
75. World Bank, "Data Base: Military Expenditure (% of GDP)," https://data.worldbank.org/indicator/MS.MIL.XPND.GD.ZS?locations=CN-IN-US.
76. CIA, *World Factbook*.
77. EIA, *International Energy Outlook 2019*.

78. If India, by itself, wanted to maintain effective parity with China, a defense spending rate of 2.5 percent of China's GDP would translate to a 4.5 percent rate for India in 2039. In the alliance structure, India would be committed to spend about 3 percent of its GDP, a considerably lower burden than attempting to go solo. It is unlikely that China would seek to get into a defense spending race with such an alliance. From India's perspective, an alliance with the US would be an effective way to resolve its guns versus butter dilemma. India gets more security (through the alliance) and more development (a lower defense spending burden can translate to a higher spending rate for economic development and growth). The fact that India's GDP of $30 trillion will be ahead of US GDP of $26.5 trillion by 2039 (per EIA) suggests that a partnership of equals is a realistic expectation.
79. *Global Firepower 2021*, https://www.globalfirepower.com/.
80. Assuming, in the future, reflecting the increasingly close energy ties between Moscow and Beijing, Russia allocates 60 percent of its oil and gas exports to China then in 2039 Russia would supply the Middle Kingdom 4.7 mbpd of oil and 6.6 Tcf of gas representing 37 percent of China's total oil imports of 12.5 mbpd and 100 percent of China's total gas imports of 6.6 Tcf. In that year, China's total oil consumption is projected to be 16.7 mbpd. For China to successfully prosecute a major war with oil supplies sufficient to meet only 53 percent of its total oil requirements (Russian oil imports of 4.7 mbpd together with domestic oil production of 4.2 mbpd) would be extraordinarily difficult and most likely impossible. See EIA, *International Energy Outlook 2019*, Table A5 (oil consumption), A6 (gas consumption), and G2 (oil production). See *IEO 2017* for natural gas imports (Table I4). Exports calculated as the excess of production over consumption. Imports calculated as the excess of consumption over production.
81. North Atlantic Treaty Organization (NATO), "The North Atlantic Treaty, 4 April 1949," https://www.nato.int/cps/en/natolive/official_texts_17120.htm. Ambiguous language such as in the US–Japan mutual defense treaty (which is silent on the option of a military response) or declaratory statements affirming a special relationship (such as non-binding US congressional resolutions and US presidential statements on Israel) is unlikely to deter China as such deliberately vague formulations would reinforce doubts about the likelihood of US intervention in the event of Sino-Indian conflict. In fact, it could encourage Beijing to gamble that such ambiguity is merely a bluff, and that Washington would not respond militarily to a limited attack on India such as a Chinese move to seize part of the disputed state of Arunachal Pradesh (South Tibet) or to extend westward Aksai Chin's border with Ladakh by wresting

control over portions of the Kargil-Leh-Nyoma sector. Similarly, there would be doubt about the likelihood of Indian military support to the United States in the event of Sino-American conflict in the disputed international waters of the South China Sea.

82. For different perspectives on the likely trajectory of US–India relations, see Robert D. Blackwill and Ashley J. Tellis, "New Delhi Remains Washington's Best Hope in Asia," *Foreign Affairs*, vol. 98, no. 5, September/October 2019, 173–183; Rajesh Rajagopalan, "U.S.-India Relations Under President Trump: Promise and Peril," *Asia Policy*, vol. 24, July 2017, 39–45; and Sumit Ganguly, "Has Modi Truly Changed India's Foreign Policy?" *Washington Quarterly*, vol. 40, no. 2, Summer 2017, 131–143.
83. The Biden Administration's Indo-Pacific strategy envisions a growing US–India strategic partnership. See, The White House, *Indo-Pacific Strategy of the United States, February 2022*, 13 and16, https://www.whitehouse.gov/wp-content/uploads/2022/02/U.S.-Indo-Pacific-Strategy.pdf.
84. "Text of the Prime Minister's Address to the Joint Session of U.S. Congress," *Hindu*, 8 June 2016, https://www.thehindu.com/news/resources/Text-of-the-Prime-Ministers-address-to-the-Joint-Session-of-U.S.-Congress/article14391856.ece.
85. White House, "Joint Statement: The United States and India: Enduring Global Partners in the 21st Century," 7 June 2016, https://obamawhitehouse.archives.gov/the-press-office/2016/06/07/joint-statement-united-states-and-india-enduring-global-partners-21st; and "United States and India: Prosperity Through Partnership," 26 June 2017, https://www.whitehouse.gov/briefings-statements/united-states-india-prosperity-partnership/.
86. Bruce Stokes, Dorothy Manevich and Hanyu Chwe, "Three Years In, Modi Remains Very Popular," 15 November 2017, Pew Research Center, https://www.pewresearch.org/global/2017/11/15/india-modi-remains-very-popular-three-years-in/.
87. Ibid.
88. Bruce Stokes, "India and Modi: The Honeymoon Continues," Pew Research Center, 19 September 2016, https://www.pewresearch.org/global/2016/09/19/india-and-modi-the-honeymoon-continues/.
89. CIA, *World Factbook*.
90. Global Firepower 2021, https://www.globalfirepower.com/.
91. US Department of Defense, *Annual Report to Congress: Military and Security Developments Involving the People's Republic of China 2019*, 31, https://media.defense.gov/2019/May/02/2002127082/-1/-1/1/2019_CHINA_MILITARY_POWER_REPORT.pdf.
92. EIA, *IEO 2019*.

93. Center for Strategic and International Studies (CSIS), "Defining Our Relationship with India for the Next Century: An Address by U.S. Secretary of State Rex Tillerson," 18 October 2017, https://csis-prod.s3.amazonaws.com/s3fs-public/event/171018_An_Address_by_U.S._Secretary_of_State_Rex_Tillerson.pdf?O0nMCCRjXZiUa5V2cF8_NDiZ14LYRX3m.
94. White House, *The National Security Strategy of the United States of America, December 2017*, 25, https://www.whitehouse.gov/wp-content/uploads/2017/12/NSS-Final-12-18-2017-0905.pdf.
95. Ibid., 46 and 50.
96. Laura Silver, Kat Devlin and Christine Huang, "U.S. Views of China Turn Sharply Negative Amid Trade Tensions," 13 August 2019, Pew Research Center, https://www.pewresearch.org/global/2019/08/13/u-s-views-of-china-turn-sharply-negative-amid-trade-tensions/.
97. Siddharth Varadarajan, "Interview: There Is a New China in the NSG and India Needs to Find a Way to Deal with It," *The Wire* (India), 30 June 2016, https://thewire.in/external-affairs/interview-there-is-a-new-china-in-the-nsg-and-india-needs-to-find-a-way-to-deal-with-it. Also see Shyam Saran, "An India Allying with None," *Business Standard*, 20 January 2013, https://www.business-standard.com/article/opinion/shyam-saran-an-india-allying-with-none-112032100104_1.html.
98. Japan, Australia, and France are allies or, more accurately, security dependents of the United States. Vietnam and Singapore are increasing their military cooperation with America. It is reasonable to assume that the defense relationships of these countries with the United States would take precedence over any security cooperation arrangements these countries may have with India. Even more radically, if New Delhi were to craft major energy and defense cooperation agreements with Russia and Iran (as an alternative to an Indo-American alliance), these arrangements would not redress the adverse power imbalance relative to China. Both Russia and Iran are increasingly dependent on China for their economic security, so ultimately their relationship with Beijing would trump their arrangements with New Delhi when it matters most—a future Sino-Indian conflict. For example, it is unlikely that either Russia or Iran would suspend energy exports to China in the event of a war between India and China. Moreover, if India continues to rely on Moscow for a major portion of its imports of military equipment, New Delhi could not expect a continued flow of such equipment during a war with the Middle Kingdom.
99. "Nehru Correspondence, November 1962: 11–19," John F. Kennedy Library Archives, https://www.jfklibrary.org/Asset-Viewer/Archives/JFKNSF-111-016.aspx.

100. Ministry of External Affairs (India), "Treaty of Peace, Friendship and Cooperation Between the Government of India and the Government of the Union of Soviet Socialist Republics, 9 August 1971," https://mea.gov.in/bilateral-documents.htm?dtl/5139/Treaty+of+.
101. Shortly after the commencement of the Sino-Indian border war, the United States stated it recognized the McMahon Line as India's northeastern boundary while remaining silent on Aksai Chin and the northwestern boundary. This continues to be the American position. See "Memorandum from the President's Deputy Special Assistant for National Security Affairs (Kaysen) to President Kennedy, 26 October 1962" (Document no. 181) in Office of the Historian, *Foreign Relations of the United States, 1961–1963, Volume 19, South Asia*, https://history.state.gov/historicaldocuments/frus1961-63v19/d181.
102. Hannah Ellis-Peterson, "China and India Move Troops as Border Tensions Escalate," *Guardian* (UK), 27 May 2020, https://www.theguardian.com/world/2020/may/27/china-and-india-move-troops-as-border-tensions-escalate; and Archana Chaudhary, "Why Chinese and Indian Troops Clash in the Himalayas," *Washington Post*, 2 July 2021, https://www.washingtonpost.com/business/why-chinese-and-indian-troops-clashin-the-himalayas/2021/06/29/0cd73f20-d892-11eb-8c87-ad6f27918c78_story.html. Ultimately, China's strategic ambitions may be to push Aksai Chin's border with Ladakh deeply westward following the Indus River along a line running through the Kargil-Leh-Nyoma sector by 2025–2030 in advance of the prospective completion of the Iran to China energy pipeline in the 2035–2039 timeframe. Seizure of such a significant swathe of territory currently under Indian administration most likely could only be achieved through war. India has yet to recognize that it is in the Middle Kingdom's crosshairs because of the potential geostrategic threat it poses to China's energy security.
103. Ministry of Commerce and Industry (India), "Trade Statistics: Export Import Data Bank: Annual, 2018–2019, Total Trade," https://commerce-app.gov.in/eidb/.
104. Ibid.
105. Since China supplies close to 14 percent of India's total imports of $514.1 billion (FY 2019), New Delhi will have to find alternative foreign suppliers or produce such goods domestically. Import substitution will boost the domestic economy. The loss of imports from China will not have an adverse impact on India's national security as the imported goods are not defense related.
106. For 2019 trade figures (exports and imports) see Central Intelligence Agency (CIA), *The World Factbook*, https://www.cia.gov/the-world-factbook/.

107. See "Memorandum of Conversation, 10 December 1971" (Document no. 274) in Office of the Historian, *Foreign Relations of the United States, 1969–1976, Volume 11, South Asia Crisis*, https://history.state.gov/historicaldocuments/frus1969-76v11/d274.
108. See Kautilya, *The Arthashastra*, edited and translated by L. N. Rangarajan (New Delhi: Penguin Books, 1992), 505–634; Lord Curzon, *The Place of India in the Empire* (London: John Murray, 1909), 11–14, https://babel.hathitrust.org/cgi/pt?id=umn.319510023281092;view=1up;seq=16; and K. M. Panikkar, *India and the Indian Ocean: An Essay on the Influence of Sea Power on Indian History*, 2nd ed. (London: G. Allen & Unwin Ltd., 1951), https://catalog.hathitrust.org/Record/001250787.
109. It will take time, probably 5–10 years, to crystallize the political will to consummate such an alliance of equals. India will have to develop the self-confidence to operate as an equal partner and America will have to adjust from being *primus inter pares* to equal partner. Obviously, India or US indecision and procrastination favors China. Clearly, Beijing will seek to dissuade New Delhi from committing to a formal Indo-American military alliance.

CHAPTER 3

# China's Grand Strategy: Reincarnation of the Middle Kingdom

The People's Republic of China (PRC), born on 1 October 1949, is still at the growing, young adult stage in terms of the long arc of Chinese history.[1] It will probably take another 15–20 years for the PRC to reach prime maturity and restore the Middle Kingdom, of which the PRC is the modern reincarnation, to its traditional position as Asia's regional hegemon. China is the world's largest economy with gross domestic product (GDP) in terms of purchasing power parity of $22.5 trillion in 2019, and is expected to further reinforce its economic leadership position with GDP growing to $53.4 trillion by 2039.[2] For the remainder of the twenty-first century, Beijing's grand strategy is likely to focus on the pursuit of 5 vital national interests: (1) energy security through access to foreign energy resources in order to safeguard its economic and military security as well as political independence, given the reality of the country's heavy reliance on oil and gas imports for the foreseeable future; (2) the restoration of the territorial integrity of the Middle Kingdom and reconstitution of a singular national identity through (a) resolution with India of the final status of Aksai Chin (currently under Chinese administration) and Arunachal Pradesh/South Tibet (currently under Indian administration), (b) the reintegration of Taiwan, (c) the return of the Senkaku/Diaoyu Islands (currently under Japanese administrative control) and recognition of Chinese sovereignty over them, and



S. Tata, *Reflections on Grand Strategy*,
https://doi.org/10.1007/978-981-19-3773-6_3

(d) acquiescence to the so-called "nine-dash" line as the basis of demarcating China's de facto maritime boundary in the South China Sea; (3) acceptance of an exclusive Chinese sphere of influence representing a "Greater China" that serves as a *cordon sanitaire* protecting the Middle Kingdom's "core" territory; (4) economic security through access to foreign markets, reflecting the continued reliance on exports as a driver of economic growth; and (5) freedom of navigation and connectivity in the global commons as one of the world's leading trading nations.

## Energy Security

The Middle Kingdom's "Achilles' heel" is its overwhelming dependence on oil and gas imports. China's economic and military security as well as its political independence are inextricably intertwined with its energy security. According to the Energy Information Administration (EIA), the statistical arm of the US Department of Energy, in 2019 China imported 10.1 million barrels per day (mbpd) of oil to satisfy about 70 percent of total oil consumption of 14.5 mbpd and 4.6 trillion cubic feet (Tcf) of gas to meet nearly 43 percent of total natural gas consumption requirements of 10.8 Tcf.[3] By 2039, the EIA projects that Chinese oil imports will rise to 12.5 mbpd in order to meet about 75 percent of the country's total oil consumption requirements of 16.7 mbpd, while gas imports will increase to 6.6 Tcf to satisfy about 39 percent of total natural gas consumption needs of 16.8 Tcf.[4] According to the US Department of Defense (DoD or Pentagon), in 2019 about 77 percent of China's oil imports and 10 percent of its natural gas imports transited through the Malacca Straits—China's jugular vein—to the South China Sea on the final leg to various ports on the country's east coast.[5]

Manifestly, China is extraordinarily dependent on maritime transport with respect to oil imports, which are primarily from the Persian Gulf and Africa (about 62 percent in 2019).[6] The US Navy, which dominates the global maritime commons, controls the energy trade's crucial sea lines of communication and maritime chokepoints of the Indian Ocean—from the Strait of Hormuz in the Persian Gulf and the Bab al-Mandab Strait in the Gulf of Aden to the Malacca, Sunda, and Lombok Straits that are the gateways to the South China Sea.[7] The Pentagon estimates that at least for the next 15 years (until about 2035), China will remain dependent on maritime routes for a significant portion of its oil imports.[8] Clearly, for the foreseeable future energy security will loom large as a vital national interest for China.

The Middle Kingdom's challenge with respect to energy security has three facets.[9] First, Beijing must have friendly, reliable suppliers collectively capable of meeting China's oil and gas import requirements over the long term. Friendly means that the supplying countries do not have vital national interests that conflict with or adversely affect China's vital national interests. Reliable means that the energy supplying countries have the capacity to ensure internal stability as well as protect themselves against external threats, so that there are no major, lengthy energy supply disruptions. Second, China must be able to demonstrate to its energy suppliers that it can ensure their economic security. This will require Chinese long-term purchase contracts to quantify assured energy demand; and the provision of substantial capital resources and technological expertise to help energy producers explore and develop oil and gas reserves, expand production, and build associated infrastructure. Third, the routes over which the oil and gas supplies are transported from the producing countries to China—energy trade connectivity—must be secure. Accordingly, the transit countries through which the energy imports flow (via pipeline, road, or rail) must be friendly and reliable; and, to the extent that the energy imports are sea-borne, freedom of navigation must prevail with respect to the relevant maritime oil and gas trade routes within the global commons.

## China's Energy Quintet: Russia, Kazakhstan, Turkmenistan, Iran, and Iraq

From Beijing's perspective, Russia represents the ideal combination of geographic propinquity, energy reserves, reliability, and friendship essential to resolving China's energy security dilemma. China shares a 4133 km border (in the northeast) and 46 km border (in the northwest) with Russia.[10] According to EIA's country analysis brief, Russia had proved reserves of 80 billion barrels of oil and 1688 Tcf of gas (the world's largest) at year-end 2016.[11] In that year, Russia exported about 7 mbpd of oil and 7.5 Tcf of gas based on total production of 11.2 mbpd of oil and 21 Tcf of gas. Yet, oil exports to China accounted for only 14 percent of Russia's 2016 total oil exports, while gas exports to China were negligible.[12] By 2039, the EIA projects that Russia will export 7.8 mbpd of oil and 15.6 Tcf of gas based on total production of 11.3 mbpd of oil and 31.2 Tcf of gas.[13] In 2039, as noted earlier, Chinese energy import requirements will be 12.5 mbpd of oil and 6.6 Tcf of gas. If Russia were to allocate 60 percent of its energy exports to China, then in 2039 about 37 percent of the Middle Kingdom's oil import requirements and 100 percent of its gas import requirements would be satisfied.[14] Simply put, such energy imports from Russia together with domestic energy production, would enable China to meet about 53 percent of its total oil consumption needs and all of its gas consumption needs. Moreover, Beijing does not have to worry about the physical security of the energy transport corridor as the land routes (pipelines, roads, and rail) from Russia's oil and gas fields to the Chinese border would run entirely through Russian territory, while the maritime route—the arctic Northern Sea Route from the Yamal Peninsula to Vladivostok—is dominated by the Russian Navy.[15]

The building blocks for an enduring Sino-Russian energy partnership are being put in place in a systematic manner on the basis of a simple bargain: energy security for China in return for economic security for Russia. The crucial major effort that is required to transform Russia into the Middle Kingdom's keystone energy supplier is the expansion of the existing energy pipeline networks connecting Russia's eastern Siberia oil and gas fields to northeastern China. By 2039, the capacity of the East Siberia-Pacific Ocean (ESPO) pipeline network (current planned capacity of 1.6 mbpd as of 2020) will have to be tripled to 4.8 mbpd and the Power of Siberia (POS) gas pipeline network (current planned capacity of 3.3 Tcf as of 2020) would have to be doubled to 6.6 Tcf.[16] These oil and gas pipeline expansion projects are undoubtedly ambitious and aggressive, but they are realistic and reasonable considering the 15-to 20-year time frame for completion (with completion anticipated by 2035–2039). Russia has the energy reserves; exploration, development, and production technology and expertise; and pipeline construction skills. China, with foreign currency reserves of about $3.2 trillion (2020), has the capital to fund these projects.[17] Both countries are highly motivated to cement the nascent energy partnership. For Moscow, assured Chinese demand supported by long-term purchase contracts would virtually guarantee Russian economic security without political strings attached (such as the sanctions imposed by the United States and the European Union following Russia's annexation of Crimea in 2014 and the even more onerous sanctions that were imposed in the wake of Russia's February 2022 reinvasion of Ukraine).[18] For Beijing, assured energy supply is an existential necessity. The mutual interdependence is strongly symmetrical, which is essential for a stable, long-term partnership of strategic equals.

Kazakhstan (with respect to oil) and Turkmenistan (with respect to natural gas)—two former Central Asian Republics of the erstwhile Soviet Union—have important supplementary roles to play in support of the rapidly developing Sino-Russian energy partnership. Kazakhstan's 2017 proved oil reserves amounted to 30 billion barrels of oil.[19] In 2017, according to EIA's country analysis brief, Kazakhstan produced 1.8 mbpd of oil, of which 1.3 mbpd was exported, mostly to Europe. Exports to China were miniscule—about 52,000 barrels per day (representing 4 percent of oil exports).[20] While there is an existing Kazakhstan to China (Urumqi in Xinjiang province) oil pipeline with a capacity of 400,000 barrels per day, currently mostly Russian oil destined for China flows through this pipeline, given the small volume of Kazakh oil exports to China. Undoubtedly, there is an attractive opportunity to significantly ramp up Kazakh oil production. China, with proved reserves (2014) of about 24.6 billion barrels of oil, produced 4.6 mbpd of oil in 2014.[21] Accordingly, it would be reasonable to assume that over the next twenty years, Kazakhstan, which has proved reserves that are slightly larger than that of China, could double the amount of oil produced to a level of 3.6 mbpd in 2039 (reflecting an annual growth rate in production of 3.625 percent).[22] Likewise, if domestic oil consumption (about 400,000 barrels per day currently) were assumed to grow at a rate of 5 percent per annum, then by 2039 oil consumption would be 1.1 mbpd. In 2039, the amount of oil available for export (the difference between production and consumption) would be 2.5 mbpd. Assuming further that 60 percent of such oil exports are allocated to China, then Kazakhstan could supply 1.5 mbpd of oil to meet about 12 percent of China's 2039 oil import requirements. Of course, the existing pipeline connection would have to be quadrupled from 0.4 mbpd to 1.6 mbpd to accommodate the growth in Kazakh oil exports to the Middle Kingdom. China would not have to worry about the security of the energy pipeline connection. Kazakhstan shares borders with China (1765 km), Russia (7644 km), Uzbekistan (2330 km), and Turkmenistan (413 km).[23] In extremis, Russia, which considers the former Soviet Central Asian Republics to be firmly within its sphere of influence, would safeguard Kazakhstan, Uzbekistan, and Turkmenistan against internal and external threats.

Turkmenistan's total proved natural gas reserves amounted to 265 Tcf as of 2017.[24] In that year, natural gas exports were 1.3 Tcf based on production of 2.7 Tcf of dry natural gas.[25] Over 70 percent of Turkmenistan's natural gas exports flowed to China (Urumqi in Xinjiang province) through pipelines connected to Kazakhstan's pipeline system (including a pipeline transiting through Uzbekistan). Accordingly, in 2017, gas imports from Turkmenistan met about 35 percent of China's total gas import requirements.[26] If, over the next 20 years, Turkmenistan can double its production of dry natural gas to 5.4 Tcf (reflecting an annual compound growth rate of 3.625 percent) while keeping the growth rate of domestic gas consumption at a similar 3.625 percent per annum, then in 2039 the amount of Turkmen gas available for export will be 2.6 Tcf.[27] Assuming further that Turkmenistan continues to allocate 70 percent of its gas exports to China (given Turkmenistan's limited access to alternative export markets), then in 2039 Turkmenistan would satisfy 27 percent (1.8 Tcf) of China's total gas import needs (6.6 Tcf).[28] The forecast assumptions are conservative and reasonable.[29] Indeed, the US Department of Defense estimates that by the end of 2020, Turkmenistan's gas exports to China will jump to 2.8 Tcf and that the existing gas pipeline system will be expanded accordingly.[30] Turkmenistan shares a 413 km border with Kazakhstan, a 1793 km border with Uzbekistan, an 804 km border with Afghanistan, and a 1148 km border with Iran.[31] Given that Turkmenistan, Uzbekistan, and Kazakhstan are part of Russia's sphere of influence, and that both Turkmenistan and Uzbekistan share borders with Kazakhstan, which in turn shares a long border with China, it is unlikely that Beijing will have to fret over the security of the energy pipelines connecting these Central Asian republics to the Middle Kingdom.

Strategic prudence suggests that China would seek to hedge its energy partnership with Russia. Iran is the only other major oil and gas exporter possessing significant enough oil and gas reserves to satisfy a substantial portion of both China's oil *and* gas import requirements on a sustainable basis via land-based pipelines that would completely bypass the maritime energy trade routes dominated by the American navy. Iran's 2020 proved oil reserves amounted to 209 billion barrels (about 2.6 × the amount of Russia) and its proved natural gas reserves totaled 1200 Tcf (the world's second largest after Russia).[32] In 2017 (the year before the United States reimposed sanctions on Iran's oil trade), Iran exported about 3 mbpd of oil and 0.3 Tcf of gas based on production of 4.7 mbpd of oil and 7.2 Tcf of dry gas.[33] If, over the next two decades, Tehran can boost oil production (using 2017 oil production of 4.7 mbpd as the base) at an annual growth rate of 3.625 percent while restraining domestic oil consumption to an annual growth rate of 2.5 percent, then in 2039 Iran will be able to export 6.6 mbpd of oil based on production of 9.4 mbpd.[34] With respect to natural gas, if production can be increased at an annual growth rate of 6.5 percent while limiting the rate of growth in domestic consumption to 5 percent per annum, then in 2039 Tehran will be in a position to export 7.1 Tcf of gas based on production of 25.4 Tcf of dry gas.[35] Further assuming Tehran allocates 60 percent of its energy exports to the Middle Kingdom (reflecting prudent diversification), then in 2039 Iran would be able to satisfy 32 percent of China's oil import requirements and 65 percent of its gas import needs.[36] Tehran and Beijing have no conflicting vital national interests and have no history of tension or animosity, while there is an obvious mutuality of interest in a long-term economic security/energy security bargain. Clearly, from China's perspective, transforming the potential of the Persian energy security hedge into reality will be an enormous undertaking (in terms of finance as well as technical expertise) over the next 15–20 years and a critical test of Beijing's strategic patience, given that the cumulative impact of American economic sanctions imposed on Iran as a consequence of long-running US–Iran tensions (since the 1979 Iran revolution) has severely hobbled Iran's oil and gas industry.[37]

Iran shares a 959 km border with Pakistan (southwestern Pakistan's Baluchistan province), while Pakistan (northwestern Pakistan's Gilgit-Baltistan region) shares a 438 km border with China (Xinjiang province in western China).[38] Iran has had friendly relations with Pakistan since the latter's birth in 1947, and Pakistan and China have been de facto allies for over a half century. Beijing is planning an economic corridor connecting Pakistan's Gwadar port (to be built and operated by China) in Baluchistan province to Kashgar in Xinjiang province—the so-called China–Pakistan Economic Corridor (CPEC).[39] The strategic centerpiece of CPEC is a proposed energy pipeline system connecting Iranian oil and gas fields to China's energy terminal in Kashgar.[40] An energy pipeline linking Iran to the Pakistan border is in place, although it would have to be significantly expanded. The pipeline system connecting Gwadar (Pakistan) to Kashgar (China) has yet to be built; however, there is an existing highway, which will have to be expanded and upgraded. A rail link is envisaged as well. Beijing has committed to invest $46 billion in the CPEC project. Assuring security for the network of roads, railways, and pipelines running through Pakistan—the critical infrastructure of CPEC—will be a major challenge. The Pakistani army is battling a separatist movement in Baluchistan province along the Iran–Pakistan border, and radical Sunni fundamentalist groups such as ethnic Pashtun Pakistani Taliban along the Afghanistan–Pakistan border.[41] Islamabad has established a special 15,000-person security force specifically to safeguard CPEC.[42] Pakistan is a nuclear-armed state, with a well-trained, highly disciplined, professional army. Pakistan is fully capable of defending itself against internal and external threats. The strategic importance of CPEC is that it provides the Middle Kingdom an energy transit corridor that is outside the control of both Moscow and Washington, as Beijing and Islamabad are longstanding allies (with China as the senior partner). For Islamabad, CPEC will provide substantial transit fees which will help finance Pakistan's economic growth and development, and the corridor's strategic importance to China will ensure an enduring security commitment to Pakistan.[43]

Iraq, as the Mesopotamian supplement to Beijing's Persian hedge, has a major role to play to reinforce and significantly enhance China's oil security. As of 2020, Iraq's total proved oil reserves were 145 billion barrels (almost 70 percent as large as Iran's reserves).[44] In 2019, Iraq's oil production was about 4.7 mbpd and oil consumption was about 0.9 mbpd, which implied a net export capacity of about 3.8 mbpd.[45] If, over the next 20 years, Iraq can increase oil production at an annual growth rate of 3.625 percent while limiting domestic oil consumption to the same rate of growth as production, then in 2039 Iraq would have 7.6 mbpd of oil available for export.[46] Assuming further that 60 percent of Iraqi oil exports are allocated to China, then in 2039 Iraqi oil exports of 4.6 mbpd would satisfy about 37 percent of China's oil import requirements of 12.5 mbpd for that year.

Iraq and Iran share a 1599 km border, while Iran shares a 959 km border with Pakistan and a 1148 km border with Turkmenistan.[47] Tehran and Baghdad have had very close ties since the overthrow of the Iraqi dictator Saddam Hussein in 2003 following the US invasion and occupation of Iraq, and the relationship has grown and strengthened since then to such an extent as to be characterized as a de facto alliance. Iran has been particularly useful in helping Baghdad combat Sunni fundamentalist insurgencies and Kurdish separatism that have threatened Iraq's stability.[48] Accordingly, a pipeline from Iraq's southern oilfields (which have no significant security issues) connecting (or running parallel) to the proposed Iran–China oil pipeline via Pakistan could be built as part of an expanded CPEC project.[49] Such a development would be enormously attractive: China would gain access to Iraqi oil via a land-based pipeline system that bypasses the maritime routes dominated by the American navy; Iran and Iraq's strategic partnership would be further reinforced, and the strategic importance of the Iran–Iraq energy combine for the Middle Kingdom would be significantly boosted; Iran would earn substantial oil transit fees; and Pakistan's oil transit fee income would nearly double by virtue of the additional volume of oil flowing through the CPEC pipeline network, while Islamabad's strategic importance for Beijing would be further magnified.

While China has embedded its energy security strategy within the architecture of the One Belt, One Road (or New Silk Road) Initiative, which includes other objectives such as connectivity, trade and commerce, economic growth and development, political and diplomatic relationships, as well as possible security partnerships and military options, the overarching centrality of energy security to China's grand strategy is obvious and cannot be overlooked.[50] The Pentagon estimates that it will take China about 15 years to sufficiently develop alternative land routes for its energy imports so that the Middle Kingdom would no longer be dependent on maritime routes for its energy trade: "Despite China's efforts to diversify energy suppliers, the sheer volume of oil and liquified natural gas imported from the Middle East and Africa will make securing strategic SLOCs a priority for at least the next 15 years."[51] Although it is certainly true that in the short to medium term China will have to rely on maritime energy trade routes to carry oil and gas imports, it would be a grave mistake to assume that the Middle Kingdom will continue to do so over the long term. China is focused on getting around the obstacle posed by American sea power, not in trying to confront and overwhelm the US Navy in the global commons. China's energy security strategy reflects a quintessentially soft power approach to addressing the reality of American naval supremacy. For the Middle Kingdom, failure is not an option in executing and implementing its energy security strategy designed to link China to reliable and friendly oil and gas producers via land-based pipelines that completely circumvent maritime trade routes ultimately controlled by the United States. The foregoing analysis strongly suggests, with a very high degree of confidence, that within a generation (by 2035–2039) the Middle Kingdom will succeed in safeguarding its energy security.

## Territorial Integrity and a Singular National Identity

The PRC's approach to the Sino-Indian border dispute is deeply rooted in geostrategic necessity and realpolitik, rather than the emotional well-springs of territorial integrity and national identity that shape its approach to Taiwan, Diaoyu Islands, and the South China Sea. At the time of its establishment in 1949, the PRC's administrative control over its western provinces of Xinjiang and Tibet, with substantial non-ethnic Chinese (Han) indigenous populations, was tenuous although its sovereignty with respect to the provinces was not seriously contested (either internally or externally). Indeed, sizable military garrisons continue to be needed to maintain the government's control.[52]

The Aksai Chin region of Ladakh (claimed by India as part of the erstwhile princely state of Kashmir) is a sparsely populated, remote geographic salient that separates the southwestern junction of Xinjiang and Tibet. During the 1950s, the PRC constructed a strategically vital military highway linking Xinjiang and Tibet via Aksai Chin. The Indian government was unaware of this activity as it did not send military patrols to what it considered to be a barren and desolate area. By 1959, when it woke up to what was a fait accompli, the Government of India protested what it viewed as Chinese trespassing into Indian territory. Beijing in turn rejected New Delhi's position of unilaterally using the so-called Johnson Line (1865), which was not demarcated, as India's northwestern border between Kashmir and China. Beijing also raised the ante by counterclaiming that Arunachal Pradesh in India's northeast was historically a part of southern Tibet, and the McMahon Line which served as the boundary between Tibet and India was illegitimate since it was imposed on Tibet in 1914 by the British (who were then in control of India) without the written consent of China. The PRC suggested that de facto administrative control rather than de jure sovereignty claims should be the criterion for resolving the border dispute. The Government of India as successor to British India considered its inherited borders to be non-negotiable.[53]

On 20 October 1962, against the backdrop of the Cuban Missile crisis, China and India went to war over their territorial quarrels. As Chinese military forces rolled over a poorly equipped Indian army, Prime

Minister Jawaharlal Nehru appealed for American military assistance. President John F. Kennedy promptly agreed to provide such aid.[54] The United States also recognized the McMahon Line as India's northeastern border but remained silent on India's northwestern border, including Aksai Chin.[55] The Chinese unilaterally decided to withdraw completely from Arunachal Pradesh (although maintaining their sovereignty claim) but remain in Aksai Chin. Prudently, since 1962, New Delhi has made no attempt to recover Aksai Chin—an implicit acknowledgment that such a venture would fail.

Given the centrality of CPEC (particularly the Gwadar to Kashgar energy pipeline connecting Iran's oil and gas resources to China) to the Middle Kingdom's energy security, a final resolution of the status of Aksai Chin looms large in China's grand strategy. Kashgar, which would be the terminus for the land pipeline linking Iranian oil and gas via Pakistan, would be vulnerable to an attack by India through Aksai Chin (claimed by India but administered by China) or Gilgit-Baltistan (claimed by India but administered by Pakistan). Clearly, Beijing will strive over the next 5–10 years (2025–2030) to ensure that India not only recognizes Chinese sovereignty with respect to Aksai Chin, but that the final border separating the Chinese territory of Aksai Chin from India's union territory of Ladakh is militarily defensible so that India could not successfully attack Kashgar via Aksai Chin. Undoubtedly, safeguarding Kashgar as the prospective energy entrepot and terminus of the Iran to China oil and gas pipeline transiting through CPEC will be a vital national interest for China.[56] Against the backdrop of the COVID-19 pandemic, China surprised an inattentive and complacent India and between May and June 2020 effectively shifted westward the notional and yet to be defined and demarcated Line of Actual Control (LAC) separating Aksai Chin from Ladakh by occupying areas previously patrolled intermittently and symbolically by India.[57] Conscious of its relative weakness, India has made no military move to reclaim control over the incremental territory gained by China.

Obviously, Beijing views Aksai Chin, given its geostrategic importance, to be part of the Middle Kingdom's territorial core. By contrast, it considers Arunachal Pradesh/South Tibet to be akin to a potential "hostage"—territory that the Chinese could seize at will and use as a bargaining chip to ensure tacit Indian acquiescence with respect to Chinese vital national interests. Beijing is acutely aware that whoever controls Arunachal Pradesh controls northeastern India—indeed, using

Arunachal Pradesh as a base, the whole of northeastern India could be cut off from the rest of the country. As long as Chinese seizure of Arunachal Pradesh remains a credible threat, India will be deterred from seriously challenging Beijing.

The People's Republic of China was not fully formed at birth—the result of a frozen civil war with the Republic of China (ROC), the pretender to the Middle Kingdom, which continues to remain in control of the offshore island province of Taiwan. The province was ceded by the Middle Kingdom to Japan in 1895 and was retroceded to the ROC, then the recognized government of China, in 1945 at the end of World War II. In the subsequent civil war between the Communists, under the leadership of Mao Tse-tung, and the Kuomintang (Nationalist) forces of the ROC, under the leadership of Chiang Kai-shek, the latter's forces were defeated on the mainland and withdrew to Taiwan. The outbreak of the Korean War in June 1950 resulted in a de facto suspension of the efforts of the PRC to gain control of Taiwan.[58] This status quo prevails. Both the PRC and ROC consider the province of Taiwan to be an integral part of the territory of China. The Shanghai Communiqué of 27 February 1972, which was issued jointly on the last day of President Richard M. Nixon's historic visit to China, articulated and memorialized this "One China" consensus: "The United States acknowledges that all Chinese ... maintain there is but one China and that Taiwan is part of China ... It [the United States] reaffirms its interest in the peaceful settlement of the Taiwan question by the Chinese themselves."[59] In a subsequent joint communiqué of 15 December 1978, issued in connection with US recognition of the People's Republic of China as the sole legal government of China, the understanding on Taiwan was reaffirmed: "The Government of the United States of America acknowledges the Chinese position that there is but one China and Taiwan is part of China."[60]

The Shanghai Communiqué reflects the Middle Kingdom's fundamental decision to opt for strategic patience with respect to extending its administrative control over Taiwan, given that the PRC's sovereignty claim is uncontested.[61] As of 2022, reunification of the island province with the mainland remains unconsummated—73 years since the establishment of the PRC and 50 years after the issuance of the Shanghai Communiqué. The centenary of the founding of the Chinese Communist Party is 2021, while the centenary of the PRC's establishment will be in 2049. It is quite likely that sometime before 2049, reflecting China's progress in achieving energy security as well as modernizing and strengthening its military capabilities, Beijing's strategic patience will be exhausted with respect to Taipei's acceptance of the former's administrative control. In this context, the US Department of Defense expects that China will achieve substantially its military modernization goals by 2035. As already argued, it seems reasonable to project that China will achieve its energy security goals by the 2035–2039 timeframe. Without a clear horizon for the end of the long frozen civil war, Chinese nationalism will be difficult to manage and could metastasize into irredentism and jingoism, and short circuit the slow, incremental process of Taiwan's organic reintegration into the Middle Kingdom.[62] Accordingly, barring an unanticipated move by Taiwan to unilaterally declare independence, the window for the province's peaceful reunification with the mainland is likely to remain open at most for the next two decades, after which (about 2039) the Middle Kingdom can be expected to exercise its option to use military force (including a possible naval blockade and air "no fly" zone).[63] Taiwan reunification will finally end China's civil war and complete the Middle Kingdom's singular national identity.

From a purely geostrategic perspective, Taiwan's critical importance as an integral part of China's "core" territory should not be overlooked or discounted. The island province straddles the passageway connecting the East China Sea to the South China Sea and its southern tip overlooks the Luzon Strait (which links the South China Sea to the Philippine Sea and the western Pacific Ocean). Once Taiwan returns to the Middle Kingdom's fold, the island will serve as China's sentinel guarding a maritime arc between northern Philippines and Japan's Ryukyu Islands chain (which includes Okinawa, where most of the American troops in Japan are based).

Closely linked to Taiwan are the five uninhabited islands known as the Diaoyu Islands in China and the Senkaku Islands in Japan. The strategic importance of the Diaoyu/Senkaku Islands is that they help demarcate Taiwan's and China's maritime boundaries. Taiwan, Japan, and China each separately claim sovereignty over these East China Sea islands (or rocks), which are located about 200 kilometers northeast of Taiwan and southwest of the Ryukyu Islands.[64] The United States has taken no position with respect to the various sovereignty claims but has recognized Japan's administrative control.[65] Japan exercised sovereignty over the Senkakus from the 1895 cession of Taiwan to the end of the Second World War, and was granted administrative control over the island chain by the United States in 1972 following the formal end of the American occupation of Japan.[66] The three-way tussle over sovereignty claims with respect to the Diaoyu/Senkaku Islands is unlikely to be resolved prior to the commencement of Taiwan's reunification with China, barring a sudden move by Japan to militarize the nature of its administrative control over the islands. Once Taiwan rejoins China, however, it is doubtful that Beijing will tolerate continued Japanese administrative control of the Diaoyu/Senkaku Islands. At that time, the US–Japan mutual defense treaty notwithstanding, it is quite likely that in case of Tokyo's refusal to accede to a peaceful takeover of the disputed islands, Beijing would seize the rocks, particularly if the Middle Kingdom, as expected, has made substantial progress with respect to energy security and military modernization.[67]

The most challenging part of Beijing's effort to restore and reconstitute the territorial integrity of the Middle Kingdom, is gaining acquiescence to the use of the so-called nine-dash line as at least a de facto maritime boundary in the South China Sea.[68] The nine-dash line (originally eleven-dash line) was introduced in official maps in 1948 by the Republic of China as part of the Kuomintang-led government's attempt to demarcate the Middle Kingdom's boundaries.[69] At the time of its establishment in 1949, the People's Republic of China inherited this demarcation of the South China Sea maritime boundary. Both Taipei and Beijing have continued to insist on this line as the proper basis for delineation of the Middle Kingdom's maritime claims in the South China Sea.

Beijing is systematically reinforcing its claims to various islands, rocks, and reefs in the South China Sea that fall within the nine-dash line through a program of artificially extending these outcroppings mainly through reclamation involving dredging, excavation, and landfills, and then constructing dual-use features such as lighthouses, radar stations, docks, and air strips.[70] The United States, in connection with its vital national interest in safeguarding freedom of navigation, has rejected the use of the nine-dash line as the basis of demarcating China's maritime boundary in the South China Sea. The Middle Kingdom has offered bilateral negotiations to each of the countries with which it has overlapping claims in the South China Sea: Philippines, Malaysia, Brunei, Indonesia, and Vietnam. China's approach of incrementally creating "facts" in the South China Sea while rhetorically reiterating its maritime claims and rejecting protests to such claims appears to be succeeding in gaining grudging acquiescence to the Middle Kingdom's territorial reach. China is unlikely to jeopardize its vital national interests in achieving energy security, Taiwan reunification, and the return of the Diaoyu Islands for the sake of restricting freedom of navigation in the South China Sea. Instead, Beijing will wait patiently until China is no longer vulnerable to an energy embargo imposed by the US Navy and has gained sufficient *local* naval strength relative to other powers before attempting to enforce the Middle Kingdom's narrow interpretation of navigation rights within the South China Sea. Accordingly, there is a 20-to 25-year window for a peaceful resolution of the various maritime claims and freedom of navigation issues with respect to the South China Sea.

## The Middle Kingdom's Security Envelope

The contours of the Middle Kingdom's sphere of influence or security envelope—a work that is very much in progress—are clearly visible. As discussed in the preceding section above, it is crucially important to recognize that the territorial core of the PRC is incomplete. Only China's territorial claim with respect to Arunachal Pradesh/South Tibet can be considered a non-core issue that does not rise to the level of a vital national interest. Accordingly, the de facto territorial core around which the Middle Kingdom appears to be constructing its security envelope consists of: (1) the territory under the administrative control of the PRC (including the seas within 12 nautical miles of the shoreline as per customary international law), (2) the area beyond the traditional 12 nautical mile limit encompassing the nine-dash line maritime boundary in the South China Sea (contested sovereignty and partial Chinese administrative control), (3) Taiwan (uncontested sovereignty but under local, non-PRC administrative control), and (4) Diaoyu/Senkaku Islands (contested sovereignty but under Japanese administration). When the project of completing the Middle Kingdom's territorial core is realized, in addition to the land features (natural and reclaimed) there will be as part of the PRC's territorial waters a formidable albeit virtual maritime great wall, stretching from the Yellow Sea through the East China Sea to the South China Sea, safeguarded by an array of powerful onshore defenses and patrolled by the Chinese Navy.

The security envelope around this de facto territorial core consists of two layers. The first layer is a *cordon sanitaire* comprising the following countries with which China shares borders: Mongolia (north central);

North Korea (northeast); Vietnam and Laos (southwest); and Pakistan (west). The purpose of the *cordon sanitaire* is to create a territorial buffer to protect against a possible invasion via these countries.[71] Accordingly, for the remainder of the twenty-first century (and beyond), the Middle Kingdom is unlikely to tolerate the establishment of a government that is hostile to the PRC in any of the countries comprising the *cordon sanitaire*. Similarly, such buffer states would not be allowed to grant long-term basing rights to foreign military forces of states whose interests are inimical to those of the PRC. Ultimately, the countries within the *cordon sanitaire*, as constituent members of a "Greater China," will be expected to constrain their sovereignty and subordinate their vital national interests to those of the Middle Kingdom.[72] The PRC will make sure that there is no doubt that it will be prepared to safeguard the sanctity of the *cordon sanitaire* by military force, if necessary. The second layer of the security envelope is an outer perimeter designed to provide "early warning" of emerging national security threats. This early warning system consists of Cambodia (which shares borders with Vietnam and Laos) and the following relatively weak countries with which the PRC shares borders: Burma (southwest), Nepal and Bhutan (south), and Afghanistan (west). The two critical concerns of Beijing would be (a) internal instability in one or more of these countries that could have adverse "spill-over" effects necessitating Chinese intervention, and (b) the use of these countries to host anti-China covert activities by hostile foreign states.[73] Except for Cambodia, which has very close economic, political, and military ties to the Middle Kingdom, this "early warning" layer of China's sphere of influence is relatively flimsy and contested with India (which, as successor to British India, is trying to retain Nepal, Bhutan, Burma, and Afghanistan within its own sphere of influence).[74] Over the remainder of the twenty-first century, these four countries that were tied previously to the sphere of influence of the British Raj, will be the focus of a "great game" between India and China.

Although not part of its security envelope or sphere of influence, the centrality of the Middle Kingdom's economic importance to other Asian countries creates a penumbra that could extend selectively China's sphere of influence. This penumbra covers, to varying degrees, Iran and Iraq in West Asia; Bangladesh and Sri Lanka in South Asia; and the Philippines, Thailand, Indonesia, Malaysia, Singapore, and Brunei in Southeast Asia.

As already discussed, Iran and Iraq are critical to China's energy security strategy. Beijing, however, will be reluctant to be involved directly with Iraq's internal challenges with its Sunni Arab and Kurdish minorities, or Iran's external challenges with the United States—Saudi Arabia—Israel triple axis. Instead, Beijing would prefer that Tehran and Baghdad resolve their problems by themselves or with the assistance of Russia (which has its own vital national interests at stake that do not conflict with those of the Middle Kingdom).[75] Accordingly, China can be expected to extend substantial economic and diplomatic support to Iran and Iraq (particularly with respect to developing their oil and gas industries to ensure energy exports) but stop short of major military assistance (although Beijing may underwrite a significant portion of Russia's military costs incurred in supporting these two countries). In extremis, such as an American air campaign to cripple Iran's oil and gas fields and associated infrastructure, or invasion and occupation of Iran, Beijing is likely (in coordination with Moscow) to supply Tehran with sophisticated arms, ammunition, and other military equipment via Pakistani and Central Asian routes—along the lines of American support for Afghanistan to counter the Soviet Union during the Cold War.[76] Barring such possible but not probable scenarios, Beijing's expectation over the long-term is that Iran and Iraq would be attached to the Middle Kingdom's sphere of influence on the strength of the economic security/energy security bargain and the lack of any other credible alternatives for addressing vital national interests.

With respect to Bangladesh and Sri Lanka, Beijing will be in an extended competition with New Delhi to gain predominant influence. While geographic propinquity and historical ties favor India, the promise of substantial economic assistance and military support are impressive Chinese calling cards. In the case of Sri Lanka, Beijing provided critical military equipment, supplies, and training to ensure the Sri Lankan government's victory in the 27-year war against Tamil separatists. And, following the end of the civil war, Beijing has extended significant economic aid and infrastructure finance to Colombo, including the development of a major new port at Hambantota as part of the maritime Silk Road initiative.[77] Similarly, China is playing an increasingly large role both as a provider of economic aid and infrastructure finance as well as a supplier of military equipment to Bangladesh.[78] Beijing's ace is its half century commitment to Pakistan as an example of the benefits that would accrue by choosing to partner with the Middle Kingdom.

Trade with China coupled with the prospect of significant economic assistance (including as part of the One Belt, One Road Initiative) is the powerful gravitational force attracting the countries of Southeast

Asia to the orbit of the Middle Kingdom. China unquestionably is the economic engine of Southeast Asia—having displaced both the United States and Japan as the most important trading partner of each of the ASEAN countries.[79] China is the single largest provider of bilateral foreign aid to them.[80] In addition, China is sponsoring multilateral institutions such as the Asian Infrastructure Investment Bank (AIIB), New Development Bank (NDB or BRICS Bank), and the BRICS Contingent Reserve Arrangement (BRICS CRA) to further reinforce and identify its central role in funding Asian economic development.[81] In the wake of the collapse of the proposed Trans-Pacific Partnership (TPP) as a result of President Donald Trump's decision to terminate US participation in the initiative, Beijing has resurrected and is promoting assiduously its own regional free trade alternative, the Comprehensive Regional Economic Partnership (CREP).[82] Moreover, there is an important cultural dimension that enhances Beijing's economic soft power as there are significant minority ethnic Chinese communities with deep local roots and prominent commercial roles in each of the Southeast Asian countries (with ethnic Chinese constituting the majority population of Singapore).[83]

Memories of the erstwhile Empire of Japan's earlier ill-fated effort to forge a Greater East Asia Co-Prosperity Sphere no doubt will act as a powerful brake as countries in the region seek to find the right balance between close, mutually beneficial economic ties with China on the one hand, and safeguarding political independence and sovereignty on the other hand.[84] In this context, the issues raised by China's maritime and territorial claims associated with the Middle Kingdom's nine-dash line demarcation of its maritime boundary in the South China Sea are a major challenge for Vietnam, the Philippines, Indonesia, Malaysia, and Brunei—each of whom have varying, competing, and overlapping claims that could impede China's efforts to construct a robust security envelope around its core territory.

Ultimately, given the asymmetry in power between China and its rival claimants, it will be up to the Middle Kingdom to demonstrate that it is a buddy and not a bully and forge an acceptable compromise. In each case, the solution is likely to be different. For example, China may consider that by virtue of giving up its claims in the Gulf of Tonkin (by reducing the original eleven-dash line to the nine-dash line) it has already compromised with Vietnam (which it considers to be part of the Middle Kingdom's *cordon sanitaire*).[85] Beijing is holding out the promise of major economic aid and infrastructure investment to persuade the Philippines to shelve its

South China Sea claims, which were upheld by an international arbitration tribunal in July 2016.[86] Indeed, shortly after the favorable arbitration decision, President Rodrigo Duterte of the Philippines, during his visit to China in October 2016, underscored his interest in putting aside differences over maritime claims in the South China Sea in favor of promoting increased bilateral trade and greater Chinese investment in the Philippines.[87] Beijing rewarded him by promising $24 billion for infrastructure projects and easier access for Philippine fishermen to the disputed waters in the South China Sea.[88] In addition to anesthetizing the South China Sea issue, the Middle Kingdom's strategic objective is to wean Manila from its security agreement with the United States and encourage the Philippines, a former American colony, to opt for neutrality. The security agreement, albeit deliberately vague and ambiguous, provides a legal basis for US intervention on behalf of the Philippines.[89] Crucially, with the Philippines as a base, American forces could threaten the eastern seaboard of China. If Beijing is successful and Manila shifts to neutrality and terminates the American security agreement, then, at best, the United States would be a supplier of defensive military equipment to the Philippines.

In dealing with Thailand, which also has a security understanding with the United States, the Middle Kingdom can be expected to follow an approach patterned after its Philippines game plan.[90] The objective in this case would be to persuade Bangkok to remain neutral in the event of US–China conflict so that American forces could not use Thailand as a base to block China's access to the Malacca Strait. Indonesia, Malaysia, Singapore, and Brunei do not have security agreements or understandings with the United States or any other country whose vital national interests would conflict with Chinese interests. Accordingly, Beijing will seek to preserve the status quo and nudge these Southeast Asian countries to formal declarations of neutrality while spinning its web of commercial and financial links further binding their economies to the Middle Kingdom. Simply put, Beijing is likely to speak softly and rely on the allure of its soft power and economic power to coax the Philippines, Thailand, Indonesia, Malaysia, Singapore, and Brunei to follow a path of strategic prudence and embrace neutrality. Such a zone of neutrality, although not a formal part of its envisaged security envelope, would provide a crucial buffer for the Middle Kingdom's soft southern underbelly.

## Foreign Trade and Connectivity: The Keys to Economic Security

China is the world's largest trading nation, with two-way merchandise trade amounting to $4.7 trillion in 2020.[91] China relies heavily on exports to drive economic growth and will continue to do so for the foreseeable future. In 2020, merchandise exports of $2.6 trillion contributed about 17.7 percent of the Middle Kingdom's GDP.[92] The United States is the most important market for Chinese products, accounting for about 17 percent of Chinese exports.[93] A closure of the American market would lop off about 3 percentage points from China's GDP, which would be a painful blow.[94] Clearly, over the next two decades, the Middle Kingdom can be expected to make a major effort to leverage its One Belt, One Road Initiative to shift the destination of its exports from the United States to Europe, the Middle East and Africa. The challenge for China will be to achieve this trade rebalancing in an orderly manner.

Foreign trade is inseparably conjoined with freedom of navigation and connectivity. It is estimated that almost 70 percent by value (80 percent by volume) of global foreign trade is carried over maritime routes.[95] China's foreign trade is overwhelmingly sea-borne—as is true of most other major trading nations. As has already been highlighted, according to the Pentagon, about 77 percent of China's strategically vital oil imports are transported over maritime routes dominated by the US Navy—SLOCs passing through the critical chokepoints of Malacca, Sunda, and Lombok Straits before entering the South China Sea.[96] A similar dependency prevails with respect to China's exports. For example, it is estimated that in 2016 about 44 percent of China's total exports ($874 billion of China's total exports of $1.99 trillion) flowed through the South China Sea (including the three chokepoints).[97] While a significant portion of Chinese foreign trade (principally oil imports) passing through the South China Sea (and its Malacca, Sunda, and Lombok chokepoints) will have alternative land routes once the new Silk Roads of the OBOR Initiative are operational (expected within 20 years), the South China Sea, reflecting its military and (albeit to a lesser degree) economic importance, will remain a vital national interest for the Middle Kingdom for the foreseeable future.[98] Accordingly, to safeguard this interest China can be expected to build up its naval capability to establish dominance in the South China Sea over the next two decades.

Given the importance of foreign trade for China's economic security coupled with the Middle Kingdom's overwhelming reliance on energy imports for its economic and military security, ***connectivity*** is a sine qua non for preserving China's sovereignty and independence. Freedom of navigation writ large, which is so central to American grand strategy, is beyond the Middle Kingdom's reach for the foreseeable future since the harsh reality is that China cannot hope to achieve naval superiority over the United States in the global maritime commons.[99] So, if connectivity cannot be achieved by sea, then it must be achieved by land. The PRC has found the answer to its strategic dilemma by turning to the Middle Kingdom's past—the ancient Silk Roads which served as land-based trade corridors. The One Belt, One Road Initiative—the New Silk Roads—is China's soft power response to get around the reality of American naval supremacy. The OBOR Initiative is not an attempt to create an alternate pathway for the projection of Chinese hard power. Russia and (to a lesser extent) Pakistan, both crucial land corridors for the New Silk Roads, are nuclear-armed and are unlikely to allow Chinese military forces to transit through their territories unless such Chinese military activities serve their respective vital national interests (or at least do not jeopardize respective Russian or Pakistani vital national interests). As a practical matter, neither Russia nor Pakistan (currently or for the foreseeable future) have vital national interests that would conflict with Chinese vital national interests.[100] Consequently, economic and diplomatic cooperation rather than military confrontation and intimidation are likely to be the means by which the Middle Kingdom preserves connectivity for the remainder of the twenty-first century.

## China's Capabilities: Closing the Gap Between Potential and Real Power

China is on a trajectory to great power status and Asian hegemony. It ranks first globally with respect to the size of its national economy (GDP calculated on purchasing power parity basis), international merchandise trade, and accumulated foreign exchange reserves. It is the biggest trading partner of each of the countries within its envisioned sphere of influence.[101] By 2039, according to EIA projections, China's economy is expected to grow to \$53.4 trillion, which will make it about 2 times larger than the US economy (\$26.5 trillion) and 1.8 times larger than India's economy (\$30 trillion).[102] Quite simply, China's slight edge over the United States in terms of GDP (PPP basis) of $2 trillion in 2019 will have widened massively into a virtually insurmountable lead of $26.9 trillion by 2039. Without a doubt, the Middle Kingdom's position as the world's predominant economic power will be further reinforced and entrenched over the next two decades.

China's hard power, however, does not yet match its latent or potential power and it is likely to take a generation to correct this asymmetry. Currently, in terms of military power, China is ranked third (after the United States and Russia but ahead of India).[103] The PRC has the world's largest standing army, which is rapidly modernizing, and it is a nuclear power with intercontinental delivery capability by land, air, and sea. Over the next two decades, China's focus on its military capabilities will be to ensure sufficient dominance within its envisioned sphere of influence so that an adversary would be deterred from launching an attack. Such a capability would require China to be able to field a quantitatively superior and qualitatively adequate military force that could inflict unacceptable losses so that an adversary would be dissuaded from attacking the Middle Kingdom's security envelope in the first place.[104]

China's navy is pursuing an aggressive new building and modernization program (in conjunction with onshore anti-ship and anti-aircraft defenses) to achieve dominance within its maritime great wall, and the merchant marine is now the largest among the world powers.[105] The Middle Kingdom's air force (again together with onshore anti-aircraft and anti-ballistic missile defenses) is also making major strides to ensure that it controls the skies over China's territorial core and *cordon sanitaire*. According to the Pentagon: "The PLAAF [People's Liberation Army Air Force] … is rapidly catching up to Western air forces. This trend is gradually eroding longstanding and significant U.S. military technical advantages vis-à-vis the PRC in the air domain."[106]

China spent about 1.9 percent of GDP on defense in 2019.[107] By comparison, in 2019 military expenditures as a percentage of GDP for the United States and India amounted to 3.4 percent and 2.4 percent, respectively.[108] If China wanted to achieve parity with the United States in terms of defense spending, then in 2019 it would have had to allocate 3.1 percent of GDP for military expenditures.[109] Clearly, there is a gap in defense spending (both quantitative and qualitative) that the Middle Kingdom will seek to close to achieve effective parity with the United States. It is reasonable to assume that to ensure dominance within its sphere of influence, the Middle Kingdom will gradually increase its defense spending over the next two decades to about 2.5 percent of GDP.[110] It is unlikely that China will seek significant conventional power projection capabilities beyond its sphere of influence (other than retaliatory capabilities that could inflict painful damage but not necessarily unacceptable losses on an adversary), as the cost of doing so would be beyond its resources (given the demands for domestic economic growth and development).

The end goal of the Middle Kingdom's grand strategy is Asian hegemony, not global hegemony. Certainly, China anticipates that within a generation it will be able to defeat any conventional challenge mounted by the United States to the Middle Kingdom's envisioned Asian sphere of influence. China already has the capability to defeat India in any conventional conflict. Other than the United States and India, China has no credible rivals. A possible US–India alliance could serve as an effective and credible counterweight to the Middle Kingdom, but the consummation of such a security partnership would have to overcome deeply entrenched mutual hesitations and is by no means a foregone conclusion.

Ensuring that the PRC will have the resources to support the capabilities needed to pursue the 5 vital national interests outlined above will be challenging enough, given that the Middle Kingdom's potential adversaries are likely to be the United States and India. Beijing is expected to have other pressing needs that will constrain defense spending. China is projected to face a pension and social security bomb by 2050. The combined impact of a low fertility rate (1.56) and skewed male to female ratio at birth (1.18–1) means that, "unlike the rest of the developed world, China will grow old before it gets rich."[111] As Nicholas Eberstadt, a leading demographics expert, has pointed out: "By 2040, China could have twice as many elderly people [over the age of 65] as children under the age of 15 ... these unfavorable demographic trends are creating heavy winds for the Chinese economy."[112] The financial requirements of providing a safety net for its growing elderly population will force Chinese decision-makers to carefully align the Middle Kingdom's vital national interests with the limited resources that will be available to fund the capabilities needed to safeguard such interests.[113] The success of the One Belt, One Road Initiative, the central pillar of China's grand strategy, depends upon cooperation and mutual interdependence, not on conflict and coercion. Consequently, Beijing may very well be receptive to a modus vivendi that carves out an Asian sphere of influence for the Middle Kingdom.

China is confident of its own power and acts accordingly as a great power and Asia's presumptive hegemon. All other states will have to deal with this reality in their relationships with the Middle Kingdom. Henry Kissinger, who together with President Richard Nixon helped pave the way for détente and rapprochement with China, has astutely pointed out: "By the time the Chinese reach … [2049, the PRC's centenary], they will be, by their own estimate, the equal of any other country in the contemporary world, and will, by their reckoning, be able to insist on absolute material and strategic equality, including with America."[114] Accordingly, from China's perspective, 2035–2049 may be the ideal time frame to negotiate a modus vivendi with its two most important potential adversaries—the United States and India. By then, China will have achieved its energy security and military modernization objectives, but it also would be facing the daunting challenge of an adverse demography. Whether China, the United States, and India have the collective will and creative imagination to forge a sustainable modus vivendi remains to be seen. War or peace hangs in the balance.

## Notes

1. For example, the Qing Dynasty, the last imperial dynasty of the Middle Kingdom, had a lifespan of about 268 years (1644–1912). See Warren I. Cohen, *East Asia at the Center: Four Thousand Years of Engagement with the World* (New York: Columbia University Press, 2000), 216–244.
2. For 2019 GDP figure see Central Intelligence Agency (CIA), *The World Factbook*, https://www.cia.gov/the-world-factbook/. For 2039 GDP projection see Energy Information Administration (EIA), *International Energy Outlook 2019* (IEO 2019), "Table A3: World Gross Domestic Product (GDP) by Region Expressed in Purchasing Power Parity (Reference Case) 2015–2050," https://www.eia.gov/outlooks/aeo/data/browser/#/?id=3-IEO2019&sourcekey=0.
3. Energy Information Administration (EIA), *Country Analysis Brief: China*, 30 September 2020, https://www.eia.gov/international/analysis/country/CHN.
4. See EIA, *International Energy Outlook 2019* (IEO 2019) for projections of oil consumption (Table A5), natural gas consumption (Table A6), and oil production (Table G2), https://www.eia.gov/outlooks/archive/ieo19/tables_ref.php. Oil imports is calculated as the excess of oil consumption over oil production. IEO 2019 did not provide country level data on natural gas production for China although the same was provided in prior IEOs. See EIA, *International Energy Outlook 2017*

(IEO 2017) for projections of natural gas imports (Table I4), https://www.eia.gov/outlooks/archive/ieo17/ieo_tables.php.

5. US Department of Defense, Office of the Secretary of Defense, *Annual Report to Congress: Military and Security Developments Involving the People's Republic of China 2020*, 133–134, https://media.defense.gov/2020/Sep/01/2002488689/-1/-1/1/2020-DOD-CHINA-MILITARY-POWER-REPORT-FINAL.PDF.
6. EIA, *Country Analysis Brief: China*, 30 September 2020, https://www.eia.gov/international/analysis/country/CHN.
7. EIA, *World Oil Transit Chokepoints*, 25 July 2017, https://www.eia.gov/international/analysis/special-topics/World_Oil_Transit_Chokepoints.
8. US Department of Defense, Office of the Secretary of Defense, *Annual Report to Congress: Military and Security Developments Involving the People's Republic of China 2020*, 133–134, https://media.defense.gov/2020/Sep/01/2002488689/-1/-1/1/2020-DOD-CHINA-MILITARY-POWER-REPORT-FINAL.PDF.
9. There is another dimension—domestic energy policy—that is beyond the scope of the analytical framework with respect to grand strategy, which focuses on the cross-border aspects of energy security. China's domestic energy policy includes expanding renewable sources of energy: nuclear, wind, and solar; developing shale oil and gas reserves so that production is technologically and commercially feasible; developing clean coal technology to exploit the country's significant coal reserves; and conservation efforts to reduce the growth of energy demand.
10. CIA, *World Factbook.*
11. EIA, *Country Analysis Brief: Russia*, 31 October 2017, https://www.eia.gov/international/analysis/country/RUS.
12. Ibid.
13. EIA, *IEO 2019*, Tables A5, A6, G2 and I1. Exports is calculated as the excess of production over consumption.
14. EIA does not project destinations of Russian energy exports.
15. See Total, "Yamal LNG: The Gas That Came In From the Cold," https://www.total.com/en/energy-expertise/projects/oil-gas/lng/yamal-lng-cold-environment-gas and Bruce Jones, "Russia Activates New Arctic Joint Strategic Command, *Jane's Defence Weekly*, 2 December 2014, https://www.janes.com/article/46577/russia-activates-new-arctic-joint-strategic-command. Also see, Congressional Research Service, *Changes in the Arctic: Background and Issues for Congress*, 4 March 2019, (R41153), https://fas.org/sgp/crs/misc/R41153.pdf and Harriet Moynihan, "Expert Comment: China Expands Its Global Governance Ambitions to Arctic," 15 October 2018, Chatham House,

https://www.chathamhouse.org/expert/comment/china-expands-its-global-governance-ambitions-arctic.
16. For current planned capacity (2020) see EIA, *Country Analysis Brief: Russia*.
17. International Monetary Fund (IMF), "International Reserves and Foreign Currency Liquidity: China," https://data.imf.org/regular.aspx?key=61280813.
18. Assuming Russia allocated 60 percent of its energy exports to China, the balance of 40 percent of its energy exports would provide Moscow with significant diversification opportunities.
19. EIA, *Country Analysis Brief: Kazakhstan*, 7 January 2019, https://www.eia.gov/international/analysis/country/KAZ.
20. Ibid.
21. EIA, *Country Analysis Brief: China*.
22. Base year (2019) oil production and oil consumption assumed same as 2017.
23. CIA, *World Factbook*.
24. EIA, *Country Analysis Brief: Turkmenistan*, July 2016, https://www.eia.gov/international/analysis/country/TKM.
25. Dry natural gas production is gross natural gas produced net of flared gas and gas reinjected into oil wells to enhance oil production.
26. Based on estimated Turkmenistan gas exports to China of 0.91 Tcf (70 percent of Turkmenistan exports of 1.3 Tcf) per EIA's country analysis brief for Turkmenistan and China's estimated gas imports for 2017 of 2.6 Tcf per *IEO 2017*.
27. Base year (2019) gas production and gas consumption assumed same as 2017.
28. Based on Turkmenistan gas exports to China of 1.8 Tcf (70 percent of 2.6 Tcf total gas exports) and China total gas imports of 6.6 Tcf.
29. Per EIA's country analysis brief on Turkmenistan, existing contractual commitments require Turkmenistan to deliver 2.3 Tcf of gas to China in 2020. Current pipeline capacity (Turkmenistan to China via Uzbekistan and Kazakhstan) is 1.9 Tcf.
30. US Department of Defense, Office of the Secretary of Defense, *Annual Report to Congress: Military and Security Developments Involving the People's Republic of China 2020*, 134.
31. CIA, *World Factbook*.
32. EIA, *Country Analysis Brief: Iran*, 20 July 2021, https://www.eia.gov/international/analysis/country/IRN.
33. EIA, *Country Analysis Brief*, 7 January 2019, https://www.eia.gov/international/content/analysis/countries_long/Iran/archive/pdf/iran_2019.pdf. In 2017, gross natural gas produced amounted to 9.4 TCf, of which 0.6 Tcf was flared and 1.6 Tcf was reinjected in oil wells to

enhance oil production. Dry gas production of 7.2 Tcf is net of flared gas and gas reinjected in oil wells.

34. Assumed base year (2019) oil production of 4.7 mbpd and oil consumption of 1.7 mbpd (same as 2017).
35. Assumed base year (2019) dry gas production of 7.2 Tcf and dry gas consumption of 6.9 Tcf (same as 2017). In 2017, Iranian gas production jumped by 9 percent over the previous year, so a 6.5 percent per annum production growth rate appears to be reasonable.
36. Based on projected Iranian oil and gas exports to China of 3.96 mbpd and 4.26 Tcf, respectively, in 2039, and total China oil and gas import requirements of 12.5 mbpd and 6.6 Tcf, respectively, for the same year.
37. Kenneth Katzman, *Iran Sanctions*, 22 April 2019, (RS 20871), Congressional Research Service, 12–23 and 67–72, https://fas.org/sgp/crs/mideast/RS20871.pdf. Ultimately, the key challenge to ensuring Iranian oil and gas export capacity is not so much production (which has been hobbled by the legacy of sanctions); rather, it is limiting domestic consumption of fossil fuels so that a significant portion of the oil and gas produced is available for exports. This requires an alternative source of renewable energy—nuclear power—to satisfy domestic energy requirements while optimizing oil and gas export capacity. Given the dual use nature of nuclear energy, Iran's program to develop a domestic nuclear power capacity for electricity generation has raised fears of a potentially nuclear-armed Iran—an outcome which Washington has declared it is determined to prevent by any means necessary, including war.
38. CIA, *World Factbook*.
39. President Xi Jinping, "Full Text of President Xi Jinping's Speech to the Parliament in Pakistan," 21 April 2015, http://issi.org.pk/wp-content/uploads/2015/07/Pak-China_Year_of_Friendly_Exchange_Doc-1.docx.pdf. See also Daniel S. Markey and James West, "Expert Brief: Behind China's Gambit in Pakistan," Council on Foreign Relations, 12 May 2016, https://www.cfr.org/expert-brief/behind-chinas-gambit-pakistan.
40. Zafar Bhutta, "Pakistan Working on Gwadar-China Oil Pipeline," *Express Tribune* (Pakistan), 13 July 2016, https://tribune.com.pk/story/1140506/crude-export-pakistan-working-gwadar-china-oil-pipeline/; and Zafar Bhutta, "From Gwadar-Kashgar: Crude Oil Pipeline Requires $10 Billion Investment," *Express Tribune* (Pakistan), 18 May 2018, https://tribune.com.pk/story/1712888/2-gwadar-kashgar-crude-oil-pipeline-requires-10-billion-investment/.
41. It also should be noted that the final stretch of CPEC to the Pakistan–China border runs through Gilgit-Baltistan, which is part of Pakistan-held Kashmir. Gilgit-Baltistan is the only part of Pakistani-administered territory that borders China. India claims sovereignty over

Gilgit-Baltistan (as part of its claim to all of Kashmir) and has objected to routing CPEC through this area. Apart from lodging official protests, New Delhi has taken no action targeting CPEC.

42. Raza Khan, "15,000 Troops of Special Security Division to Protect CPEC Projects, Chinese Nationals," *Dawn*, 12 August 2016, https://www.dawn.com/news/1277182.
43. While in the long-term Pakistan's CPEC corridor would serve as the ideal transit route for Iranian energy exports to China, there is a possible alternate transit route via Turkmenistan and Kazakhstan that could be used in the short term (and, in the long term, as a hedge against temporary supply disruptions). An oil pipeline could be constructed linking Iranian oil fields via Turkmenistan to the underutilized existing Kazakhstan–China oil pipeline (current capacity of 0.4 mbpd). Similarly, a gas pipeline could be built linking Iranian gas fields to the existing Turkmenistan–China gas pipeline network.
44. EIA, *Country Analysis Brief: Iraq*, 24 February 2021, https://www.eia.gov/international/analysis/country/IRQ.
45. EIA, *Country Analysis Brief: Iraq*, 24 February 2021, https://www.eia.gov/international/analysis/country/IRQ.
46. Assumed base year (2019) oil production of 4.7 mbpd and oil consumption of 0.9 mbpd (same as 2019). Restraining the rate of growth of oil consumption will be a challenge, given that Iraq has experienced a 6 percent annual growth rate in oil consumption over the past decade (per EIA's country analysis brief). Obviously, political stability will be critical for Iraq's viability as a major oil exporter.
47. CIA, *World Factbook*.
48. Martin Chulov, "Iran Sends Troops Into Iraq to Fight Against ISIS Militants," *Guardian* (UK), 14 June 2014, https://www.theguardian.com/world/2014/jun/14/iran-iraq-isis-fight-militants-nouri-maliki; and Martin Chulov, Julian Borger and Kamali Dehghan, "US Military Rushes to Defuse Looming Crisis in Kirkuk After Iraqi Army Advances," Guardian (UK), 16 October 2017, https://www.theguardian.com/world/2017/oct/16/iraq-kurdish-forces-army-us-military.
49. Tehran and Baghdad are developing a close energy partnership initially with respect to Iraq's northern oil fields (which potentially could be extended to Iraq's southern oil fields). See, Bozorgmehr Sharafedin, "Iraq and Iran Swap Kirkuk Oil in Strategic Boost for Tehran," *Reuters*, 3 June 2018, https://www.reuters.com/article/us-oil-iran-iraq-idUSKCN1IZ0QA; and "Update 1- Iraq, Iran Consider Building Pipeline to Export Kirkuk Crude," *Reuters*, 20 February 2017, https://www.reuters.com/article/iraq-iran-oil-idUSL8N1G53FT.
50. For the formal announcements by President Xi Jinping of the One Belt, One Road Initiative see Ministry of Foreign Affairs of the People's

Republic of China, "President Xi Jinping Delivers Important Speech and Proposes to Build a Silk Road Economic Belt with Central Asian Countries", 7 September 2013, http://www.fmprc.gov.cn/mfa_eng/topics_665678/xjpfwzysiesgjtfhshzzfh_665686/t1076334.shtml; and Wu Jiao and Zhang Wunbi, "Xi in call for building new 'maritime silk road'", *China Daily*, 4 October 2013, http://usa.chinadaily.com.cn/china/2013-10/04/content_17008940.htm. See also Jack Farchy, James Kynge, Chris Campbell and David Blood, "The New Trade Routes: Silk Road Corridor," *Financial Times*, 14 September 2016, https://ig.ft.com/sites/special-reports/one-belt-one-road/.

51. US Department of Defense, Office of the Secretary of Defense, *Annual Report to Congress: Military and Security Developments Involving the People's Republic of China 2020*, 133–134, https://media.defense.gov/2020/Sep/01/2002488689/-1/-1/1/2020-DOD-CHINA-MILITARY-POWER-REPORT-FINAL.PDF.
52. Thomas Lum, "In Focus: Uyghurs in China," 6 March 2019, (IF 10,281), Congressional Research Service, https://fas.org/sgp/crs/row/IF10281.pdf; Lily Kuo, "China Says That it has Arrested 13,000 Terrorists in Xinjiang," *Guardian* (UK), 18 March 2019, https://www.theguardian.com/world/2019/mar/18/china-says-it-has-arrested-13000-terrorists-in-xinjiang; and John Sudworth, "China's Hidden Camps: What's Happened to the Uighurs of Xinjiang," *BBC News*, 24 October 2018, https://www.bbc.co.uk/news/resources/idt-sh/China_hidden_camps. See also, "Tibet Profile," *BBC News*, 26 April 2019, https://www.bbc.com/news/world-asia-pacific-16689779; and Susan V. Lawrence, *The Tibetan Policy Act of 2002: Background and Implementation*, 5 November 2014, (R 43781), Congressional Research Service, https://fas.org/sgp/crs/row/R43781.pdf.
53. For background analysis (in 3 chronological parts) see CIA, *The Sino-Indian Border Dispute, Section 1*, https://www.cia.gov/library/readingroom/docs/polo-07.pdf; *The Sino-Indian Border Dispute, Section 2*, https://www.cia.gov/library/readingroom/docs/polo-08.pdf; and *The Sino-Indian Border Dispute, Section 3*, https://www.cia.gov/library/readingroom/docs/polo-09.pdf. Also see collection of primary documents, "Sino-Indian Border War, 1962," in "Digital Archive: International History Declassified," Wilson Center, https://digitalarchive.wilsoncenter.org/collection/71/sino-indian-border-war-1962.
54. John F. Kennedy Library, "Nehru Correspondence, November 1962", https://www.jfklibrary.org/Asset-Viewer/Archives/JFKNSF-111-016.aspx. For an incisive account of President Kennedy's decision to extend American assistance to India, see Bruce Riedel, *JFK's Forgotten Crisis: Tibet, the CIA, and the Sino-Indian War* (Washington, DC: Brookings Institution Press, 2015).

55. US Department of State, Office of the Historian, "Memorandum From the President's Deputy Special Assistant for National Security Affairs (Kaysen) to President Kennedy, 26 October 1962 (Document no. 181)" in *Foreign Relations of the United States, 1961–1963, Volume XIX, South Asia*, https://history.state.gov/historicaldocuments/frus1961-63v19/d181.
56. Accordingly, China's strategic ambitions may be to push Aksai Chin's border with Ladakh deeply westward following the Indus River along a line running through the Kargil-Leh-Nyoma sector by 2025–2030 in advance of the prospective completion of the Iran to China energy pipeline in the 2035–2039 timeframe. Seizure of such a significant swathe of territory currently under Indian administration most likely could only be achieved through war. India has yet to recognize that it is in the Middle Kingdom's crosshairs because of the potential geostrategic threat it poses to China's energy security.
57. Hannah Ellis-Peterson, "China and India Move Troops as Border Tensions Escalate," *Guardian* (UK), 27 May 2020, https://www.theguardian.com/world/2020/may/27/china-and-india-move-troops-as-border-tensions-escalate; and Archana Chaudhary, "Why Chinese and Indian Troops Clash in the Himalayas," *Washington Post*, 2 July 2021, https://www.washingtonpost.com/business/why-chinese-and-indian-troops-clashin-the-himalayas/2021/06/29/0cd73f20-d892-11eb-8c87-ad6f27918c78_story.html.
58. Chen Jian, *Mao's China and the Cold War* (Chapel Hill, NC: University of North Carolina Press, 2001), 55.
59. See "Joint Statement Following Discussions with Leaders of the People's Republic of China, Shanghai, 27 February 1972" in Office of the Historian, US Department of State, *Foreign Relations of the United States, 1969–1972, Volume VIII, China, 1969–1972*, Document No. 203, https://history.state.gov/historicaldocuments/frus1969-76v17/d203.
60. Embassy of the People's Republic of China in the United States, "Joint Communiqué on the Establishment of Diplomatic Relations between the People's Republic of China and the United States of America" (16 December 1978), http://www.china-embassy.org/eng/zmgx/doc/ctc/t36256.htm.
61. China's strategic patience with respect to Taiwan reunification was memorably highlighted in an emphatic declaration by Mao Tse-tung in a meeting on 17 February 1973 with Henry Kissinger, then President Nixon's national security advisor: "I say that we can do without Taiwan for the time being, and let it come after one hundred years. Do not take matters on this world so rapidly. Why is there need to be in such great haste?" See Henry Kissinger, *On China* (New York: Penguin Press, 2011), 280.

62. Chen Jian, *Mao's China and the Cold War*, 280.
63. The Middle Kingdom's claim of sovereignty over Taiwan is settled; the challenge for Beijing is how to enforce it without provoking a coercive American response. The basis for an American intervention in response to a coercive Chinese takeover of Taiwan is rooted in the Taiwan Relations Act of 1979. The Act declares that the use of coercion to achieve Taiwan's reunification with the mainland would be considered "a threat to the peace and security of the Western Pacific area and a grave concern to the United States." See American Institute in Taiwan, "Taiwan Relations Act, 1 January 1979," http://www.ait.org.tw/en/taiwan-relations-act.html. While the nature of an American response is purposefully vague and ambiguous, the option of a military response is not off the table. Indeed, in March 1996 President Bill Clinton sent a naval force steaming through the Taiwan Strait in response to Chinese military threats (which were provoked by pro-independence Taiwanese rhetoric in the run up to local elections). See James Risen, "U.S. Warns China on Taiwan, Sends Warships to Area," *Los Angeles Times*, 11 March 1996, http://articles.latimes.com/1996-03-11/news/mn-45722_1_taiwan-strait, and Barton Gellman, "U.S. and China Nearly Came to Blows in '96," *Washington Post*, 21 June 1998, https://www.washingtonpost.com/archive/politics/1998/06/21/us-and-china-nearly-came-to-blows-in-96/926d105f-1fd8-404c-9995-90984f86a613/.
64. BBC, "How Uninhabited Islands Soured China-Japan Ties," *BBC News*, 10 November 2014, http://www.bbc.com/news/world-asia-pacific-11341139.
65. Mark E. Manyon, *The Senkakus (Diaoyu/Diaoyutai) Dispute: U.S. Treaty Obligations*, 14 October 2016, (R 42761), Congressional Research Service, 5–7, https://fas.org/sgp/crs/row/R42761.pdf.
66. See "Text of U.S.-Japanese Treaty Restoring Okinawa and Nearby Islands to Tokyo," *New York Times*, 18 June 1971, https://www.nytimes.com/1971/06/18/archives/text-of-usjapanese-treaty-restoring-okinawa-and-nearby-islands-to.html; and editorial "Okinawa's Reversion," *New York Times*, 15 May 1972, https://www.nytimes.com/1972/05/15/archives/okinawas-reversion.html.
67. For text of US–Japan mutual defense treaty see Ministry of Foreign Affairs of Japan, "Treaty of Mutual Cooperation and Security between Japan and the United States of America,19 January 1960," http://www.mofa.go.jp/region/n-america/us/q&a/ref/1.html. Article V of the Treaty states: "[E]ach Party recognizes that an armed attack against either Party in the territories under the administration of Japan would be dangerous to its own safety and declares it would act to meet the common danger." What action the United States might take is shrouded

in ambiguity. A China that has achieved substantially its military modernization and energy security objectives may be emboldened to seize the disputed islands by force on the basis of a strategic calculation that the United States would not be willing to respond militarily to a takeover of barren rocks.

68. Gaining *de jure* recognition of the nine-dash line is unlikely given the 2016 unanimous ruling of an international arbitration tribunal in favor of the Philippines in its dispute with China over Scarborough Shoal and the Spratly Islands in the South China Sea. The tribunal specifically rejected the validity of the nine-dash line as a basis of demarcating China's maritime boundaries in the South China Sea. See Permanent Court of Arbitration (The Hague), "PCA Case No. 2013–19: In the Matter of the South China Sea Arbitration," 12 November 2016, 67–117, https://pcacases.com/web/sendAttach/2086. China did not participate in the tribunal's proceedings and rejected its ruling. See Tom Phillips, Oliver Holmes and Owen Bowcott, "Beijing rejects tribunal's ruling in South China Sea case," *Guardian* (UK), 12 July 2016, https://www.theguardian.com/world/2016/jul/12/philippines-wins-south-china-sea-case-against-china.
69. For copies of the original eleven-dash line map and the revised nine-dash line map, see Permanent Court of Arbitration South China Sea ruling, 75 and 77, https://pcacases.com/web/sendAttach/2086.
70. US Department of Defense, *Annual Report to Congress: Military and Security Developments Involving the People's Republic of China 2019*, 73–75, https://media.defense.gov/2019/May/02/2002127082/-1/-1/1/2019_CHINA_MILITARY_POWER_REPORT.pdf. Also see Brad Lendon, "China Tests Anti-Ship Missile in South China Sea—Pentagon Says," *CNN News*, 3 July 2019, https://www.cnn.com/2019/07/03/asia/south-china-sea-missile-test-intl-hnk/index.html; and Reuters, "China Deploys Cruise Missiles on South China Sea Outposts—Reports," *Guardian* (UK), 3 May 2018, https://www.theguardian.com/world/2018/may/03/china-deploys-cruise-missiles-on-south-china-sea-outposts-reports.
71. For example, Russia could launch an attack on China (Xinjiang province) by sending troops through Mongolia (which historically was part of the Soviet Union's sphere of influence). Likewise, the US could launch an invasion against the Chinese mainland (Xinjiang province) by marching expeditionary forces through Pakistan along the CPEC route. Also, the United States could use Vietnam as a launching pad for a pincer move against the southwestern island of Hainan, a major Chinese naval base. It should be recalled that the approach of US troops to the Yalu River bordering North Korea and China (Liaoning and Jilin provinces) in

November 1950 triggered Chinese military intervention in the Korean War.

72. With respect to the Korean Peninsula, China is likely to welcome future reunification of North and South Korea if accompanied by neutralization of a unified Korea and irrespective of the nuclear weapons status of the unified country. From the Middle Kingdom's perspective, the nuclearization of the Korean Peninsula is a fait accompli that is irreversible, so the sine qua non of unification would be neutralization of the unified country to ensure that no foreign power could use Korea as a base from which to threaten China.
73. Except for Nepal and Bhutan, none of these countries would be likely invasion routes for an attack against China. It is possible, though not probable, for India to send its troops through Nepal and Bhutan in a major conflict with China. Of course, from India's perspective, Nepal, Bhutan, and Burma are possible invasion routes for a Chinese attack on India. Clearly, sensitivities run high on both sides as underscored by the Doklam "stand-off" in 2017 between Chinese and Indian troops near the tri-junction of the borders of Bhutan, China, and India. See Michael Safi, "Chinese and Indian Troops Face Off in Bhutan Border Dispute," *Guardian* (UK), 5 July 2017, https://www.theguardian.com/world/2017/jul/06/china-india-bhutan-standoff-disputed-territory; and Josy Joseph, "What is the Doklam Issue All About?" *Hindu*, 27 January 2018, https://www.thehindu.com/news/national/what-is-the-doklam-issue-all-about/article22536937.ece.
74. Iran and Pakistan also have vital national interests at stake with respect to a stable Afghanistan, their common neighbor.
75. Russia has a vital national interest in safeguarding its southern flank—stretching from Ukraine, the Black Sea, the Caucasus, the Caspian Sea, and the former Soviet Central Asian republics. An Iran–Iraq–Syria land bridge enables Russia to outflank Turkey (a NATO member), gain a warm-water outlet to the Eastern Mediterranean, and add a protective "early warning" fold shielding Moscow's sphere of influence over Central Asian oil and gas producing states bordering the Caspian—Azerbaijan, Turkmenistan, and Kazakhstan.
76. The consequence (whether unintended or not) of such an American war against Iran would be to destroy China's Persian energy hedge. Clearly, Beijing would not allow such a result to stand and, short of direct military intervention (which would mean fighting US troops in Iran—a logistically daunting proposition making such a clash unlikely), the Middle Kingdom can be expected to supply conventional weapons to Tehran on a scale sufficient to enable Iran to defend itself by itself. Also, to neuter credible threats of devastating US military attacks against Iran, China is likely to acquiesce in an effort by Tehran to achieve nuclear

weapons latency (similar to Japan and Germany) and, if American threats persist over an extended period, Beijing may tolerate the emergence of a nuclear-armed Iran (just as it has accepted the emergence of Pakistan and North Korea as nuclear weapons states).

77. See Peter Popham, "How Beijing Won Sri Lanka's Civil War," *Independent* (UK), 23 May 2010, https://www.independent.co.uk/news/world/asia/how-beijing-won-sri-lankas-civil-war-1980492.html; Kiran Stacey, "China Signs 99-Year Lease on Sri Lanka's Hambantota Port," *Financial Times*, 11 December 2017, https://www.ft.com/content/e150ef0c-de37-11e7-a8a4-0a1e63a52f9c; and Michael Safi and Amantha Perera, "'The Biggest Game Changer in 100 years': Chinese Money Gushes into Sri Lanka," *Guardian* (UK), 25 March 2018, https://www.theguardian.com/world/2018/mar/26/the-biggest-game-changer-in-100-years-chinese-money-gushes-into-sri-lanka.
78. Kiran Stacey, "Chinese Investment in Bangladesh Rings India Alarm Bells," *Financial Times*, 6 August 2018, https://www.ft.com/content/1ab2ebe6-85c3-11e8-96dd-fa565ec55929; and Nilanthi Samaranayake, "Special Report: China's Engagement with Smaller Asian Countries, April 2019," 8–9, United States Institute for Peace, https://www.usip.org/sites/default/files/2019-04/sr_446-chinas_engagement_with_smaller_south_asian_countries.pdf.
79. Association of Southeast Asian Nations, *External Trade Statistics*, Table 20, https://asean.org/wp-content/uploads/2016/11/Table20_as-of-6-dec-2016.pdf.
80. Neil Renwick, *China as a Development Actor in Southeast Asia*, Institute of Development Studies (UK), April 2016, https://assets.publishing.service.gov.uk/media/57a08960ed915d3cfd0001f2/ER187_ChinaasaDevelopmentActorinSoutheastAsia.pdf.
81. Molly Elgin-Cossart and Melanie Hart, "China's New International Financing Institutions," Center for American Progress, 22 September 2015, https://www.americanprogress.org/issues/security/reports/2015/09/22/121668/chinas-new-international-financing-institutions/. Also see Brazil Ministry of External Relations, "Treaty for the Establishment of a BRICS Contingent Reserve Arrangement," 15 July 2015, http://brics.itamaraty.gov.br/media2/press-releases/220-treaty-for-the-establishment-of-a-brics-contingent-reserve-arrangement-fortaleza-july-15.
82. Office of US Trade Representative, "The United States Officially Withdraws from the Trans-Pacific Partnership," January 2017, https://ustr.gov/about-us/policy-offices/press-office/press-releases/2017/january/US-Withdraws-From-TPP. See also, Alex Ward, "The Trans-Pacific Pact has Been Resurrected—And It's Happening Without the US," *Vox*,

23 November 2017, https://www.vox.com/2017/11/11/16637826/trump-trans-pacific-partnership; and Jane Perlez, "Asian Nations Plan Trade Bloc That, Unlike U.S.'s, Invites China," *New York Times*, 20 November 2012, http://www.nytimes.com/2012/11/21/world/asia/southeast-asian-nations-announce-trade-bloc-to-rival-us-effort.html.

83. Indonesia, however, has a strong undercurrent of anti-Chinese ethnic tension, which exploded in violent anti-Chinese riots at the beginning and end of President Suharto's regime. See Norman G. Owen (editor), *The Emergence of Modern Southeast Asia* (Honolulu: University of Hawaii Press, 2005), 434–435; and John M. Glionna, "In Indonesia, 1998 Violence Against Ethnic Chinese Remains Unaddressed," *Los Angeles Times*, 4 July 2010, https://www.latimes.com/archives/la-xpm-2010-jul-04-la-fg-indonesia-chinese-20100704-story.html.
84. The original version of the Greater East-Asian Co-Prosperity Sphere was articulated in August 1940 by Japanese militarists to serve as the rationale for the expansion of the Japanese Empire. See Warren I. Cohen, *East Asia at the Center: Four Thousand Years of Engagement with the World*, 352.
85. Hannah Beech, "Just Where Exactly Did China Get the South China Sea Nine-Dash Line From?" *Time*, 19 July 2016, https://time.com/4412191/nine-dash-line-9-south-china-sea/. See also Robert D. Kaplan, "The Vietnam Solution," *Atlantic*, June 2012, https://www.theatlantic.com/magazine/archive/2012/06/the-vietnam-solution/308969/.
86. Martin Perry and Neil Jerome Morales, "China's Xi Visits Philippines as Duterte Pressed to Take Tougher Line," *Reuters*, 19 November 2018, https://www.reuters.com/article/us-philippines-china/chinas-xi-visits-philippines-as-duterte-pressed-to-take-tougher-line-idUSKCN1NP0BR; and John Reed and Grace Ramos, "China and Philippines Sign Offshore Oil and Gas Deal," *Financial Times*, 20 November 2018, https://www.ft.com/content/a4bf926e-ecb9-11e8-89c8-d36339d835c0.
87. Tom Phillips and Oliver Holmes, "China Courts Philippines Leader Duterte Amid Signs of US Rift," *Guardian* (UK), 17 October 2016, https://www.theguardian.com/world/2016/oct/17/china-courts-philippines-leader-duterte-amid-signs-of-us-rift; Reuters, "Duterte: Philippines is Separating from US and Realigning with China," *Guardian* (UK), 20 October 2016, https://www.theguardian.com/world/2016/oct/20/china-philippines-resume-dialogue-south-china-sea-dispute; and Associated Press, "Philippines to 'Set Aside' South China Sea Tribunal Ruling to Avoid Imposing on Beijing," *Guardian* (UK), 17 December 2016, https://www.theguardian.com/world/2016/dec/17/philippines-to-set-aside-south-china-sea-tribunal-ruling-to-avoid-imposing-on-beijing.

88. Ralph Jennings, "Once-Distrusted China Pledges Millions More to Philippines," *Voice of America News*, 13 April 2018, https://www.voanews.com/east-asia/once-distrusted-china-pledges-millions-more-philippines.
89. For the text of the Philippines mutual defense treaty see Avalon Project, Yale Law School, "Mutual Defense Treaty Between the United States and the Republic of the Philippines, 30 August 1951," http://avalon.law.yale.edu/20th_century/phil001.asp.
90. For text of US bilateral assurance to Thailand see the Dean Rusk-Thanat Khoman Joint Statement of 6 March 1962 in US Department of State, *Foreign Affairs Current Documents 1962*, 1091–1093, https://babel.hathitrust.org/cgi/pt?id=mdp.39015013346716;view=1up;seq=1175.
91. Two-way merchandise trade consists of merchandise exports, $2.59 trillion (2020), and merchandise imports, $2.06 trillion (2020). See World Bank, "Data Bank: Merchandise Exports (current US$)," https://data.worldbank.org/indicator/TX.VAL.MRCH.CD.WT; and World Bank, "Data Bank: Merchandise Imports (current US$)," https://data.worldbank.org/indicator/TM.VAL.MRCH.CD.WT.
92. Based on 2020 GDP of $14.7 trillion (current US$). See World Bank, "Data Bank: GDP", https://data.worldbank.org/indicator/NY.GDP.MKTP.CD?locations=CN.
93. CIA, *World Factbook*.
94. Of the 17.7 percentage points of GDP accounted by exports, 17 percent or about 3 percentage points ($17.7 \times 0.17 = 3.0$) reflects exports to the United States.
95. China Power Team, "How Much Trade Transits the South China Sea?" China Power Project at the Center for Strategic and International Studies (CSIS), 27 October 2017, https://chinapower.csis.org/much-trade-transits-south-china-sea/.
96. US Department of Defense, *Annual Report to Congress: Military and Security Developments Involving the People's Republic of China 2020*, 133.
97. For estimated Chinese exports flowing through South China Sea see China Power Team, "How much trade transits the South China Sea?" China Power Project at the Center for Strategic and International Studies (CSIS). For total China exports see CIA, *World Factbook*.
98. By contrast, only an estimated 5 percent of total US foreign trade flows through the South China Sea per the China Power Project estimates. For the United States, freedom of navigation with respect to the South China Sea is strategically important to reinforce American control over SLOCs and the maritime global commons (and not because the South China Sea is critical economically for US trade).
99. Foregoing any ambitions to become a global sea power does not mean that the Middle Kingdom will not seek to be the dominant naval power

within the maritime wall comprising the South China, East China, and Yellow Sea; nor does it mean that China will not seek to challenge the Indian Navy's domination of the Indian Ocean.

100. The Central Asia routes of the Silk Road are controlled by Russia as they are within its sphere of influence, while Pakistan controls the CPEC route. Russia and Pakistan may allow transit of Chinese military supplies in the event of an American attack on Iran. Also, Pakistan, which considers India an adversary, may allow Chinese troops to pass through its territory in the event of a Sino-Indian war. Pakistan, given its military and economic dependence on China, is a decidedly junior partner and therefore will have to subordinate its vital national interests to those of China to a far greater extent than would Russia, which is a strategically equal partner of the Middle Kingdom.
101. In fact, China is also the largest trading partner of the United States as well as each of America's formal strategic partners in Asia—Australia, Japan, South Korea, Philippines, and Thailand. Although they are formal strategic partners of America, these countries will strive to balance military security against economic security, and therefore, absent an imminent military threat, will be very cautious in engaging in economic warfare against China. See CIA, *World Factbook*.
102. For 2019 GDP figure see CIA, *The World Factbook*, https://www.cia.gov/the-world-factbook/. For 2039 GDP projection see EIA, *International Energy Outlook 2019* (IEO 2019), "Table A3: World gross domestic product (GDP) by region expressed in purchasing power parity (reference case) 2015–2050," https://www.eia.gov/outlooks/aeo/data/browser/#/?id=3-IEO2019&sourcekey=0.
103. See "2021 Military Strength Ranking," *Global Firepower*, https://www.globalfirepower.com/countries-listing.php.
104. US Department of Defense, Office of the Secretary of Defense, *Annual Report to Congress: Military and Security Developments Involving the People's Republic of China 2020*, 30–31, https://media.defense.gov/2020/Sep/01/2002488689/-1/-1/1/2020-DOD-CHINA-MILITARY-POWER-REPORT-FINAL.PDF.
105. For China's naval progress see Ronald O'Rourke, "China Naval Modernization: Implications for U.S. Navy Capabilities—Background and Issues for Congress, 7 October 2021, (CRS Report no: RL33153)," *Congressional Report Service*, https://sgp.fas.org/crs/row/RL33153.pdf; US Department of Defense, *Annual Report to Congress: Military and Security Developments Involving the People's Republic of China 2020*, 44–49; and David Lague and Benjamin Kang Lim, "The China Challenge: Ruling the Waves," *Reuters*, 30 April 2019, https://www.reuters.com/investigates/special-report/china-army-navy/. For merchant navy comparative statistics see CIA, *World Factbook*.

106. US Department of Defense, *Annual Report to Congress: Military and Security Developments Involving the People's Republic of China 2020*, 50.
107. World Bank, "Data Bank: Military expenditure (% GDP)," https://data.worldbank.org/indicator/MS.MIL.XPND.GD.ZS?locations=CN-IN-US.
108. Ibid.
109. In 2019 China's GDP of $22.5 trillion was 1.1 times larger than US GDP of $20.5 trillion. Accordingly, to achieve parity with the US defense spending of 3.4 percent of GDP, China's defense spending would have to be 3.1 percent of its GDP (3.1 × 1.1 = 3.4). For 2019 GDP see CIA, *World Factbook.*
110. According to the World Bank, Chinese defense spending peaked at about 2.5 percent of GDP in 1992. See World Bank, "Data Bank: Military expenditure (% GDP)".
111. See "Demography: China's Achilles Heel," *Economist*, 12 April 2012, https://www.economist.com/china/2012/04/21/chinas-achilles-heel; and "China's Population: The Most Surprising Demographic Crisis," *Economist*, May 5, 2011, https://www.economist.com/asia/2011/05/05/the-most-surprising-demographic-crisis.
112. Nicholas Eberstadt, "With Great Demographics Comes Great Power: Why Population Will Drive Geopolitics," *Foreign Affairs*, vol. 98, no. 4, July/August 2019, 150.
113. In a bid to mitigate the damage done to China's demographics by the PRC's one-child policy designed to limit population growth, the government belatedly terminated the misguided policy in 2015. See Patti Waldmeir, "China Scraps One-Child Policy After More Than Three Decades," *Financial Times*, 29 October 2015, https://www.ft.com/content/4f966d1a-7e2d-11e5-98fb-5a6d4728f74e; and Lily Kuo and Xueying Wang, "Can China Recover from Its Disastrous One-Child Policy?" *Guardian* (UK), 2 March 2019, https://www.theguardian.com/world/2019/mar/02/china-population-control-two-child-policy.
114. See interview with Jeffrey Goldberg, "The Lessons of Henry Kissinger" *Atlantic*, December 2016, http://www.theatlantic.com/magazine/archive/2016/12/the-lessons-of-henry-kissinger/505868/.

CHAPTER 4

# Re-Emerging Russia's Grand Strategy: Twixt Tsar and Commissar

The Russian Federation (Russia), representing an evolution beyond tsar and commissar, is the third incarnation of the state of the Russian people. It rose on 25 December 1991 from the ashes of the Union of Soviet Socialist Republics (USSR or Soviet Union), which in turn was created on 30 December 1922 after a five-year period of turmoil, chaos, and civil war between Communist and non-Communist forces following the collapse of the Russian Empire triggered by the abdication of Tsar Nicholas II on 2 March 1917. The Russian Empire, which was founded by Tsar Peter I (Peter the Great) on 22 October 1721, lasted for nearly two centuries. Viewed through the prism of grand strategy, perhaps the most appropriate symbol for the Russian Federation is the phoenix rather than the Soviet bear or the Tsarist eagle. The supreme vital national interest of the Russian Federation, which is still emerging from the dissolution of the Soviet Union, is to ensure Russia's continued, sustainable existence as a viable political entity preserving its five structural features: territory, people, identity, sovereignty, and independence. Russian grand strategy, as it has evolved so far, has been characterized by realism, restraint, and pragmatism. It is driven by realpolitik, not Tsarist expansionism or Soviet revisionism. As such, the grand strategy of the Russian Federation is still very much a work in progress.



S. Tata, *Reflections on Grand Strategy*,
https://doi.org/10.1007/978-981-19-3773-6_4

## Territory

At the time of its birth, the territorial scope of the Russian Federation was clear and there were no conflicting or competing claims with the other previous member republics of the erstwhile USSR. Accordingly, Russia had no unrequited irredentist or revanchist ambitions that needed to be realized for the state to be considered whole and complete with respect to land, people, or national identity.[1] Rather, the Russian Federation's challenge was to ensure that it could exercise effective control over its existing extensive territory.[2] Russia is the world's largest country in terms of territory, covering 17.1 million square kilometers (km) spanning 11 time zones.[3] By comparison, the next three largest countries are significantly smaller: Canada, 10 million square km; the United States, 9.8 million square km; and China, 9.6 million square km.[4]

Yet, on 21 March 2014 the Russian Federation formally annexed Crimea following a 16 March referendum in which the local population opted to secede from Ukraine and rejoin Russia. The referendum was called by the regional government of Crimea, presumably with Moscow's covert encouragement and support, shortly after the collapse of Ukraine's central government led by President Viktor Yanukovych (who favored closer relations with Russia) on 21 February 2014 in the wake of three months of protests (sometimes violent) in the capital city of Kiev and in parts of western Ukraine against the government's decision of 21 November 2013 to terminate negotiations for a closer association with the European Union and opt for stronger ties with Russia.[5]

Understanding Moscow's rationale for annexation is crucial to deciphering Russia's grand strategy. To frame Russia's action as a reflection of irredentist or revanchist expansionism would be a grave mistake. Rather, annexation was a carefully crafted strategic response to preempt a perceived imminent existential threat to Russia's national security posed by the likely accession of Ukraine to the NATO (North Atlantic Treaty Organization) military alliance and the attendant loss of Russia's long-term lease (scheduled to expire in 2042) of the naval base at Sevastopol in Crimea.[6] In his speech on 18 March 2014 to the Duma, President Vladimir Putin underscored the national security dimension of annexation: "[W]e have already heard declarations from Kiev about Ukraine soon joining NATO... It would have meant that NATO's navy would be right there [Sevastopol] ... and this would create not an illusory but a perfectly real threat to the whole of southern Russia."[7] In fact, since

2007 Moscow had repeatedly and explicitly warned against further NATO planned expansion to Ukraine that would bring the military alliance to Russia's highly vulnerable southwestern border.[8] Finally, to preempt any possibility of Ukraine slipping out of Russia's sphere of influence and into the embrace of NATO, on 24 February 2022 President Putin launched an invasion of Ukraine, declaring: "*Any further expansion of the North Atlantic alliance's infrastructure or the ongoing efforts to gain a military foothold of the Ukrainian territory are unacceptable for us.*"[9]

## People and National Identity

As a Eurasian state stretching across Europe, Central Asia, and the Far East, diversity is embedded in the overarching national identity of the Russian Federation. A profile of the country's people would indicate that (1) in terms of ethnicity, Russians account for about 78 percent of the population, with the balance representing nearly 200 different minorities; (2) in terms of language, Russian is the primary language of about 86 percent of the population, with the balance reflecting the primary non-Russian languages of various minority ethnic groups; and (3) in terms of religion, although a majority of the population do not practice any religion, about 15–20 percent of the population claim to be Russian Orthodox Christians and another 10–15 percent follow Islam, while small minorities adhere to Judaism, Buddhism, and other Christian sects.[10] As the continuing struggle to integrate Chechnya's Muslim-majority population demonstrates, the Russian Federation's project of forging a singular national identity that transcends the various sub-identities of its people is far from complete. By the same token, the Russian Federation does not claim to have any extraterritorial vital national interest with respect to ethnic Russians of the former Soviet Union who are living outside the Federation's territorial boundaries. Nevertheless, President Vladimir Putin has highlighted the historical continuity in the evolution of Russian national identity: "Russia is a country with a history that spans more than a thousand years and has practically always used the privilege to carry out an independent foreign policy."[11] From the perspective of Russian grand strategy, territory, people, and national identity are congruent.

## Sovereignty and Independence

Russia insists on its sovereignty and rejects as illegitimate the conception of unipolarity espoused by the United States following the end of the Cold War. In a seminal speech in Munich in 2007, President Vladimir Putin argued:

> [W]hat is a unipolar world? … [I]t refers to one type of situation, namely one center of authority, one center of force, one center of decision-making … It is a world in which there is one master, one sovereign … [T]his is pernicious not only for all those within this system, but also for the sovereign itself because it destroys itself from within … I consider that the unipolar model is not only unacceptable but impossible in today's world.[12]

As already pointed out, in 2014 Russia extended its sovereignty over Crimea via annexation after the region separated from Ukraine. Russia will safeguard its sovereignty over Crimea because the loss of control over exclusive access to the Sevastopol naval base is unacceptable given its vital geostrategic importance for national security, which is the same rationale Moscow has articulated to justify annexation.[13] Although Ukraine continues to claim sovereignty over Crimea, it has made no serious attempt to recover the lost territory.[14]

Safeguarding independence of the Russian Federation looms large as a vital national interest given the state's overwhelming dependence on energy exports for its economic security. Accordingly, for Russia independence has three critical dimensions: (1) capability to be a reliable keystone supplier of significant amounts of oil and gas in quantities sufficient to meet a substantial portion of the energy requirements of major energy importing countries; (2) the reciprocal dependency of major importing countries on Russian energy supplies reflecting their lack of alternative comparable energy suppliers; and (3) ability to leverage revenues generated by energy exports to significantly diversify the country's economy (a) through import substitution of manufactured goods, agricultural products, and services, and (b) through exports of military and commercial manufactured goods and services with a technological and qualitative edge.

Russian independence is primarily a function of its economic security, which, in turn, is dependent largely upon the ability to generate revenues from oil and gas exports to finance economic growth and development. According to the International Monetary Fund (IMF), in 2019 oil and gas exports represented about 14.1 percent of Russia's GDP and accounted for nearly 49 percent of the country's total exports.[15] Clearly, dependence on energy exports is Russia's "Achilles' heel." Simply put, if a Russian government attempts to pursue policies that it believes safeguards or furthers the state's vital national interests but which are disapproved by Moscow's major energy customers, there is a possibility that it could face economic pressure in the form of boycotts or sanctions imposed or supported by such customers. Immunizing the Russian Federation against such economic coercion in order to safeguard its independence will be a major objective of Moscow for the remainder of the twenty-first century.

Russia is one of the world's largest energy exporters and is expected to remain so for the foreseeable future. According to the Energy Information Administration (EIA), the statistical arm of the US Department of Energy, Russia's total proved oil and gas reserves at year-end 2016 amounted to 80 billion barrels of oil and 1688 trillion cubic feet (Tcf) of gas.[16] In that year, Russia exported about 7 million barrels per day (mbpd) of oil and 7.5 Tcf of gas based on total production of 11.2 mbpd of oil and 21 Tcf of gas.[17] By 2039, the EIA projects that Russia will export 7.8 mbpd of oil and 15.6 Tcf of gas based on total production of 11.3 mbpd of oil and 31.2 Tcf of gas.[18]

Currently, its status as a leading energy exporter notwithstanding, Russia is highly vulnerable to economic coercion in the form of embargoes on and sanctions with respect to its energy exports because its principal importing countries have alternate sources of supply. In 2016, the European member countries of the Organization for Economic Cooperation and Development (OECD) accounted for about 44 percent of Russia's oil exports (3.1 mbpd) and 75 percent (5.6 Tcf) of its gas exports, which satisfied about 33 percent and 70 percent of OECD's total oil and gas import requirements respectively.[19] This energy trade interdependence, however, is highly asymmetric because these European energy customers have the ability to substitute relatively easily and quickly other energy suppliers (principally from the Middle East and Africa) in lieu of Russia. On the other hand, Russia has limited options with respect to alternative buyers, and it would require significant investment in terms of time and money to put in place the infrastructure required to redirect Russia's energy exports. Not surprisingly, the sanctions placed on Russia's energy sector by the European Union (and the United States) in response to the 2014 annexation of Crimea have adversely impacted the Russian economy. According to the IMF, the Russian economy suffered a sharp recession in 2015 and 2016 with real GDP contracting about 2 percent, reflecting primarily the combined impact of sanctions and declining oil prices, and then a gradual recovery over 2017–2018 reflecting slightly improved oil prices, so that over the five-year 2014–2018 period average GDP growth was essentially flat at 0.5 percent per annum as compared to the previous five-year 2009–2013 period (pre-sanctions, stable oil prices but low demand) during which the average annual growth rate was 1.2 percent.[20]

Moscow has recognized its strategic vulnerability and has moved to diversify and rebalance Russia's energy exports away from Europe to China in order to forge a more robust and symmetrical mutual interdependency based on a de facto bargain of energy security for the Middle Kingdom in return for economic security for Russia. China has not supported the US and EU energy sanctions imposed to punish Russia for the annexation of Crimea. Undoubtedly, Russia has the capability to satisfy a substantial portion of China's energy import requirements. In 2016, given Moscow's focus on the European energy market, China accounted for only about 14 percent of Russia's oil exports and a negligible amount of its gas exports.[21] By 2039, the EIA projects that Chinese oil imports will rise to 12.5 mbpd in order to meet about 75 percent of the country's total oil consumption requirements of 16.7 mbpd, while gas imports will increase to 6.6 Tcf to satisfy about 39 percent of total natural gas consumption needs of 16.8 Tcf.[22] As already noted, in 2039 Russia is projected to export 7.8 mbpd of oil and 15.6 Tcf of gas.[23] If Moscow were to pivot completely to Beijing, it could satisfy about 62 percent of China's oil import needs and all of China's gas import requirements. More realistically, if Russia were to hedge its relationship with the Middle Kingdom and allocate 60 percent of energy exports to China (with the balance allocated to other countries for prudent diversification), in 2039 Russia would be able to meet about 37 percent of China's oil import requirements and all of China's gas import needs. Moreover, although it will take significant investment in energy infrastructure over the next two decades, Russian energy exports could be delivered securely via land-based pipelines directly connecting Russian oil and gas fields to China, which would fit seamlessly with Beijing's Silk Roads project (announced in 2013) designed to reduce dramatically the Middle Kingdom's reliance on sea-borne energy imports and circumvent American control of the global maritime commons.[24]

From Moscow's perspective, China would be a reliable purchaser of Russia's oil and gas exports over the long term with sufficient demand to help anchor the Russian economy, while from Beijing's perspective, Russia would be a reliable supplier capable of satisfying a substantial portion of China's energy import requirements over the long term thereby ensuring the Middle Kingdom's energy security. No country other than Russia can provide such energy security for China, and no country other than China can provide such economic security for Russia. Accordingly, the mutual interdependence would be symmetrical, and Russia would need China just as much as China would need Russia. The burgeoning China–Russia energy partnership, which is likely to take a generation to fully develop and mature, is a strategic relationship that will be a cornerstone of the grand strategies of both Russia and China for the foreseeable future.

The third dimension of Russian independence relates to the diversification of the country's economy to reduce the dependency on energy exports. Both the IMF and the World Bank have consistently emphasized the critical importance of a diversified economy for Russia's future growth prospects, but the challenge is yet to be met.[25] For Russia, the primary driver of economic diversification will be import substitution so that the country is not dependent on foreign goods and services that could be withheld at the discretion of foreign suppliers (or more accurately, the home countries of such suppliers) who do not agree with Russian foreign or domestic policies. Clearly, there is a significant element of mercantilism and associated economic inefficiency reflecting the subordination of economic comparative advantage to the imperatives of safeguarding Russian independence. While currency depreciation and import barriers may be necessary (at least in the short and medium term) to protect import substitution industries, such measures are not sufficient. Russian decision-makers have yet to clearly articulate an import substitution strategy and demonstrate the political will to embrace major reforms with respect to the labor market, financial and capital markets, taxation, and regulatory streamlining that would be required to stimulate and nurture the domestic production of goods and services that are currently imported. Likewise, other than promoting sales of military equipment and nuclear reactors for electricity generation, the government has not made a significant effort to encourage the development of an export market for goods and services where Russia may have a comparative advantage such as information technology services (for example, cyber security) or otherwise efficiently channel and utilize the entrepreneurial talents of its well-educated work force.[26] Unquestionably, using and leveraging energy export revenues to finance the diversification of the Russian economy (instead of simply funding imports of goods and services that, at least in the short and medium term, may be cheaper or better than those that might be produced domestically) will be a critical challenge for the balance of the twenty-first century.

## Stitching a Russian Security Envelope

As an enfeebled Russia re-emerged from the rubble of the erstwhile Soviet Union, Moscow faced the task of patching together a security envelope or sphere of influence to protect the new state's territorial core. The harsh reality was that the dissolution of the Soviet Union and disbanding of the Warsaw Pact meant that Russia lost the shield provided by other former member republics of the USSR as well as the deep buffer zone provided by the other former members of the Warsaw Pact military alliance (Albania, Poland, Hungary, Czechoslovakia, Romania, Bulgaria, and East Germany). Over the past two decades, the Russian Federation has made considerable progress in stitching together a sphere of influence, but the ongoing project remains incomplete, and the security envelope constructed so far is fragile.

Russia has been most successful in crafting a *cordon sanitaire* in Central Asia to protect its southcentral border and preserve Moscow's control over access to the energy resources of the Caspian Sea littoral states that were former republics of the erstwhile Soviet Union. This *cordon sanitaire* consists of the three energy-rich Caspian Sea littoral states—Azerbaijan, Kazakhstan, and Turkmenistan—and the adjacent Central Asian states of Uzbekistan, Kyrgyzstan, and Tajikistan.[27] Quite simply, with respect to these six Central Asian states, Moscow is unlikely to tolerate any government that is considered hostile to the vital national interests of the Russian Federation (or any foreign intervention, either overt or covert, in support of such a hostile government).

Russia continues to struggle to establish an effective *cordon sanitaire* along its highly vulnerable European southwestern flank, which has been the historic invasion route followed by hostile attacking forces during the Napoleonic War (1812), Crimean War (1853), First World

War (1914), and Second World War (1941). The precarious southwestern *cordon sanitaire* that the Russian Federation has patched together consists of five former Soviet republics: Belarus, Ukraine, Moldova, Georgia, and Armenia (including the northern and eastern shores of the Black Sea). Reflecting the significant asymmetry in power between a weakened Russia and the even weaker group of neighboring states, Moscow has not hesitated to bring to bear considerable coercive pressure, primarily the leverage of residual Russian military presence in these states (a holdover of the legacy of the USSR ostensibly to help tamp down ethnic tensions in these erstwhile Soviet republics) and its position as a monopoly supplier of oil and gas, to ensure that these five states would not act in a manner that conflicted with the Russian Federation's vital national interests. Indeed, from 1992 until 2006, the United States, NATO, and the European Union did not object to Moscow's efforts to carve out this European sphere of influence along the Russian Federation's southwestern underbelly.[28] It was only at the 2006 NATO Summit in Riga and the following 2008 NATO Summit in Bucharest that the United States and its NATO allies challenged Russia's southwestern *cordon sanitaire* by declaring that NATO would be receptive to the accession of these five European former Soviet republics to the military alliance and specifically encouraged Georgia and Ukraine to intensify their preparations for NATO membership.[29] As already noted, over the course of 2007–2008, Moscow repeatedly drew a bright red line against such a proposed NATO expansion along the Russian Federation's sensitive southwestern flank. Certainly, President Putin did not mince any words when he declared: "We view the appearance of a powerful military bloc on our borders ... as a direct threat to the security of our country."[30] In fact, Moscow's military operations against Georgia in 2008 and Ukraine in 2014 have underscored its determination to preserve Russia's fragile European *cordon sanitaire*.[31] Russia's February 2022 reinvasion of Ukraine is a continuation of its effort to secure its southwestern flank—which the more limited 2014 annexation of Crimea failed to accomplish.

Moscow has not indicated any intention to expand Russia's sphere of influence beyond the existing *cordon sanitaire*. Rather than seeking an expanded buffer zone, the Russian Federation appears focused on ensuring stability with its neighbors along its southeastern and northwestern territorial borders, and security along its northern maritime boundary in the Arctic Ocean (stretching from the Barents Sea in the northwest to the Chukchi Sea and Bering Strait in the northeast).

Following the collapse of the Soviet Union, Moscow made a concerted effort over a decade to peacefully resolve Russia's territorial disputes along its 4179 km southeastern border with China, and also accepted the shift of Mongolia and North Korea from the erstwhile Soviet sphere of influence to the Chinese *cordon sanitaire*.[32] Likewise, Moscow has offered to resolve Japanese claims to the Kuril Islands in the Sea of Okhotsk, which were occupied by the erstwhile Soviet Union at the end of WWII and has been under Soviet and then Russian administration since then.[33] In sharp contrast to the peace and stability prevailing along the Russian Federation's lengthy southeastern border, the decade-long calm generally prevailing along Russia's short northwestern border with its Baltic neighbors—Estonia, Latvia, and Lithuania—from the 2004 accession of these three former Soviet republics to the NATO military alliance (a move accepted grudgingly by Moscow) has become increasingly tense since 2014 as Russia has intervened militarily in Ukraine to preserve the *status quo* with respect to the southwestern *cordon sanitaire* and prevent Kiev from following in the footsteps of the Baltic republics and break the strategic ties with the Russian Federation and join NATO. In response to Russia's annexation of Crimea, NATO (pursuant to an American initiative) has bolstered the alliance's military presence in the Baltics, and Moscow has reacted in a "tit for tat" fashion with increased military activity along Russia's borders with the Baltic states.[34] It should be stressed, however, that neither in its rhetoric nor in its actions has Moscow given any revanchist indication that it seeks to reverse the *status quo* along Russia's northwestern borders and extend its sphere of influence to the Baltics.[35] The reality is that the Russian exclave of Kaliningrad, sandwiched between Lithuania and Poland, is effectively hostage to NATO, and any Russian move against Estonia, Latvia or Lithuania would be countered by a NATO squeeze on Kaliningrad. In terms of safeguarding its territorial integrity, Russia's major focus since 2014 has been not on its northwestern land border with the Baltics but on its northern maritime border stretching along the Arctic Ocean.[36] In fact, the strategic importance of Russia's northern maritime border is expected to increase dramatically over the next two decades as climate warming makes the hitherto frozen Northern Sea Route (which passes through Russian territorial waters linking the Pacific and Atlantic Oceans via the Arctic Ocean) a commercially viable SLOC for maritime trade (including Russia's energy trade).[37]

## Potential Adversaries

From the perspective of Moscow, the United States, particularly in her leadership role as *primus inter pares* in the NATO military alliance, has emerged since 2006 as the primary potential adversary which could have both the intention as well as the capability to challenge the vital national interests of the Russian Federation. At America's behest, at each of NATO's biannual summits beginning with the 2006 NATO Summit in Riga, the military alliance has encouraged the five former Soviet republics (Belarus, Ukraine, Moldova, Georgia, and Armenia) that form Russia's southwestern *cordon sanitaire* to move out of the orbit of the Russian Federation and become members of NATO, Moscow's objections notwithstanding. Indeed, specifically with respect to the geo-strategically critical Black Sea littoral states of Ukraine and Georgia, the 2008 NATO Summit in Bucharest issued an unambiguous declaration: "NATO welcomes Ukraine's and Georgia's Euro-Atlantic aspirations for membership in NATO. We agreed today that these countries will become members of NATO."[38] Clearly, Russia's military moves against Georgia in 2008 and Ukraine in 2014 have not deterred the United States and its NATO allies from pursuing the expansion of the military alliance to Russia's southwestern borders. Indeed, a decade after the Bucharest Summit, the 2018 NATO Summit in Brussels reaffirmed NATO's intention to offer membership to the five former Soviet republics on Russia's vulnerable southwestern underbelly, including specifically Ukraine and Georgia.[39] From the Kremlin's perspective, the 2014 annexation of Crimea failed to dent NATO's expansionist aspirations, and in February 2022, Russia launched a major reinvasion of Ukraine to preempt any possibility of the country slipping out of its sphere of influence.

Moscow cannot ignore the repeated and consistent declarations of the intentions of the United States and its NATO allies.[40] Quite simply, the strategic calculus is not in Russia's favor in terms of both latent as well as actual conventional military power. According to the CIA, Russia's GDP (measured on a purchasing power parity basis) was $4 trillion in 2019, which amounted to a mere 19.5 percent of America's GDP of $20.5 trillion, while Russia's population of 142.3 million persons (2021) was only 42.5 percent of the US population of 335 million persons.[41] In terms of conventional military power, Russia also is at a distinct disadvantage in the air and at sea: Russia has a total of 1531 fighter and attack aircraft (the United States, 2717) and 538 attack helicopters (the United States, 904), while at sea Russia has only 1 aircraft carrier (the United States, 11) and 64 submarines (the United States, 68). On land, however, Russia likely has an edge compared to the United States: Russia can muster 13,000 tanks (the United States, 6100) and 27,100 armored fighting vehicles (the United States, 40,000).[42] Russia's active military personnel total 1 million persons compared to 1.4 million persons for the United States.[43] Although in 2019 Russian defense spending was 3.9 percent of GDP compared to 3.4 percent of GDP for the United States, reflecting the fact that the US economy was almost 5.1 times larger than that of Russia, to achieve parity with respect to defense spending Russia would have had to allocate about 17.3 percent of GDP for such purposes, which clearly would be an unsustainable burden.[44] For the foreseeable future, Russia will have to craft its grand strategy based on the reality of an adverse, asymmetric power imbalance relative to the United States. Certainly, with respect to Russia's *cordon sanitaire*, Moscow cannot take American forbearance for granted.

## Potential Strategic Partners

Russia will have to forge a strategic partnership with another powerful state that also has vital national interests that are being challenged by the United States. China is such a strategic partner.

As discussed above, Beijing and Moscow have a compelling basis to forge a strategic partnership of equals that ensures energy security for the Middle Kingdom and economic security for the Russian Federation, regardless of whether there is a shared perception of America as a common adversary. Arguably, a US challenge to Russia's effort to preserve a *cordon sanitaire* along its southwestern border with Crimea as the strategic centerpiece, and China's attempt to carve a maritime *cordon sanitaire* (stretching from the South China Sea through the East China Sea to the Yellow Sea) with Taiwan as the strategic centerpiece, will be seen by Moscow and Beijing as a threat to their respective vital national interests, and, therefore, the United States will be perceived as a common foe. Although an attack by the United States on the territory of either Russia or China is unlikely, it is possible. American attacks on Chinese forces in Taiwan attempting to reintegrate the "renegade" province or on Russian forces in Crimea could materialize as an unintended consequence of an escalatory spiral in connection with Taiwanese efforts to declare independence unilaterally or Ukrainian efforts to recover Crimea. Accordingly, Beijing and Moscow could carefully tailor a military partnership to deal with such an eventuality. For example, such a military pact could declare that an armed attack by the United States on the Russian Federation or the People's Republic of China in territory under their respective administration or on vessels or craft of either country in international waters or air space, would be considered as an attack on both countries, and accordingly the strategic partners would respond jointly and severally to such an attack using all appropriate means, including military force. For the purposes of the defense agreement, Taiwan would be deemed to be part of China and treated as if it were under the PRC's administrative control.[45] Such a strategic military partnership would be a strong deterrent to any US attempt to keep Ukraine or the South China Sea out of the respective spheres of influence of Russia and China.

The vital national interests of Russia and China are not likely to conflict for the foreseeable future, so a Moscow-Beijing strategic partnership of equals can be expected to crystallize and take shape over the next two decades in response to the converging shared threat perception with respect to the United States.[46]

To hedge the security of its southcentral *cordon sanitaire* Russia is trying to forge a strategic partnership with Iran. A friendly Iran will not allow activities to be conducted within its territory that would threaten the vital national interests of the Russian Federation. While Russia dominates the northern, eastern, and western shores of the Caspian Sea, Iran, by virtue of its geostrategic location overlooking the southern shore of the Caspian, can cover a crucial gap in the Central Asian *cordon sanitaire* of the Russian Federation.[47] Iran, which since the 1979 revolution overthrowing the US-supported monarch, Shah Mohammed Reza Pahlavi, has developed significant indigenous unconventional military capabilities and possesses the national will to resist and ultimately defeat foreign control, is unlikely to be part of a Russian *cordon sanitaire* so the only option for Moscow is to craft a mutually satisfactory strategic partnership with Tehran. However, reflecting the substantial asymmetry with respect to both conventional military power and mutual interdependence in favor of Russia, the embryonic partnership can be characterized as one in which Moscow is the senior partner and Tehran is the junior partner.

The catalyst for the emerging strategic partnership is the convergence of the perception of the United States as a threat to the respective vital national interests of Russia and Iran. In this context, the United States is seen as attempting to gain control over access to the global oil and gas markets via the use of economic sanctions as a weapon to prevent Russia and Iran, as major energy exporters, from gaining access to foreign markets for their oil and gas products and thereby threatening their economic security. Additionally, in the case of Iran, the United States has repeatedly and explicitly threatened an armed attack to prevent the development of a nuclear weapon or long-range missile capable of delivering such a weapon and, albeit more ambiguously, to prevent Tehran from providing military and financial assistance to foreign proxies engaged in activities inimical to the vital national interests of America's strategic partners in the Middle East.[48] Ultimately, these Iranian activities jeopardize US control over access to Persian Gulf oil and gas resources. In the event an American attack on and invasion of Iran were to materialize, Moscow would be faced with the prospect of US military forces on the southern shores of the Caspian, which would then pose a direct threat to the Russian Federation's southcentral *cordon sanitaire*. Russia most likely would supply Iran with enough military equipment both in terms of quantity and quality needed to help defeat American expeditionary forces.

To further reinforce the Iranian buffer to its southcentral *cordon sanitaire* as well as provide a hedge to its southwestern *cordon sanitaire*, Russia is strengthening its ties to Iran's key allies—Iraq and Syria.[49] The Iran–Iraq–Syria land bridge connecting the Caspian Sea to the Mediterranean Sea is strategically important to Moscow as the only route to outflank NATO's eastern bastion, Turkey, which controls the southern shore of the Black Sea. In the event NATO, under US leadership, attempts to use military force to pry loose Ukraine or Georgia from Russia's sphere of influence, Moscow could use the land bridge to funnel Russian military forces to attack Turkey.[50] A "hub and spoke" security architecture connecting Russia to Iran, Iraq, and Syria is at an embryonic stage, but it could gestate over the next twenty years into a serious strategic partnership to deter further NATO expansion to the southwestern and southcentral borders of Russia.

## Russia's Quest for Internal Restraints on NATO Expansion

Much to the Kremlin's chagrin, NATO refuses to wither away and instead, spurred on by America, adamantly continues to insist on expanding the military alliance to the borders of the Russian Federation. Russia's plan A of constructing a sphere of influence and forging strategic partnerships with China and Iran (and its allies—Syria and Iraq) while necessary for any credible effort to deter the United States and its NATO allies, may not be sufficient to trigger a NATO reset and reconsideration of the alliance's planned expansion. After all, for over a decade the United States and its fellow members of NATO have consistently refused to acknowledge the red lines against encroaching on Russia's sphere of influence that President Vladimir Putin publicly declared in his 2007 Munich speech. Ultimately, NATO restraint must come from within and not as a response to external pressure. Not surprisingly, Moscow is pursuing also a plan B designed to persuade two key members of NATO—Turkey and Germany—that certain of their respective vital national interests which are not supported sufficiently by the United States and other members of NATO could be furthered better through cooperation with Russia, and, although not explicitly linked in exchange for the benefits of such cooperation, Ankara and Berlin could reciprocate by opposing further expansion of the military alliance to Russia's borders on the basis that such expansion would be an obstacle to achieving a *modus vivendi* with the Russian Federation. Among the NATO member countries, Turkey has the second largest military force and Germany has the second largest economy.

Safeguarding Turkey's territorial integrity and sovereignty against the threat of Kurdish separatism is a key vital national interest that in Ankara's view is not sufficiently shared by the United States, since Washington has formed strategic partnerships with certain separatist Kurdish groups in neighboring Syria and Iraq (that share the aspirations of Kurdish separatist groups within Turkey) as part of American efforts to support regime change in Syria and combat IS (Islamic State), a radical Sunni fundamentalist group attempting to establish a regional Islamic caliphate in parts of Iraq and Syria.[51] The Kurdish region of Turkey shares common borders with the Kurdish regions of Syria, Iraq, and Iran, and all four countries, albeit to varying degrees, face the challenge of Kurdish separatism as many Kurds across all four countries aspire to have ultimately their own nation-state.[52] In order to ensure its access to the Iran–Iraq–Syria land bridge,

Russia has agreed to support the government of Bashar al-Assad in its efforts to preserve the territorial integrity and sovereignty of the Syrian state against a motley assortment of rebel groups with disparate aims, including seeking variously regime change, the dismemberment of the Syrian state and the inclusion of part of its territory in a regional Islamic caliphate, and a separate Kurdish state.[53] In sharp contrast to Washington's apparent disregard of Ankara's concerns, Moscow has reached out to Ankara and cooperated and coordinated with Turkey with respect to military activities along the Turkey–Syria border. Indeed, Russian and Turkish forces jointly patrol the Kurdish areas along the Syrian border with Turkey to prevent the establishment of insurgent safe havens.[54] Moreover, Moscow clearly is seeking to ensure that Russian–Turkish cooperation extends beyond short-term operational matters to long-term strategic concerns. For example, Russia will supply Turkey with the S-400 antimissile defense system and build the country's first nuclear powered electricity generation plant.[55] Also, Russia has agreed to supply natural gas directly to Turkey via the new Turk Stream pipeline (which passes underneath the Black Sea) with a possible second phase to supply gas (via Turkey) to southern Europe.[56]

As the centerpiece of its strategic approach to Germany, Russia is trying to address Berlin's concerns with respect to energy security as a vital national interest. Germany is Europe's largest economy with 2019 GDP (purchasing power parity basis) of $4.5 trillion, with exports accounting for about 47 percent of 2019 GDP.[57] Germany has no significant oil and gas resources, so critical to its economic success is the availability of reliable, low-cost energy. Russia is Germany's largest supplier of oil and gas. In 2017, Russia met about 40 percent of Germany's total import requirements for natural gas and about 37 percent of its total import requirements for oil.[58] All of Russia's oil and gas exports to Germany are delivered via pipeline either directly in the case of gas via the Nord Stream pipeline system which passes under the Baltic Sea in international waters, or in the case of oil via the Druzhba pipeline system transiting through Belarus and Poland. Russia also can deliver oil directly to Germany (bypassing Belarus and Poland) via sea-borne tankers from oil terminals near St. Petersburg on the Gulf of Finland transiting through international waters to the German port of Wilhelmshaven on the North Sea. So, in addition to reliability and low cost, Moscow can deliver energy to Germany via secure routes that would circumvent the Russian

Federation's southwestern *cordon sanitaire* (thereby insulating Germany's energy security from instability in Ukraine and Belarus).

Although Germany has alternative sources of supply to meet its energy import requirements that could replace Russia permanently, Berlin appears hesitant to proceed along such a path because it would entail significant new energy infrastructure expenditures, reliability in terms of timeliness and quantity could be more uncertain, and oil and gas prices likely could be more volatile.[59] While recognizing the implied *quid pro quo* of energy security for Germany in return for economic security for Russia, both Berlin and Moscow have struggled to resolve the tension between the Russian Federation's insistence on a sphere of influence along its southwestern underbelly and NATO's insistence on expanding its membership to include explicitly Ukraine and Georgia. Germany has tried to craft a compromise that holds out the promise of future accession of Ukraine and Georgia but provides no assurances as to the expected time frame for NATO membership. The numerous NATO declarations with respect to ultimate membership of Ukraine and Georgia reflect the German approach. Unfortunately, from the Kremlin's perspective, such German reciprocity falls short since Moscow will have to continue dealing with the uncertainty of the NATO threat to the integrity of the Russian Federation's southwestern *cordon sanitaire*.[60]

Germany, by itself, cannot cut the "Gordian knot" of further NATO expansion to the east; only the United States as the military alliance's ultimate security guarantor can do so. It is for this reason that since 2014 Moscow has expressed a serious interest in a reset of Russia's relations with the United States in order to achieve a *modus vivendi* and remove the specter of a Cold War 2.0.[61] America's response to Russia's overtures has not been reassuring and, indeed, in late January 2022, the United States categorically refused to rule out future Ukraine membership in NATO.[62] Rather than continuing to live with the strategic uncertainty of a "glass half full, half empty" embedded in the German compromise formulation with respect to possibility of further NATO encroachment on its *cordon sanitaire*, Russia once again opted to preemptively enforce its red line against Ukraine membership in NATO by invading (or more accurately, reinvading) the country on 24 February 2022. As President Vladimir Putin explained: "[I]n December 2021, *we made yet another attempt to reach agreement with the United States and its allies on the principles of European security and NATO's non-expansion. Our efforts were in vain. The United States has not changed its position.*"[63] The specter of Cold War 2.0 is on the brink of becoming reality.

## Notes

1. In sharp contrast, the People's Republic of China and the State of Israel were established as incomplete states with significant irredentist claims that to date have yet to be fully realized (Taiwan in the case of China; East Jerusalem, the West Bank and Gaza—all of which are considered to be part of the Land of Israel or Eretz Israel—in the case of Israel).
2. In fact, even after two major military campaigns (1994–1996 and 1999–2000) against separatists in Chechnya, Russia continues to struggle to establish the central government's control over the Muslim-majority province in the northern Caucasus. For example, see Luke Harding, "Russia Ends anti-Terrorism Operations in Chechnya," *Guardian* (UK), 16 April 2009, https://www.theguardian.com/world/2009/apr/16/russia-chechnya-anti-terrorism; and Andrew Roth, "Chechnya Attacks Carried Out by Children as Young as 11, Say Officials," *Guardian* (UK), 21 August 2018, https://www.theguardian.com/world/2018/aug/21/chechnya-attacks-carried-out-by-children-as-young-as-11-say-officials.
3. Other than the small exclave on the Baltic Sea of Kaliningrad, sandwiched between Lithuania and Poland, Russia's territorial expanse is contiguous and, in the case of offshore islands, within territorial waters. Kaliningrad, the former Konigsberg (the erstwhile capital of Prussia), was detached from Germany (with the agreement of the United Kingdom, France, and the United States) at the end of World War II.
4. Central Intelligence Agency (CIA), *World Factbook*, https://www.cia.gov/the-world-factbook/.
5. Sergei L. Loiko, "Ukraine Protestors Take Kiev Without a Shot as Yanukovich Flees," *Los Angeles Times*, 22 February 2014, https://www.latimes.com/world/worldnow/la-fg-wn-kiev-opposition-20140222-story.html; Shawn Walker, "Ukraine's Former PM Rallies Protestors After Yanukovych Flees Kiev," *Guardian* (UK), 22 February 2014, https://www.theguardian.com/world/2014/feb/22/ukraine-president-yanukovych-flees-kiev; and Ian Traynor and Oksana Grytsenko, "Ukraine Suspends Talks on EU Trade Pact as Putin Wins Tug of War," *Guardian* (UK), 21 November 2013, https://www.theguardian.com/world/2013/nov/21/ukraine-suspends-preparations-eu-trade-pact. American sympathy and support for the anti-government protests was expressed by both US government officials as well as leading politicians. See CBS, "Top U.S. Official Visits Protestors in Kiev as Obama Admin. Ups Pressure on Ukraine president Yanukovich," *CBS News*, 11 December 2013, https://www.cbsnews.com/news/us-victoria-nuland-wades-into-ukraine-turmoil-over-yanukovich/; Guardian staff and agencies, "John McCain Tells Protesters: 'We Are Here to Support Your Just Cause,'" *Guardian* (UK),

15 December 2013, https://www.theguardian.com/world/2013/dec/15/john-mccain-ukraine-protests-support-just-cause; and BBC, "Ukraine Crisis: Transcript of Leaked Nuland-Pyatt Call," *BBC News*, 7 February 2014, https://www.bbc.com/news/world-europe-26079957.

6. Sevastopol has served as a naval base for all three incarnations of the Russian state since 1783, when Crimea originally was annexed by the Russian Empire and detached from the Ottoman Empire. Following the dissolution of the Soviet Union, the Russian Federation negotiated with Ukraine a long-term lease of the Sevastopol naval base in 1997 with an initial expiry date of 2017, which lease was subsequently extended in 2010 to 2042. See Luke Harding, "Ukraine Extends Lease for Russia's Black Sea Fleet," *Guardian* (UK), 21 April 2010, https://www.theguardian.com/world/2010/apr/21/ukraine-black-sea-fleet-russia; and "Crimea: Divided Peninsula Plays Host to Russian Warships and Ukrainian Pride," *Guardian* (UK), 15 September 2008, https://www.theguardian.com/world/2008/sep/16/ukraine.russia.
7. Office of the President, "Address by President of the Russian Federation, 18 March 2014," http://en.kremlin.ru/events/president/news/20603.
8. See for example, Office of the President, "Speech and the Following Discussion at the Munich Conference on Security Policy, 10 February 2007," http://en.kremlin.ru/events/president/transcripts/24034; "Press Statement and Answers to Journalists' Questions Following a Meeting of the Russia—NATO Council, 4 April 2008," http://en.kremlin.ru/events/president/transcripts/24903; and Unian Information Agency, "Text of Putin's Speech at NATO Summit (Bucharest, April 2, 2008)," https://www.unian.info/world/111033-text-of-putin-s-speech-at-nato-summit-bucharest-april-2-2008.html. For a US perspective regarding NATO expansion reflecting ideological sentiments rather than strategic concerns, see George W. Grayson, *Strange Bedfellows: NATO Marches East* (Lanham, MD: University Press of America, 1999) and Michael Kirk, "Frontline: 'The Putin Files', Interview with Victoria Nuland," *PBS News*, 14 June 2017, https://www.pbs.org/wgbh/frontline/interview/victoria-nuland/.
9. The Print Team, "Full Text of Vladimir Putin's Speech Announcing 'Special Military Operation' in Ukraine," *Print (India)*, 24 February 2022, https://theprint.in/world/full-text-of-vladimir-putins-speech-announcing-special-military-operation-in-ukraine/845714/.
10. CIA, *World Factbook*.
11. Office of the President, "Speech and the Following Discussion at the Munich Conference on Security Policy, 10 February 2007," http://en.kremlin.ru/events/president/transcripts/24034.

12. Office of the President, "Speech and the Following Discussion at the Munich Conference on Security Policy, 10 February 2007," http://en.kremlin.ru/events/president/transcripts/24034.
13. In May 2018, Russia built the Kerch Strait Bridge linking Crimea to mainland Russia, thereby assuring territorial contiguity and connectivity. See Andrew Roth, "Putin Opens 12-Mile Bridge Between Crimea and Russian Mainland," *Guardian* (UK), 15 May 2018, https://www.theguardian.com/world/2018/may/15/putin-opens-bridge-between-crimea-and-russian-mainland.
14. Ukraine's deep-rooted political fissures will make a restoration of the *status quo* highly unlikely. See, Eve Conant, "How History, Geography Help Explain Ukraine's Political Crisis," *National Geographic*, 31 January 2014, https://www.nationalgeographic.com/news/2014/1/140129-protests-ukraine-russia-geography-history/. Having encouraged Ukraine to pivot away from its nearly three centuries of close association with Russia in favor of Euro-Atlantic aspirations, the challenge of helping Ukraine (presumably sans Crimea) safeguard its military, economic, and political security is largely with the United States, the European Union, and NATO. Shortly after Russia's annexation of Crimea, President Barack Obama acknowledged that US vital national interests were not adversely impacted: "Our economy is not closely integrated with Ukraine's. Our people and our homeland face no direct threat from the invasion of Crimea. Our own borders are not threatened by Russia's annexation." The White House, "Remarks by the President in Address to European Youth, 26 March 2014," https://obamawhitehouse.archives.gov/the-press-office/2014/03/26/remarks-president-address-european-youth.
15. International Monetary Fund (IMF), *Russian Federation: Staff Report for the 2020 Article IV Consultation*, 19 January 2021, 30 and 36–39, https://www.imf.org/en/Publications/CR/Issues/2021/02/08/Russian-Federation-2020-Article-IV-Consultation-Press-Release-Staff-Report-50068.
16. Energy Information Administration (EIA), *Country Analysis Brief: Russia*, 31 October 2017, https://www.eia.gov/international/analysis/country/RUS.
17. Ibid.
18. EIA, *International Energy Outlook, 2019* (*IEO 2019*), https://www.eia.gov/outlooks/archive/ieo19/. See Tables A5, A6, G2 and I1. Exports is calculated as the excess of production over consumption.
19. EIA, *Country Analysis Brief: Russia*.
20. IMF, *2019 Russian Federation Article IV Staff Report*, 50, https://www.imf.org/en/Publications/CR/Issues/2019/08/01/Russian-Federation-2019-Article-IV-Consultation-Press-Release-Staff-Report-48549. See also World Bank Database, " GDP growth (annual %)—Russian Federation,"

https://data.worldbank.org/indicator/NY.GDP.MKTP.KD.ZG?locations=RU.
21. EIA, *Country Analysis Brief: Russia.*
22. See EIA, *International Energy Outlook 2019* (IEO 2019) for projections of oil consumption (Table A5), natural gas consumption (Table A6), and oil production (Table G2), https://www.eia.gov/outlooks/archive/ieo19/tables_ref.php. Oil imports is calculated as the excess of oil consumption over oil production. IEO 2019 did not provide country level data on natural gas production for China although the same was provided in prior IEOs. See EIA, *International Energy Outlook 2017* (IEO 2017) for projections of natural gas imports (Table I4), https://www.eia.gov/outlooks/archive/ieo17/ieo_tables.php.
23. Ibid.
24. China with about $3.2 trillion foreign exchange reserves (2020) has the capital to finance the investment required for development and production of Russia's oil and gas fields and associated transportation infrastructure. See IMF, "International Reserves and Foreign Currency Liquidity: China," https://data.imf.org/regular.aspx?key=61280813. The newly inaugurated Power of Siberia gas pipeline is the harbinger of a robust long-term energy partnership between the two countries. See Nastassia Astrasheuskaya,, "Russia Launches Gas Pipeline to China," *Financial Times*, 2 December 2019, https://www.ft.com/content/551258ca-14ed-11ea-9ee4-11f260415385; Yanan Wang and Daria Litvinova, Associated Press, "China, Russia Launch Massive Joint Gas Pipeline," *Washington Times*, 2 December 2019, https://www.washingtontimes.com/news/2019/dec/2/china-russia-launch-massive-joint-gas-pipeline/; and Olga Tanas, Anna Shiryaevskaya and Dan Murtaugh, "How Russia-China Gas Pipeline Changes Energy Calculus," *Bloomberg News*, 24 November 2019, https://www.bloomberg.com/news/articles/2019-11-25/how-russia-china-gas-pipeline-changes-energy-calculus-quicktake. Russia has also solidified its position as the largest supplier of oil to China. See Olga Yagova, "As Russia Expands Pacific Pipeline, a Third of Oil Exports Go East," *Reuters*, 21 November 2019, https://www.reuters.com/article/us-russia-oil-exports-idUSKBN1XV1LB.
25. See IMF, *2020 Russian Federation Article IV Staff Report*, *2019 Russian Federation Article IV Staff Report*; and World Bank, *Russia Economic Report*, May 2021, https://openknowledge.worldbank.org/bitstream/handle/10986/35653/Russia-Economic-Report-Russia-s-Economic-Recovery-Gathers-Pace-Special-Focus-on-Cost-Effective-Safety-Nets.pdf?sequence=7 and: *Russia Economic Report*, June 2019, http://documents.worldbank.org/curated/en/332081560895493011/pdf/Russia-Economic-Report-Modest-Growth-Focus-on-Informality.pdf.

26. For example, over the 2016–2020 five-year period, India accounted for about 23 percent of aggregate Russian arms exports of about $28.1 billion. India is unlikely to be a significant purchaser of Russian military equipment in the future, as New Delhi focuses increasingly on self-reliance and rebalancing its strategic partnership with the United States. Moscow will find it difficult to find alternative purchasers of its military goods and services (most likely customers are Iran, Iraq, Syria and Turkey). See Stockholm International Peace Research Institute (SIPRI), "Arms Transfers Database", https://www.sipri.org/databases/armstransfers.
27. According to the EIA, as of 2019 Azerbaijan, Kazakhstan, and Turkmenistan collectively have combined total proved reserves of about 37.6 billion barrels of oil and 385 Tcf of gas. These reserves are located within a hundred-mile radius of the Caspian Sea. See EIA, "International Energy Statistics: Crude Oil Proved Reserves," https://www.eia.gov/international/rankings/world?pa=106&u=0&f=A&v=none&y=01%2F01%2F2019&ev=false; "International Energy Statistics: Proved Reserves of Natural Gas," https://www.eia.gov/international/rankings/world?pa=102&u=0&f=A&v=none&y=01%2F01%2F2019&ev=false; and *Caspian Sea*, 26 August 2013, https://www.eia.gov/international/analysis/regions-of-interest/Caspian_Sea.
28. During the decade and a half following the collapse of the Soviet Union, the United States and its NATO allies and the EU were focused on the former Warsaw Pact countries and the Balkans to provide a security buffer for a unified Germany, which ultimately was accomplished by absorbing these former satellites of the Soviet Union into an enlarged NATO.
29. See North Atlantic Treaty Organization (NATO), "Riga Summit Declaration, 29 November 2006," https://www.nato.int/cps/en/natohq/official_texts_37920.htm?selectedLocale=en and "Bucharest Summit Declaration, 3 April 2008," https://www.nato.int/cps/en/natolive/official_texts_8443.htm.
30. Office of the President, "Press Statement and Answers to Journalists' Questions Following a Meeting of the Russia—NATO Council, 4 April 2008," http://en.kremlin.ru/events/president/transcripts/24903.
31. See Peter Beaumont, Matthew Collin and Helen Womack, "Russia Widens Attacks as World Pleads for Peace in South Ossetia," *Observer (UK)* and *Guardian (UK)*, 9 August 2008, https://www.theguardian.com/world/2008/aug/10/russia.georgia; Luke Harding and Ian Traynor, "Russians March into Georgia as Full-Scale War Looms," Guardian (UK), 11 August 2008, https://www.theguardian.com/world/2008/aug/11/georgia.russia13; Shaun Walker and Harriet Salem, Russian Parliament Approves Troop Deployment in Ukraine," *Observer (UK)* and *Guardian (UK)*,

1 March 2014, https://www.theguardian.com/world/2014/mar/02/russia-parliament-approves-military-ukraine-vladimir-putin; James Brooke, "Russia Moves to Send Troops into Crimea; Ukraine Puts Troops on Combat Alert," *Voice of America (VOA) News*, 1 March 2014, https://www.voanews.com/europe/russia-moves-send-troops-crimea-ukraine-puts-military-combat-alert; and British Broadcasting Corporation (BBC), "Ukraine Orders Full Military Mobilization Over Russia Moves," *BBC News*, 2 March 2014, https://www.bbc.com/news/world-europe-26405635.

32. See British Broadcasting Corporation (BBC), "Russia and China End 300 Year Old Border Dispute," *BBC News*, 10 November 1997, http://news.bbc.co.uk/2/hi/world/analysis/29263.stm; "China and Russia Sign Border Pact," *BBC News*, 9 December 1999, http://news.bbc.co.uk/2/hi/asia-pacific/556981.stm; and "China and Russia Sign Border Deal," *BBC News*, 21 July 2008, http://news.bbc.co.uk/2/hi/7517380.stm.
33. BBC, "Kuril Islands Dispute Between Russia and Japan," *BBC News*, 29 April 2013, https://www.bbc.com/news/world-asia-pacific-11664434; Radio Free Europe/Radio Liberty (RFE/RL), "Japan Demands Russia Return All Disputed Islands," *RFE/RL News*, 24 December 2004, https://www.rferl.org/a/1056568.html; and "Putin Says 'Painstaking Work' Remains on Peace Deal with Japan," *RFE/RL News*, 22 January 2019, https://www.rferl.org/a/putin-abe-kurile-islands-talks-russia-japan/29723492.html. However, in response to Japanese sanctions against Russia protesting the February 2022 invasion of Ukraine, Moscow has suspended its offer on a peace deal with Japan. See, Michelle Ye Hee Lee, "Russia Halts WWII Peace Treaty Talks with Japan in Response to Sanctions Over Ukraine Invasion," *Washington Post*, 22 March 2022, https://www.washingtonpost.com/world/2022/03/22/russia-japan-peace-treaty-ukraine-sanctions/.
34. Jonathan Saul, "Lithuania Says Russian Military Activity Stoking Tension in Baltics," *Reuters*, 1 December 2015, https://www.reuters.com/article/us-mideast-crisis-lithuania-russia/lithuania-says-russian-military-activity-stoking-tension-in-baltics-idUSKBN0TK5HF20151201, and Lucien Kim, "Near the Russian Border, U.S. and NATO Beef Up Their Presence," *NPR News*, 30 November 2016, https://www.npr.org/sections/parallels/2016/11/30/503772040/near-the-russian-border-u-s-and-nato-beef-up-their-presence.
35. Indeed, in his 24 February 2022 speech announcing "a special military operation" against Ukraine, President Vladimir Putin reiterated his acceptance of the dissolution of the Soviet Union: "*I have already said that Russia accepted the new geopolitical reality after the dissolution of the USSR.*" *See*The Print Team, "Full text of Vladimir Putin's Speech

Announcing 'Special Military Operation' in Ukraine," *Print (India)*, 24 February 2022, https://theprint.in/world/full-text-of-vladimir-putins-speech-announcing-special-military-operation-in-ukraine/845714/.

36. See Isabel Mandraud, "Russia Prepares for Ice-Cold War with Show of Military Force in the Arctic," *Guardian* (UK), 21 October 2014, https://www.theguardian.com/world/2014/oct/21/russia-arctic-military-oil-gas-putin; "Russia Establishes Arctic Military Strategic Command," *RFE/RL News*, 1 December 2014, https://www.rferl.org/a/russia-arctic-military-command/26719491.html; Mathieu Boulègue, *Russia's Military Posture in the Arctic: Managing Hard Power in a 'Low Tension' Environment*, June 2019, Chatham House, The Royal Institute for International Affairs, https://www.chathamhouse.org/sites/default/files/2019-06-28-Russia-Military-Arctic_0.pdf; and Zahra Ullah and Fred Pleitgen, "As the US and Russia Spar Over the Arctic, Putin Creates New Facts on the Ground," *CNN News*, 21 May 2021, https://www.cnn.com/2021/05/21/europe/russia-arctic-military-intl-cmd/index.html.
37. L.G., "What is the Northern Sea Route?" *Economist*, 24 September 2018, https://www.economist.com/the-economist-explains/2018/09/24/what-is-the-northern-sea-route.
38. NATO, "Bucharest Summit Declaration, 3 April 2008," https://www.nato.int/cps/en/natolive/official_texts_8443.htm.
39. NATO, "Brussels Summit Declaration, 11 July 2018," https://www.nato.int/cps/en/natohq/official_texts_156624.htm.
40. The 2021 NATO Summit in Brussels continued to reflect the unrelenting hostility to Russia. See NATO, "Brussels Summit Communique, 14 June 2021," https://www.nato.int/cps/en/natohq/news_185000.htm.
41. CIA, *World Factbook.*
42. See Global Firepower, "Military Power Comparison Results, Russia-US" in *Global Firepower 2021*, https://www.globalfirepower.com/countries-comparison-detail.asp?form=form&country1=russia&country2=united-states-of-america&Submit=COMPARE.
43. Ibid.
44. Russian defense spending peaked in 2016 at 5.5 percent of GDP. See World Bank Data Base, "Military expenditure (% of GDP)," https://data.worldbank.org/indicator/MS.MIL.XPND.GD.ZS?locations=RU-US.
45. China's sovereignty over Taiwan is acknowledged by the United States although the PRC does not exercise administrative control over the province. See "Joint Statement Following Discussions with Leaders of the People's Republic of China, Shanghai, 27 February 1972" in Office of the Historian, US Department of State, *Foreign Relations of the United States,1969–1972, Volume VIII, China, 1969–1972*, Document No. 203, https://history.state.gov/historicaldocuments/frus1969-76v17/d203.

46. With respect to such an axis, it also should be pointed out that while the asymmetry in both potential and actual military power favors China, this apparent advantage is neutralized by Russia's strategic depth in terms of geography. Simply put, Russia's Siberian oil and gas fields are far from China's borders, so *in extremis* there would be no realistic possibility for the Middle Kingdom to successfully seize these energy resources. The same is true with respect to the oil and gas fields of the Caspian littoral states within Russia's sphere of influence. These energy resources are located within a 100-mile radius of the Caspian Sea, which is too far from China's borders for any attempt to seize control of the Central Asian oil and gas fields to succeed. A strategic partnership of equals clearly is in the mutual interests of both Moscow and Beijing.
47. It is worth recalling that the Russian Empire during World War I and the Soviet Union during World War II occupied northern Iran (while Great Britain occupied southern Iran) to prevent Germany from gaining access to the oil resources of Iran and the other Caspian Sea littoral states. See William L. Cleveland, *A History of the Modern Middle East, Third Edition* (Boulder, CO: Westview Press, 2004), 147, 191.
48. See Laura MacInnis, "Obama: No Options Off the Table on Iran Nuclear Program," *Reuters*, 24 January 2012, https://www.reuters.com/article/us-usa-obama-speech-iran/obama-no-options-off-table-on-iran-nuclear-program-idUSTRE80O0B120120125; and BBC, "Trump Warns Iran of 'Obliteration' in Event of War," *BBC News*, 22 June 2019, https://www.bbc.com/news/world-us-canada-48728465.
49. BBC, "Syria conflict: Assad in Surprise Visit to Moscow," *BBC News*, 21 October 2015, https://www.bbc.com/news/world-europe-34590561.
50. The possibility of such a Russian-Turkey front emerging was demonstrated in the downing of a Russian fighter jet by Turkish forces along the Turkey-Syria border. See Kareem Shaheen, Shaun Walker, Julian Borger and David Smith, "Putin Condemns Turkey After Russian Warplane Downed Near Syrian Border," *Guardian* (UK), 24 November 2015, https://www.theguardian.com/world/2015/nov/24/turkey-shoots-down-jet-near-border-with-syria.
51. Jim Zanotti, James M. Blanchard et al., "Kurds in Iraq and Syria: U.S. Partners Against the Islamic State," 28 December 2016, Congressional Research Service, https://crsreports.congress.gov/product/pdf/R/R44513/7.
52. Jim Zanotti and Clayton Thomas, "In Focus: The Kurds in Iraq, Turkey, Syria, and Iran," 23 January 2019, Congressional Research Service, https://fas.org/sgp/crs/mideast/IF10350.pdf.
53. Andrew Osborn and Phil Stewart, "Russia Begins Syria Airstrikes in Its Biggest Mideast Intervention in Decades," *Reuters*, 30 September 2015,

https://www.reuters.com/article/us-mideast-crisis-russia/russia-begins-syria-air-strikes-in-its-biggest-mideast-intervention-in-decades-idUSKCN0RU0MG20150930.
54. Mehmet Guzel, Associated Press, "Turkey and Russia Begin Joint Patrols in Northeast Syria," *PBS News Hour*, 1 November 2019, https://www.pbs.org/newshour/world/turkey-and-russian-begin-joint-patrols-in-northeast-syria; and Brakkton Booker, "Turkey, Russia Reach Deal to Control Syrian Areas Once Patrolled by the U.S.," *NPR News*, 22 October 2019, https://www.npr.org/2019/10/22/772387023/turkey-russia-reach-deal-to-control-syrian-areas-once-patrolled-by-the-u-s.
55. Bill Chappell, "Turkey Accepts Russian S-400 Missile System, Rankling U.S. and NATO," *NPR News*, 12 July 2019, https://www.npr.org/2019/07/12/741068857/turkey-accepts-russian-s-400-missile-system-rankling-u-s-and-nato; BBC, "Turkey Signs Deal to Get S-400 Air Defense Missiles," *BBC News*, 12 September 2017, https://www.bbc.com/news/world-europe-41237812; and Tulay Karadeniz, "Erdogan, Putin Mark Start of Work on Turkey's First Nuclear Power Plant," *Reuters*, 3 April 2018, https://www.reuters.com/article/us-turkey-russia-nuclearpower-idUSKCN1HA2GI.
56. Sarah E. Guarding, Michael Ratner et al., "In Focus: TurkStream: Another Russian Gas Pipeline to Europe," 11 April 2019, Congressional Research Service, https://fas.org/sgp/crs/row/IF11177.pdf; and EIA, *Country Analysis Brief: Turkey*, 2 February 2017, https://www.eia.gov/beta/international/analysis.php?iso=TUR.
57. CIA, *World Factbook* and World Bank, "Databank: Exports as % of GDP," https://data.worldbank.org/indicator/NE.EXP.GNFS.ZS?locations=DE.
58. See Julian Wettengel, "Germany's Dependence on Imported Fossil Fuels," *Clean Energy Wire*, 29 April 2019, https://www.cleanenergywire.org/factsheets/germanys-dependence-imported-fossil-fuels; Rick Noack, "The Russian Pipeline to Germany that Trump is so Mad About, Explained," *Washington Post*, 11 July 2018, https://www.washingtonpost.com/news/worldviews/wp/2018/07/11/the-russian-pipeline-to-germany-that-trump-is-so-mad-about-explained/; EIA, "Today in Energy: Russia Exports Most of Its Crude Oil Production, Mainly to Europe,"14 November 2017, https://www.eia.gov/todayinenergy/detail.php?id=33732; and EIA, *Country Analysis Brief: Germany*, August 2016, https://www.eia.gov/beta/international/analysis.php?iso=DEU.
59. Alternative suppliers of oil and/or gas include Saudi Arabia, Kuwait, Qatar, Algeria, Libya, Nigeria, Angola, Venezuela, Canada, and the United States.
60. Certainly, in the past Germany has cooperated with Russia when it was in the German vital national interest to do so. The Reinsurance Treaty of 1887 was designed to prevent the Russian Empire from entering into an

alliance with France against the German Empire; the Molotov–Ribbentrop pact of 1939 was designed to prevent the USSR from forming an alliance with Great Britain against Germany; and the policy of "Ostpolitik" (détente with the Soviet Union) promoted by West German Chancellor Willy Brandt and his successors during the Cold War was designed to persuade the USSR not to foreclose the possibility of German reunification. Arguably, in each of these cases, Germany needed Russia more than Russia needed Germany (or at least the need for each other was comparable). Currently, with respect to preventing further NATO expansion, Russia needs Germany more than Germany needs Russia. See Norman Rich, *Great Power Diplomacy, 1814–1914* (New York: McGraw-Hill, 1992), 244–45; David MacKenzie, *From Messianism to Collapse: Soviet Foreign Policy, 1917–1991* (New York: Harcourt Brace, 1994), 86–105; and Ryan K. Beasley, Juliet Kaarbo, Jeffrey S. Lantis, and Michael T. Snarr, *Foreign Policy in Comparative Perspective: Domestic and International Influences on Sate Behavior* (Washington, DC: CQ Press, 2002), 75.

61. Alec Luhn, "Russian Foreign Minister Sergei Lavrov Calls for 'Reset' of Relations with US," *Guardian* (UK), 28 September 2014, https://www.theguardian.com/world/2014/sep/28/russian-foreign-minister-sergei-lavrov-reset-relations-us. Russia's support for US efforts to negotiate an agreement on Iran's nuclear energy program, and Russia's effort to ensure the destruction of Syria's stockpile of chemical weapons reflect Moscow's willingness to cooperate with Washington to address specific American national security concerns. See, Julian Borger, "Iran Nuclear Deal: World Powers Reach Historic Agreement to Lift Sanctions," *Guardian* (UK), 14 July 2015, https://www.theguardian.com/world/2015/jul/14/iran-nuclear-programme-world-powers-historic-deal-lift-sanctions; Reuters, "Obama Thanks Putin for Russia's Role in Iran Nuclear Deal," *NBC News*, 15 July 2015, https://www.nbcnews.com/storyline/iran-nuclear-talks/obama-thanks-putin-russias-role-iran-nuclear-deal-n392976; and David Smith, "Iran Ships 25,000 lb of Low-Enriched Uranium to Russia as Part of Nuclear Deal," *Guardian* (UK), 28 December 2015, https://www.theguardian.com/world/2015/dec/28/iran-ships-uranium-russia-nuclear-deal. Also see Dan Roberts and Julian Borger, "Syria Crisis: Obama Welcomes Russia's Chemical Weapons Proposal," *Guardian* (UK), 23 September 2013, https://www.theguardian.com/world/2013/sep/09/us-russian-proposal-syria-chemical-weapons.
62. Julian Borger, "US Holds Firm on Ukraine's Right to Join NATO in Its Response to Russian Demands," *Guardian (UK)*, 26 January 2022, https://www.theguardian.com/world/2022/jan/26/ukraine-and-russia-to-hold-paris-talks-in-latest-effort-to-ease-tensions.

63. The Print Team, "Full Text of Vladimir Putin's Speech Announcing 'Special Military Operation' in Ukraine," *Print* (India), 24 February 2022, https://theprint.in/world/full-text-of-vladimir-putins-speech-announcing-special-military-operation-in-ukraine/845714/.

CHAPTER 5

# Rediscovering the Vital National Interests of the United States of America

What are the vital national interests of the United States in the twenty-first century? That is the fundamental question, and it would come as no surprise to the Nation's founders. Alexander Hamilton, one of the Founding Fathers and President George Washington's Secretary of the Treasury, had a pithy answer to the question of America's vital national interest: "Self-preservation is the first duty of a Nation."[1] As an elegant distillation of a first principle it continues to resonate. In the twenty-first century, a more fulsome answer awaits as disoriented decision-makers with the responsibility for crafting American grand strategy painstakingly rediscover the Nation's permanent vital national interests.

The Founding Fathers firmly believed vital national interest was the north star that would guide the country's foreign relations as it navigated the treacherous waters of an anarchic world. They clearly understood that vital national interests, determined rationally and dispassionately, trumped emotion-laden values, ideology, and sentiments.[2]

John Adams (who would later become the second president of the United States), while acting as America's agent in Great Britain, absorbed the primacy of national interest: "The circumstances of modes, languages, and religion have less influence in determining the friendships and enmity of nations than other *more essential interests* [italics added]."[3] Accordingly, relations between states reflected converging or


S. Tata, *Reflections on Grand Strategy*,
https://doi.org/10.1007/978-981-19-3773-6_5

diverging national interests: "When two nations have the same interests in general they are natural allies; when they have opposite interests they are natural enemies."[4] President George Washington, in his Farewell Address, insisted that the United States should be guided by its own vital national interests and should not become hostage to the interests of other nations. He underscored that America had its own identity and own interests that superseded all other identities and interests: "Citizens by birth or choice of a common country, that country has a right to concentrate your affections. The name American, which belongs to you in your national capacity, must always exalt the just pride of patriotism, more than any appellation derived from local discriminations."[5] He particularly warned against subordinating America's interests to those of another nation because of shared emotions:

> Nothing is more essential than that permanent, inveterate antipathies against particular nations and passionate attachments for others should be excluded ... The nation which indulges toward another an habitual hatred or an habitual fondness is in some degree a slave. It is a slave to its animosity or its affection, either of which is sufficient to lead it astray from *its duty and its interest*. [italics added][6]

John Quincy Adams (who went on to become the sixth president and was John Adams' son), when he was Secretary of State under President James Monroe, took pains in a speech to Congress to make a clear distinction between America's interests and America's values, and left no doubt that with respect to its relations with other states the United States would pursue only its vital national interests:

> She [America] has abstained from interference in the concerns of others, even when conflict has been for principles to which she clings, as to the last drop that visits the heart ... Wherever the standard of freedom and Independence has been or shall be unfurled, there will her heart, her benedictions and prayers be. *But she goes not abroad, in search of monsters to destroy*. She is the well-wisher to the freedom and independence of all. *She is the champion and vindicator only of her own*. [all italics added][7]

So, what are the vital national interests of the United States? In the twenty-first century, the United States has 8 vital national interests: (1) territorial integrity and inviolability; (2) the preservation of the people's national identity as well as the protection of their physical and economic security; (3) freedom of navigation and connectivity; (4) foreign non-interference in American domestic political affairs; (5) independence; (6) sovereignty; (7) recognition of an exclusive American sphere of influence; and (8) for national security purposes, control over access of other states who are *adversaries* of America to foreign scarce natural resources, primarily crude oil and natural gas. It is this set of vital national interests that must be safeguarded against external threats to ensure America's continued, sustainable existence as a viable political entity for the foreseeable future.

## Territory

Territorial integrity and inviolability as a US vital national interest has four geographic components: (1) the contiguous 48 states and the District of Columbia; (2) the two non-contiguous states, Alaska and Hawaii; (3) the 5 US inhabited island territories: Puerto Rico, US Virgin Islands, American Samoa, Northern Marianas Islands, and Guam; and (4) the virtually uninhabited 9 US Minor Outlying Islands: Midway Islands, Wake Island, Baker Island, Howland Island, Jarvis Island, Johnston Atoll, Palmyra Atoll, Kingsman Reef, and Navassa Island.[8] The land, air, waters (including waters extending 12 miles beyond shorelines according to customary international law) and everything on, above, and below such features (including the electromagnetic spectrums) constitute the geographic scope of the four components comprising American territory. In terms of a security envelope, the foregoing territory constitutes the core and represents the geographic scope of US sovereignty. In this conception of territorial integrity and inviolability as a US vital national interest, no distinction is made between inhabited or uninhabited territory, or between geographic contiguity or non-contiguity, or the governing arrangements or political rights of the inhabitants.[9] In any conflict, the loss of any part of US territory would be considered a temporary tactical setback and there would be an open-ended strategic commitment to regain control of the territory. The ultimate means to protect the territorial integrity and inviolability of the United States is its nuclear weapons arsenal. It is for this reason that absolute clarity is required in articulating the definition of the territory of the United States.

## People

It is a vital national interest of the United States that there is no ambiguity or misunderstanding on the part of any foreign state as to who is an American and that there is only one American national identity. In the absence of such clarity, foreign states could discriminate among Americans—treating different Americans differently. The insistence on a singular American identity has been an enduring vital national interest since the Nation's founding. The infant Republic eventually went to war against Great Britain in 1812 to prevent the "impressment" of American seamen of British background by the Royal Navy, which disregarded their claims of American nationality.[10] As President James Madison complained in asking Congress to declare war:

> [T]housands of American citizens, under the safeguard of public law and of their national flag, have been torn from their country and from everything dear to them; have been dragged on board ships of war of a foreign nation and exposed, under the severities of their discipline, to be exiled to the most distant and deadly climes, to risk their lives in the battles of their oppressors, and to be the melancholy instruments of taking away those of their own brethren.[11]

In 1915, during the Armenian genocide, Secretary of State Robert Lansing, otherwise unmoved by the horror, authorized the US ambassador in Turkey, Henry Morgenthau, to try to arrange for the repatriation of Armenians holding American citizenship as well as Armenians with American relatives.[12] Currently, according to US State Department travel advisories, US citizens of Palestinian or other Arab heritage, traveling to or residing in Israel and Israeli controlled territories, are subject to different and discriminatory treatment.[13] Although US governments have acquiesced in such Israeli differentiation by ethnicity of American citizens, this practice is likely to become an increasingly nettlesome issue between the two countries in the future.

September 11, 2001 is indelibly seared in the consciousness of America. The attacks against the World Trade Center in New York and the Pentagon using US civilian aircraft hijacked by an al Qaeda cell whose members had entered the country legally on visitor visas, underscored the vital national interest in ensuring the physical safety and security of Americans against threats from non-state and state actors. As the Taliban-led government of Afghanistan was the host of the parent al Qaeda organization, the United States responded by attacking and invading the country and overthrowing the government.[14] More restrictive visa and travel documentation requirements and significantly enhanced airport security procedures will continue to be a feature of American life for the foreseeable future.[15] Obviously, such restrictions have an adverse impact on American businesses, such as technology companies that rely on foreign computer programming specialists on short-term work visas, and educational institutions that seek to recruit and enroll foreign students. America continues to struggle to find the right balance between security and ease of travel and entry into the country. Of course, the major challenge, both current and long-term, is rationalizing and modernizing US immigration policy so that America gains control over its borders while ensuring that the number and profile of immigrants is consistent with the economic and social needs and capacities of the country. While the crafting and implementation of American immigration policies is and will be a hugely contentious domestic issue, it also has significant foreign policy dimensions and will require the cooperation of major countries from which the migrants come such as Mexico, India, China, and the Philippines.[16]

In addition to preservation of the national identity and physical security of the people, the economic security of the people looms large as an element of vital national interest. The huge losses suffered by American businesses in Cuba caught in the cross-fire between Cuban rebels and Spanish expeditionary forces that had been sent to quell the local insurrection was a key factor behind the push for war against Spain in 1898.[17] When the Arab oil producers led by Saudi Arabia imposed an oil embargo on the United States in retaliation for America's military supply effort on behalf of Israel in the 1973 Yom Kippur War, the possibility of seizing Saudi oilfields to restore the flow of oil to America to protect its economy was seriously considered.[18] Today, vulnerability of US businesses to foreign cyberattacks is very significant and could cause economic havoc.[19]

## Freedom of Navigation

In the twenty-first century, it is essential that the United States reaffirm as a vital national interest freedom of navigation and connectivity in the global commons—whether on, under or above land, water, air, space, and cyberspace.[20] There are four key reasons. First, the territory of the United

States stretches far beyond the contiguous 48 states. From Washington, DC, the distance by air to Guam (west Pacific) is 7935 miles; American Samoa (south Pacific), 7005 miles; Alaska (north Pacific), 3370 miles; and Puerto Rico (east Caribbean), 1553 miles. Second, the United States, as a major trading nation, has important commercial relationships globally. In 2020, US total two-way (exports and imports) merchandise trade was the world's second largest at $3.84 trillion, of which exports were $1.43 trillion and imports, $2.41 trillion.[21] Third, the United States must have assured access to the sea lines of communication that connect it to overseas scarce resources, such as oil, gas, and rare earths that are crucial for its national security. Fourth, the United States as a global power has allies and strategic partners, with significant military, economic, commercial, and political ties, in the Americas, Europe, and Asia. Clarity with respect to freedom of navigation and connectivity is essential, as in the multipolar world of this century other major powers will seek to safeguard their own access to the global commons, and their interpretations and understandings with respect to such access may well be different from that of the United States.[22]

Since the birth of the Republic, freedom of navigation and connectivity, based on international customary law, has been considered a vital national interest—indeed an existential issue—reflecting America's geographic circumstances. Navigation rights with respect to the Mississippi River, the Great Lakes, the Caribbean Sea as well as the Atlantic Ocean were crucial to the economic viability of the young nation. Indeed, Alexander Hamilton devoted Federalist Paper No. 11 to the critical importance of maritime commerce and the necessity of protecting that trade with a credible American navy against powers such as Spain, France, and Great Britain: "There are rights of great moment to the trade of America ... I allude to the fisheries, to the navigation of the Western lakes, and to that of the Mississippi ... The necessity of naval protection to external or maritime commerce does not require a particular elucidation."[23] Hamilton held out the prize—regional primacy—that the United States would win by successfully asserting its right to freedom of navigation and connectivity:

> [O]ur situation invites and our interests prompt us to aim at an ascendant in the system of American affairs ... Let the thirteen States, bound together in a strict and indissoluble Union, concur in erecting one great American

> system, superior to the control of all transatlantic force or influence, and able to dictate the terms of the connection between the old and the new world![24]

Thrice the United States has waged war to defend its right to freedom of navigation: three separate expeditionary expeditions against the Barbary States between 1801 and 1816, which was fought in the Mediterranean Sea and Morocco, Algeria, Libya, and Tunisia; the War of 1812 against Great Britain, fought largely in America; and World War I against Germany, fought largely in France and the Atlantic.[25] What was remarkable about the Barbary Wars was that it was the United States' first overseas war; first encounter with state-sponsored piracy; first war with an Islamic state; and, save for the final phase in 1815–1816 (under President James Madison), the first war (1801–1805) initiated by a president, in this case President Thomas Jefferson, without a prior declaration of war by Congress.[26] The War of 1812 was consequential for two major reasons. First, it internalized in the American strategic psyche the profound existential implications of freedom of navigation as a vital national interest. For it was in this conflict that British forces successfully invaded the nation's capital and burned down the White House and the Capitol.[27] Second, the United States resolved never again to let the enemy fight a war on American soil; instead, in the future the United States would take the fight to the enemy and battle them on foreign soil. Following the war, America's right to freedom of navigation was not seriously challenged for a century. And, when Germany challenged America's broad and robust conception of freedom of navigation during the First World War, the United States responded forcefully and entered the fray on the side of the allies. In his speech to Congress asking for a declaration of war against Germany, President Woodrow Wilson spelled out the primacy of freedom of navigation as a vital national interest:

> International law had its origin in the attempt to set up some law which would be respected and observed upon the seas, where no nation had right of dominion and where lay the free highways of the world ... The present German submarine warfare against commerce is a warfare against mankind. It is a war against all nations. American ships have been sunk, American lives taken in ways which it has stirred us very deeply to learn of; but the ships and people of other neutral and friendly nations have been sunk and overwhelmed in the waters in the same way. There has been no discrimination. The challenge is to all mankind.[28]

Since the United States is the only major power that is not party to the United Nations Convention on the Law of the Sea, which codifies customary international law on this subject, it is vital that America spell out clearly its understanding of international customary law of the sea so that other countries are on notice. Failure to do so is an invitation to misunderstanding and conflict.

## Foreign Non-Interference in American Domestic Affairs

Safeguarding the Nation against foreign interference in American domestic affairs has been an abiding vital national interest of the United States. The controversy over alleged Russian meddling in the 2016 presidential election plagued the Trump presidency, continues to roil domestic politics and feed conspiracy theories, and is testimony of the existential fears of foreign influence subverting American independence.[29] In March 2015, during a visit to the United States which was not cleared in advance with President Barack Obama, Prime Minister Benjamin Netanyahu of Israel gave a pair of speeches in Washington, DC, excoriating President Barack Obama's proposed deal on Iran's nuclear energy program: first to the American Israel Political Affairs Committee (AIPAC) and then to a special Joint-Session of Congress.[30] And twenty years earlier, the Chinese government was accused of influence buying and attempting to tilt the 1996 elections in favor of President Bill Clinton and the Democratic Party.[31]

President George Washington in his Farewell Address warned the country not to open itself to foreign influence in its domestic politics and to vigilantly resist it: "[H]istory and experience prove that foreign influence is one of the most baneful foes of republican government."[32] And he cautioned that emotional and ideological attachments and aversions to foreign causes would be exploited by self-interested foreign governments "to tamper with domestic factions, to practice the arts of seduction, to mislead public opinion, to influence or awe the public councils."[33] His were not idle words, as Washington had to deal with the attempts of the popular Citizen Edmond Genet, the ambassador of the revolutionary government of France, to appeal directly to the American public in an effort to subvert the US government's policy of neutrality with respect to conflicts between France and Great Britain.[34]

The specter of malign foreign influence has haunted subsequent presidents. President John Adams was so panicked by the fear of foreign influence on American politics that he signed the Alien and Sedition Acts of 1798, trampling civil liberties in the process.[35] In the run-up to World War I and two years prior to US entry into the war, President Woodrow Wilson urged Congress to pass legislation to eradicate foreign subversion claiming that:

> There are some men among us, and many resident abroad who, though born and bred in the United States and calling themselves Americans, have so forgotten themselves and their honor as citizens as to put their ***passionate sympathy*** [italics added] with one or the other side in the great European conflict above their regard for the peace and dignity of the United States.[36]

Congress obliged with the passage of the Espionage Act of 1917 and its associated amendment, the Sedition Act of 1918.[37] And President Franklin D. Roosevelt issued his infamous executive orders for the internment of Japanese-Americans during the Second World War. Finding the proper balance between the national security imperative to safeguard the country's independence against foreign subversion and the civil rights of American citizens and residents will be a continuing challenge in the twenty-first century.

## Independence

The concern with respect to foreign interference—in the past, currently, and the foreseeable future—is so powerful because it strikes at the heart of the ***absolute political*** independence of the United States. It is for this reason that foreign non-interference has been treated separately above. There is, however, another distinct form of external restraint on America's independence, in the form of bilateral, multilateral, and international treaties contracted voluntarily by the United States. Ensuring that such treaties do not constrain the United States' freedom of action is a vital national interest in the twenty-first century. Accordingly, a major challenge for the United States will be to identify the treaties that raise such concerns, articulate the vital national interests that are adversely impacted, and either alleviate the restrictions or withdraw from or terminate these agreements.

Of course, parting ways with inconvenient treaties is firmly rooted in American history. Alexander Hamilton was a vigorous advocate for suspending the Treaty of Alliance (1778) between the United States and France, which eventually was terminated in 1801 by mutual agreement.[38] And, in 1939 with the likelihood of war on the horizon, President Franklin D. Roosevelt decided against renewing the 1911 trade agreement with Japan and instead allowed it to lapse.[39] As a result, the United States increased its ability to exert economic pressure on Japan, which was heavily dependent upon imports of strategic materials from America. Not surprisingly, Tokyo perceived the move as a hostile act.

A prime example of arrangements that are now considered disadvantageous from a national security perspective are the various arms control agreements between the United States and the Soviet Union (Russia as successor state). President Donald Trump announced on 1 February 2019, the US withdrawal from the Intermediate-Range Nuclear Forces Treaty (signed in 1987).[40] Earlier, on 13 December 2001, President George W. Bush announced US withdrawal from the Treaty on the Limitation of Anti-Ballistic Missile Systems (1972).[41] The third major bilateral treaty, the so-called New START or Treaty on Measures for the Further Reduction and Limitation of Strategic Offensive Arms (2010) was set to expire in February 2021, but President Joe Biden and President Vladimir Putin agreed to a five-year extension.[42] For the foreseeable future, the United States is unlikely to agree to any new treaty that would restrict America's perceived ability to defend itself by itself.

Trade reflects the reality of interdependence. Given that the United States is the world's second largest trading state and will continue to be a major trader for the foreseeable future, a vital national interest will be to ensure that such interdependence is with and among allies and friends while limiting trading relationships with adversaries. Only by doing so will America be able to safeguard its *relative economic* independence in the context of interdependence. Admittedly, this is Mercantilism 2.0 and elevates national security considerations over economic considerations of comparative advantage (where an adversary may have a relative comparative advantage over a friend or ally with respect to certain products).

For example, in 2020, about 18.6 percent of US merchandise imports were from China while only 2.2 percent came from India.[43] If the United States were to determine that India rather than China is more likely to be a friend or ally for the foreseeable future (thus the political risk of the trade relationship with India is lower than the political risk of the trade relationship with China), then significantly shifting US imports away from China and in favor of India would not only be a huge boost for India's economy (and strengthen the potential for a US–India strategic partnership) but also further America's relative economic independence over time, given the reality of interdependence and the impossibility of autarky (even though such a move may be inefficient from a purely economic point of view—assuming that Indian goods are more costly or of lower quality than comparable Chinese goods albeit still cheaper or better quality than if such goods were attempted to be made in America again). Restructuring the profile of US trading relationships to diversify and redirect trade flows (toward allies and friends, and away from adversaries) to safeguard its relative economic independence will be a critical component of American grand strategy in the twenty-first century.

## Sovereignty

In a multipolar world, anarchy reigns supreme. It is this mantra that will be invoked by the United States as it reasserts the safeguarding of its sovereignty as a vital national interest for the remainder of this century. Specifically, the United States will have to clearly articulate that its freedom of action to pursue vital national interests is not bound by international law (whether it be customary law or international or multilateral treaties and agreements or declarations) but only by domestic law. Congress, accordingly, will have a major role to play as it will have to decide what parts of international law should be specifically incorporated into domestic law and pass the appropriate legislation. By doing so, America will put other states on notice as to which parts of international law it accepts and which parts it rejects or has reservations. Such action by Congress is particularly important because, although the Constitution recognizes international treaties submitted by the President and approved by the Senate as part of the laws of the United States (Article VI), the views of the United States may have changed or, in the case of customary law, may never have been clearly articulated.

As has already been noted, the United States accepts customary international law of the sea but not the United Nations Convention on the Law of the Sea (UNCLOS), which purports to incorporate the customary international law on this subject. Since the US understanding of customary international law of the sea has not been specifically articulated through domestic legislation, there is no clarity where America stands with respect to freedom of navigation—one of its most cherished vital national interests. Similarly, article 51 of Chapter VII of the United Nations Charter recognizes the right of self-defense as part of customary international law: "Nothing in the present Charter shall impair the inherent right of individual or collective self-defense if an armed attack occurs against a Member of the United Nations."[44] In justifying the American invasion and occupation of Iraq (2003) without prior UN authorization, the United States invoked this right of self-defense. President George W. Bush declared:

> The United Nations Security Council has not lived up to its responsibilities, so we will rise to ours ... The United States of America has the sovereign authority to use force in assuring its own national security ... We are now acting because the risks of inaction would be far greater. In one year, or five years, the power of Iraq to inflict harm on all free nations would be multiplied many times over.[45]

The US National Security Strategy of 2002 issued by President George W. Bush clearly asserts the right to take preventive action as part of the right of self-defense: "And, as a matter of common sense and self-defense, America will act against such emerging threats before they are fully formed."[46] At a minimum, Congress needs to clarify its understanding of the right of self-defense in the context of customary international law since the UN Charter, as an international treaty, is part of US law. In doing so, Congress should distinguish between preemptive action against an imminent threat and preventive action against an embryonic or emerging threat. It should limit the right of self-defense to preemptive action against an imminent threat as well as action in response to an actual attack. Without such a clarification, chaos rather than anarchy will prevail.

## Sphere of Influence

In the twenty-first century, the United States needs a security envelope, called a sphere of influence, to protect its core—its territory and its people. It is a vital national interest of the United States that other major powers recognize and accept, or at least not challenge, America's sphere of influence. This sphere of influence is composed of three layers: a *cordon sanitaire*, a moat, and a fire wall.

The first layer is the *cordon sanitaire*, which has two components: (a) the other countries in the Americas and (b) the three island states in the western Pacific with which the United States has "Compacts of Free Association"—Palau, Micronesia, and the Marshall Islands. All of the other countries in the Americas are de facto protectorates of the United States by virtue of the Monroe Doctrine, a *unilateral* anti-access, area denial declaration establishing the Americas as an exclusive sphere of influence, formally articulated by President James Monroe in a message to Congress in 1823: "[W]e should consider any attempt on their part [European powers] to extend their system to any portion of this hemisphere as dangerous to our peace and safety."[47] The three Pacific Islands states are de jure protectorates via bilateral defense treaties called Compacts of Free Association. Pursuant to these separate bilateral treaties, Palau, Micronesia and the Marshall Islands each agree not to have any security relations with any state whose interests are inimical to those of the United States in return for American military protection, hosting American military facilities, and significant economic assistance.[48] The strategic importance of these three Pacific Islands states is that they are geographically vital to the defense of the most vulnerable part of America's core: Guam, the Northern Marianas, and American Samoa. For example, the distance by air between Guam and Palau is only about 580 miles. The two key features of the *cordon sanitaire* are (1) the vital national interests of the states within the *cordon sanitaire* are subordinate to those of the United States, and (2) no foreign power can have a relationship with any state in the *cordon sanitaire* without at least the implicit acquiescence of the United States. The sanctity of the *cordon sanitaire* will be protected by the United States at all costs, if necessary, by military force (including nuclear weapons). Ultimately, the states within the American *cordon sanitaire* have no discretion as to whether they want to be part of such a security envelope—they are included by American fiat because the United States has decided that the *cordon sanitaire* is essential to safeguard its territory and people.

The second layer of the security envelope has two wings attached to the *cordon sanitaire*: (1) the Pacific Ocean from the west coast of the Americas to Japan and Australia (referred to as the Western Pacific Area), and (2) the Atlantic Ocean from the east coast of the Americas to a line running from Greenland in the north Atlantic to the Azores in the central

Atlantic to the South Sandwich Islands in the south Atlantic (referred to as the Eastern Atlantic Area). These are international waters and part of the global commons that serve as moats protecting the *cordon sanitaire*. If this second layer is to serve its security purpose, the United States must be the predominant power and must be able to demonstrate maritime and air supremacy within this area so that it can credibly deny adversaries access in case of conflict.

The third layer of the security envelope, representing the fire wall or outer perimeter of the sphere of influence, consists of a subset of states with whom the United States has a formal treaty relationship providing for *mutual* defense against a common adversary: (1) Japan and Australia; and (2) the United Kingdom, and perhaps, although to a far lesser extent, France and Germany (representing the core of the European Union).[49] The strategic rationale for this layer of the sphere of influence is three-fold. First, it reflects the long-held American conviction (born from the bitter experience of the sacking of Washington, DC during the War of 1812) that the United States should carry the battle to its enemies rather than let them bring the fight to the American homeland. Second, with respect to the Western Pacific Area, Japan and Australia both have the geostrategic critical mass to serve as the landing, assembly, and launching points for American expeditionary forces confronting an Asian adversary. The United Kingdom plays the same vital role for American expeditionary forces confronting a European adversary. Third, each of the countries in this layer has significant military power sufficient to inflict heavy costs that would deter or delay an adversary, thereby providing enough time for the arrival of American forces. The strategic objective of the United States is to ensure that a single regional hegemon does not arise in either Asia or Europe because such a regional hegemonic power would then be in a position to cross the moat in the reverse direction and challenge the *cordon sanitaire*. Accordingly, the United States will expect that the countries that constitute the firewall can counterbalance and contain any such ambitious power in their respective regions. The United States, in effect, would be providing security reinsurance and would be the backstop to cover any gaps.[50]

A common feature of the relationship of these countries with the United States is that each of them is a junior partner, willingly subordinating their respective vital national interests to those of the United States within their particular areas as far as it relates to the common foe.

It is this voluntary deference to the United States in return for American security reinsurance (the scope of which in both cases is limited to the common adversary in their geographic area) that makes this layer of the security envelope a part of the sphere of influence. For example, with respect to Asia, Japan's vital national interests are subordinated to those of the United States as far as it relates to the common adversary (say, China). Similarly, in the case of the United Kingdom, London defers to Washington with respect to the common European enemy (say, Russia). These countries are junior partners to the United States because individually and collectively they have significantly less power (military, economic, and diplomatic power) compared to America. The challenge for the United States is to ensure the *mutuality* of the defense relationship. This means that the junior partners have to carry their weight to ensure a closer alignment of their individual actual power and potential power. It also means that the threat perceptions regarding the common foe are congruent. Absent a strong mutuality of interests in addressing such a common threat, it may not be possible to rely on or even have this third layer of the security envelope.

## Access to Scarce Energy Resources

For the remainder of the twenty-first century, a vital national interest of the United States will be *denial* to its adversaries that may be dependent upon energy imports, access to foreign oil and gas resources. The overriding objective for the denial of such access is to significantly impair the ability of the adversary to conduct sustained military operations, including war, against the United States and its allies.

Since the end of the Second World War, the United States, as a major oil and gas importer, has had as a vital national interest the control over access to foreign energy resources. The Persian Gulf has the world's largest concentration of proved oil and gas reserves. In 2020, the Persian Gulf accounted for about 48 percent of world total proved oil reserves and 40 percent of world total proved natural gas reserves.[51] Not surprisingly, the United States, in order to ensure its own energy security, has had a vital national interest in assured access for itself to Persian Gulf oil and gas resources. Indeed, the specter of Soviet control over access to Persian Gulf energy resources (and the resultant power to deny the US access to such resources), specifically Iranian oil and gas resources, was the primary driver of the US orchestrated coup in 1953 that overthrew the government of Prime Minister Mohammad Mossadegh, perceived to be pro-Soviet, and restored to power the more compliant Mohammad Reza Pahlavi as Shah of Iran.[52]

In response to the Soviet invasion of Afghanistan, President Jimmy Carter declared in early 1980: "An attempt by any outside force to gain control of the Persian Gulf region will be regarded as an assault on the vital national interests of the United States of America, and such an assault will be repelled by any means necessary, including military force."[53] One has to go back to the Monroe Doctrine of 1823 (with respect to the Americas) for such a bold assertion of US vital national interest in another region. The so-called Carter Doctrine was the fundamental rationale underpinning President George H. W. Bush's decision in 1990 to send US military forces to expel the Iraqi occupying army from Kuwait and reverse the Iraqi dictator Saddam Hussein's attempt to annex an oil-rich neighbor. In his speech to the Nation on 8 August 1990, President George H. W. Bush highlighted the concern over energy security: "Our country imports nearly half the oil it consumes and could face a major threat to its economic independence."[54] And in National Security Directive 45 the President spells out the basis for American intervention: "U.S. interests in the Persian Gulf are vital to the national security. These interests include access to oil … The United States will defend its vital interests in the area, through the use of military force if necessary and appropriate, against any power with interests inimical to our own."[55]

In 1990 the United States had to import oil to meet nearly half of its oil consumption requirements, and Persian Gulf imports accounted for about 25 percent of total US oil imports and met about 12.5 percent of total US oil consumption requirements.[56] Clearly, US dependency on Persian Gulf oil was significant although perhaps not existential. In 2017, reflecting a dramatic drop in US dependency on imports to meet its oil consumption requirements, Persian Gulf imports were needed to meet only about 3 percent of America's total oil consumption.[57] This represents a tectonic shift. Indeed, the Energy Information Administration (EIA), the statistical arm of the US Department of Energy, expects the United States to be a net exporter of oil beginning in 2020 and to remain a net oil exporter for the next three decades until 2050.[58] So, the strategic meaning of access to Persian Gulf oil will have a radically different implication: rather than ensuring access to Persian Gulf oil to meet the needs of the United States, the focus will shift to ***denying access to Persian Gulf energy resources to America's adversaries*** who may be dependent upon oil and gas imports. The challenge for the remainder of this century will be on how best to safeguard this new incarnation of a well-established US vital national interest.[59]

## Recalibrating American Grand Strategy

The past 30 years have been both an admonition that hubris incubates within extraordinary power and a reminder that such extraordinary power is ephemeral: *sic gloria transit mundi*—so passes the glory of the world. The momentum of a "resistance-free" global environment created by the sudden and unexpected end of the Cold War heralded by the fall of the Berlin Wall in 1989 and the voluntary dissolution of the Soviet Union in 1991, catapulted the United States to its apogee as the world's sole superpower bearing with it the glittering gift of a benign and tranquil Pax Americana overseen by a presumably benevolent and magnanimous global hegemon.[60] An awed President George H. W. Bush marveled at the enticing, munificent windfall: "By the grace of God, America won the cold war... A world once divided into two armed camps now recognizes one sole and pre-eminent power, the United States of America ... the world trusts us with power and the world is right."[61]

Yet a decade later, the September 11, 2001 terrorist attack led by al Qaeda, an Islamic fundamentalist group based in Afghanistan, on the New York World Trade Center and the Pentagon, challenged the notion of a Pax Americana at its very epicenter.[62] The continuing dismal experience in Afghanistan and Iraq, coupled with Syria's defiance of Washington's demands for regime change and the 2018 American volt face with respect to the 2015 deal on Iran's nuclear program reflect the frustrating inability of the United States to bend West Asia (or more familiarly, the greater Middle East) to its will through force or the threat of force.[63] In Europe, the 2008 Russian military intervention in Georgia and the 2014 Russian annexation of Crimea along with support for an armed rebellion in eastern Ukraine signaled that Moscow would use military force to thwart American efforts to extend its protective umbrella via NATO membership to those countries.[64] Indeed, to enforce its red line against further NATO expansion eastward, Russia once again invaded Ukraine in February 2022 despite US warnings not to do so. In East Asia, the emergence of North Korea as a nuclear weapons state in 2017, and tensions with China over freedom of navigation in the South China Sea and bilateral trade imbalances indicate that a significant American role in the region cannot be taken for granted.[65] And at home, a nearly two-decade-long festering controversy over immigration policy with respect to illegal migrants from Latin America risks eroding the nation's social cohesion and is a warning flare that not all is well.[66]

Simply put, the United States is strategically lost in a brave new multipolar world which it has yet to understand. What is the nature of this multipolar world? How does America get its bearings? Who are the key players—potential adversaries, friends, and neutrals—and what are their intentions and capabilities? What is the end state that America should seek? How does it get there given its capabilities? Only with a clear-eyed view of its vital national interests can the United States be well positioned to recalibrate American grand strategy for the multipolar world of the twenty-first century. America must and will rise to this challenge of forging a new manifest destiny.

## Notes

1. Alexander Hamilton, "Pacificus No. 3, [6 July 1793]," in "Hamilton Papers," U.S. National Archives and Records Administration, https://founders.archives.gov/documents/Hamilton/01-15-02-0055. Also cited by Norman A. Graebner, "The Pursuit of Interests and a Balance of Power," in Dennis Merrill and Thomas G. Patterson (editors), *Major Problems in American Foreign Relations, Volume 1: To 1920, Sixth Edition* (Boston: Houghton Mifflin, 2005), 14.
2. See Felix Gilbert, *To the Farewell Address: Ideas of Early American Foreign Policy* (Princeton: Princeton University Press, 1961), 96–104, and Graebner, 12–16. Alexander Hamilton, a pragmatic and hard-headed realist, skewered the idealistic romantics chasing a utopian vision of America: "Is it not time to awake from the deceitful dream of a golden age, and to adopt as a more practical maxim for the direction of our political conduct that we, as well as other inhabitants of the globe, are yet remote from the happy empire of perfect wisdom and perfect virtue?" See Alexander Hamilton (Publius), "The Federalist Papers: No. 6," http://avalon.law.yale.edu/18th_century/fed06.asp.
3. Gilbert, 86.
4. Ibid.
5. George Washington, "September 19, 1793: Farewell Address," in "Presidential Speeches: George Washington Presidency," Miller Center at University of Virginia, https://millercenter.org/the-presidency/presidential-speeches/september-19-1796-farewell-address. Washington never presented these comments through a speech, the title notwithstanding;

rather he conveyed his message to the Nation by releasing the address for publication by the press. His "Farewell Address" in effect represents the first articulation of what he considered to be America's grand strategy.

6. Ibid.
7. John Quincy Adams, "July 4, 1821: Speech to the U.S. House of Representatives on Foreign Policy," in "Presidential Speeches: John Quincy Adams Presidency," https://millercenter.org/the-presidency/presidential-speeches/july-4-1821-speech-us-house-representatives-foreign-policy.
8. For the territorial definition of the United States see "Notices," in *Federal Register*, vol. 83, no. 32, 15 February 2018, p. 6493, note 4, https://www.govinfo.gov/content/pkg/FR-2018-02-15/pdf/2018-02625.pdf. Of the 14 island territories, 11 are located in the Pacific Ocean and 3 are located in the Caribbean Sea (Puerto Rico, US Virgin Islands and Navassa). Guam is the western-most geographic point of the United States, American Samoa the southern-most point, Puerto Rico the eastern-most point, and Alaska is the northern-most geographic point.
9. Existing discriminatory anomalies, which elevate territory over people, will have to be eliminated by the US Congress over the next 20 years. For example, residents of American Samoa are not citizens of the United States, citizens resident in the District of Columbia have no voting representation in Congress, and citizen residents of Puerto Rico have no voting representation in Congress and no electoral rights with respect to the election of the US President. The population of Puerto Rico is larger than that of 21 US states. In the twenty-first century, such disparate treatment makes a mockery of what it means to be an American. See Ann M. Simmons, "American Samoans Aren't Actually American Citizens: Does That Violate the Constitution?" *Los Angeles Times*, 6 April 2018, https://www.latimes.com/nation/la-na-american-samoan-citizenship-explainer-20180406-story.html; and Antonio Weiss and Brad Setser, "America's Forgotten Colony: Ending Puerto Rico's Perpetual Crisis," *Foreign Affairs*, vol. 98, no. 4, July/August 2019, 158–168.
10. It is estimated that prior to the war, about 6000 US nationals of British heritage, while sailing in international waters in US flagged vessels, were forcibly drafted by the British to serve as seamen in the Royal Navy. See Donald R. Hickey, *The War of 1812: A Short History* (Urbana and Chicago: University of Illinois Press, 1995), 7.
11. See "June 1, 1812: Special Message to Congress on the Foreign Policy Crisis—War Message," in "Presidential Speeches: James Madison Presidency," Miller Center at University of Virginia, https://millercenter.org/the-presidency/presidential-speeches/june-1-1812-special-message-congress-foreign-policy-crisis-war.
12. See "Telegram: The Secretary of State to the Ambassador in Turkey (Morgenthau), 16 July 1915" (Document no. 1402) and "Telegram: The

Secretary of State to the Ambassador in Turkey (Morgenthau), 6 October 1915" (Document no. 1413) in US Department of State, Office of the Historian, *Papers Relating to the Foreign Relations of the United States, 1915, Supplement, The World War*, https://history.state.gov/historicaldocuments/frus1915Supp/d1402 and https://history.state.gov/historicaldocuments/frus1915Supp/d1413.

13. US Department of State, Bureau of Consular Affairs, "Travel Advisory: Israel, the West Bank and Gaza," https://travel.state.gov/content/travel/en/international-travel/International-Travel-Country-Information-Pages/IsraeltheWestBankandGaza.html.
14. President George W. Bush, "September 22, 2001: Address on the U.S. Response to the Attacks of September 11," UVA Miller Center, https://millercenter.org/the-presidency/presidential-speeches/september-22-2001-address-us-response-attacks-september-11, and "Presidential Address to the Nation, October 7, 2001," https://georgewbush-whitehouse.archives.gov/news/releases/2001/10/20011007-8.html.
15. See Thomas H. Kean, Lee H. Hamilton et al., *The 9/11 Commission Report: Final Report of the National Commission on Terrorist Attacks Upon the United States, Authorized Edition* (New York: W. W. Norton, 2004), 383–393.
16. See US Department of Homeland Security, "Press Release: Humanitarian and Security Crisis at Southern Border Reaches 'Breaking Point', 6 March 2019," https://www.dhs.gov/news/2019/03/06/humanitarian-and-security-crisis-southern-border-reaches-breaking-point; and Rajat Pandit, "India to Raise H-1B Visa Issue During '2 + 2' Dialogue with US," *Times of India*, 26 July 2018, https://timesofindia.indiatimes.com/business/india-business/india-to-raise-h-1b-visa-issue-during-22-dialogue-with-us/articleshow/65152038.cms. Also see Gustavo Lopez, Kristin Bialik and Jynnah Radford, "Key Findings About U.S. Immigrants, 30 November 2018" Pew Research Center, https://www.pewresearch.org/fact-tank/2018/11/30/key-findings-about-u-s-immigrants/.
17. President William McKinley in his message to Congress highlighted the adverse economic impact of the turmoil in Cuba: "Our trade has suffered; the capital invested by our citizens in Cuba has been largely lost." See "April 11, 1898: Message Regarding Cuban Civil War," in "Presidential Speeches: William McKinley Presidency," Miller Center at University of Virginia, https://millercenter.org/the-presidency/presidential-speeches/april-11-1898-message-regarding-cuban-civil-war. The historian Walter LaFeber has estimated that capital losses amounted to about $33 million. See Walter LaFeber, *The New Empire: An Interpretation of American Expansion, 1860–1898, Thirty-Fifth Anniversary Edition* (Ithaca and London: Cornell University Press, 1998), 334.

18. See "Memorandum of Conversation: The Middle East Conflict and U.S. Oil Interests, 10 October 1973" (Document no. 26) and "U.S. Embassy Kuwait Cable 3801 Cable to State Department, 'Atiqi Comment on OAPEC Meeting,' 18 October 1973" (Document no. 38) in William Burr, "The October War and US Oil Policy, 7 October 2003," National Security Archive at George Washington University, https://nsarchive2.gwu.edu/NSAEBB/NSAEBB98/octwar-26.pdf and https://nsarchive2.gwu.edu/NSAEBB/NSAEBB98/octwar-38.pdf; and Michael Corbett, "Oil Shock of 1973–74," Federal Reserve History, https://www.federalreservehistory.org/essays/oil_shock_of_1973_74. Also see Owen Bowcott, "UK Feared Americans Would Invade Gulf During 1973 Oil Crisis," *Guardian (UK)*, 31 December 2003, https://www.theguardian.com/politics/2004/jan/01/uk.past3; and Lizette Alvarez, "Britain Says U.S. Planned to Seize Oil in '73 Crisis," *New York Times*, 2 January 2004, https://www.nytimes.com/2004/01/02/world/britain-says-us-planned-to-seize-oil-in-73-crisis.html. The feasibility of seizing Arab oil fields was reviewed in Congress in 1975 and a report on the subject was prepared for discussion purposes by the Congressional Research Service. See Congressional Research Service, *Oil Fields as Military Objectives: A Feasibility Study* (Washington, DC: US Government Printing Office, 1975), https://babel.hathitrust.org/cgi/pt?id=mdp.39015078699306;view=1up;seq=1.
19. See Ken Dilanian, Associated Press, "Chinese Cyberattacks on U.S. Companies Continue, Despite Cyber Agreement," *PBS News*, 19 October 2015, https://www.pbs.org/newshour/economy/despite-cyberagreement-chinese-cyberattacks-u-s-companies-continue. Also see Council of Economic Advisors, *The Cost of Malicious Activity to the U.S. Economy, February 2018*, https://www.whitehouse.gov/wp-content/uploads/2018/02/The-Cost-of-Malicious-Cyber-Activity-to-the-U.S.-Economy.pdf.
20. Surprisingly, the *National Security Strategy of the United States of America, December 2017*, devotes only a passing reference to freedom of navigation. The White House, *National Security Strategy of the United States of America, December 2017*, p. 47, https://www.whitehouse.gov/wp-content/uploads/2017/12/NSS-Final-12-18-2017-0905.pdf.
21. Two-way merchandise trade consists of merchandise exports and merchandise imports. See World Bank, "Data Bank: Merchandise Exports (Current US$)," https://data.worldbank.org/indicator/TX.VAL.MRCH.CD.WT; and World Bank, "Data Bank: Merchandise Imports (Current US$)," https://data.worldbank.org/indicator/TM.VAL.MRCH.CD.WT. China ranked first in 2020 with two-way trade of about $4.65 trillion, of which exports were $2.59 trillion and imports, $2.06 trillion.

22. The United States is the only major power that is not party to the United Nations Convention on the Law of the Sea (UNCLOS), which codifies current customary international law of the sea. See U.S. Navy Judge Advocate General's Corps, "The Convention on the Law of the Sea," http://www.jag.navy.mil/organization/code_10_law_of_the_sea.htm and US Department of State, "Law of the Sea Convention," https://www.state.gov/e/oes/lawofthesea/. For the text of this international treaty, see United Nations, *United Nations Convention on the Law of the Sea*, https://www.un.org/Depts/los/convention_agreements/texts/unclos/unclos_e.pdf.
23. Alexander Hamilton (Publius), *Federalist Papers No. 11*, http://avalon.law.yale.edu/18th_century/fed11.asp.
24. Ibid.
25. See US Department of State, Office of the Historian, "Barbary Wars, 1801–1805 and 1815–1816," in *Milestones in the History of U.S. Foreign Relations, 1801–1829*, https://history.state.gov/milestones/1801-1829/barbary-wars; Donald R. Hickey, *The War of 1812: A Short History* (Urbana and Chicago: University of Illinois Press), 5–12; and Thomas G. Patterson, J. Garry Clifford and Kenneth J. Hagan, *American Foreign Relations, A History—Since 1895, Volume II, Fifth Edition* (Boston and New York: Houghton Mifflin, 2000), 68–83.
26. Samuel Flagg Bemis, *A Diplomatic History of the United States, Third Edition* (New York: Henry Holt, 1950), 176–179.
27. President James Madison, "September 14, 1814: Proclamation Upon British Depredations, Burning of the Capitol," in "Presidential Speeches: James Madison Presidency," Miller Center at University of Virginia, https://millercenter.org/the-presidency/presidential-speeches/september-1-1814-proclamation-upon-british-depredations.
28. President Woodrow Wilson, "April 2, 1917: Address to Congress Requesting a Declaration of War Against Germany," in "Presidential Speeches: Woodrow Wilson Presidency," Miller Center at University of Virginia, https://millercenter.org/the-presidency/presidential-speeches/april-2-1917-address-congress-requesting-declaration-war.
29. See Robert S. Mueller III, *Report on the Investigation into Russian Interference in the 2016 Presidential Election, March 2019*, US Department of Justice, Special Counsel's Office, https://www.justice.gov/storage/report.pdf. For the Attorney General's summary of report, see "AG March 24, 2019 Letter to House and Senate Judiciary Committees," https://apps.npr.org/documents/document.html?id=5779683-AG-March-24-2019-Letter-to-House-and-Senate.
30. See Dan Roberts, "Netanyahu Defends Decision to Address Congress: 'Today We Are No Longer Silent'," *Guardian (UK)*, 2 March 2015,

https://www.theguardian.com/world/2015/mar/02/binyamin-netanyahu-aipac-speech-defends-address-congress; and Krishnadev Calamur, "In a Speech to Congress, Netanyahu Blasts 'A Very Bad Deal' with Iran," *National Public Radio (NPR)*, https://www.npr.org/sections/thetwo-way/2015/03/03/390250986/netanyahu-to-outline-iran-threats-in-much-anticipated-speech-to-congress. For text of Netanyahu's speech, see Israel Ministry of Foreign Affairs, "PM Netanyahu's Speech to a Joint Session of the US Congress, 3 March 2015," https://mfa.gov.il/MFA/PressRoom/2015/Pages/PM-Netanyahus-speech-to-Congress-3-March-2015.aspx.

31. Eric Schmitt and Don Van Natta, Jr., "Republicans Say Clinton Risked Security for Donations," *New York Times*, 16 May 1998, https://archive.nytimes.com/www.nytimes.com/library/politics/051698campaign-fundraising.html. See also "The China Connection: Summary of the Committee's Findings Relating to the Efforts of the People's Republic of China to Influence U.S. Policies and Elections," in US Senate Committee on Governmental Affairs, *Investigation of Illegal or Improper Activities in Connection with 1996 Federal Election Campaigns, Final Report, 10 March 1998*, https://fas.org/irp/congress/1998_rpt/sgo-sir/2-18.htm.
32. See George Washington, "September 19, 1793: Farewell Address," in "Presidential Speeches: George Washington Presidency," Miller Center at University of Virginia, https://millercenter.org/the-presidency/presidential-speeches/september-19-1796-farewell-address.
33. Ibid.
34. See US Department of State, Office of the Historian, "The Citizen Genet Affair, 1793–1794," in *Milestones in the History of U.S. Foreign Relations, 1784–1800*, https://history.state.gov/milestones/1784-1800/citizen-genet; and Samuel Flagg Bemis, *Diplomatic History of the United States*, 96–99.
35. See "Transcript of Alien and Sedition Acts (1798)," Our Documents, https://www.ourdocuments.gov/doc.php?flash=false&doc=16&page=transcript.
36. See "December 7, 1915: Third Annual Message," in "Presidential Speeches: Woodrow Wilson Presidency," Miller Center at University of Virginia, https://millercenter.org/the-presidency/presidential-speeches/december-7-1915-third-annual-message.
37. See Charles Cheney Hyde, "The Espionage Act," in *American Journal of International Law*, vol. 12, January 1918, 142–146, https://ia801701.us.archive.org/0/items/jstor-2187619/2187619.pdf. The US Supreme Court upheld the constitutionality of the Acts in 1919. See *Schenk v. United States (249 U.S. 47)*, https://www.law.cornell.edu/supremecourt/text/249/47.

38. See "Treaty of Alliance with France, 1778," in Dennis Merrill and Thomas G. Patterson (editors), *Major Problems in American Foreign Relations, Volume 1: To 1920, Sixth Edition* (Boston: Houghton Mifflin, 2005), 38–39; Alexander Hamilton, "Pacificus No. 3, [6 July 1793]," in "Hamilton Papers," U.S. National Archives and Records Administration, https://founders.archives.gov/documents/Hamilton/01-15-02-0055; and Samuel Flagg Bemis, *Diplomatic History of the United States*, 122–125.
39. See "The Secretary of State to the Japanese Ambassador (Horinouchi), July 26, 1939" (Document no. 115) in US State Department, Office of the Historian, *Papers Relating to the Foreign Relations of the United States, Japan, 1931–1941, Volume II*, https://history.state.gov/historicaldocuments/frus1931-41v02/d115.
40. The White House, "President Donald J. Trump to Withdraw the United States from the Intermediate-Range Nuclear Forces (INF) Treaty, February 1, 2019," https://www.whitehouse.gov/briefings-statements/president-donald-j-trump-withdraw-united-states-intermediate-range-nuclear-forces-inf-treaty/.
41. The White House, "ABM Treaty Fact Sheet, December 13, 2001," https://georgewbush-whitehouse.archives.gov/news/releases/2001/12/20011213-2.html.
42. US Department of State, "New START," https://www.state.gov/t/avc/newstart/index.htm; and BBC News, "New Start: US and Russia Extend Nuclear Treaty," 3 February 2021, https://www.bbc.com/news/world-us-canada-55923481.
43. See US Department of Commerce, US Census Bureau, "Foreign Trade: U.S. Trade in Goods by Country," https://www.census.gov/foreign-trade/balance/index.html.
44. See, "Charter of the United Nations" in UN Codification Division, *Repertory of Practice of United Nations Organs*, http://legal.un.org/repertory/art51.shtml.
45. See "March 17, 2003: Address to the Nation on Iraq" in "Presidential Speeches: George W. Bush Presidency," Miller Center at University of Virginia, https://millercenter.org/the-presidency/presidential-speeches/march-17-2003-address-nation-iraq.
46. The White House, "Introduction," in *The National Security Strategy of the United States of America, September 2002*, https://www.state.gov/documents/organization/63562.pdf. See also pp. 15–16.
47. See "December 2, 1823: Seventh Annual Message (Monroe Doctrine)," in "Presidential Speeches: James Monroe Presidency," Miller Center at

University of Virginia, https://millercenter.org/the-presidency/presidential-speeches/december-2-1823-seventh-annual-message-monroe-doctrine. For a lucid discussion of the genesis of the Monroe Doctrine, see Samuel Flagg Bemis, *A Diplomatic History of the United States*, 202–211.

48. See US Department of State, "Compact of Free Association, Agreement Between the United States of America and Palau, January 10, 1986," https://photos.state.gov/libraries/palau/5/home/rop_cofa.pdf; and "Compact of Free Association, Agreement Between the United States of America and the Marshall Islands, April 30, 2003," https://www.state.gov/documents/organization/173999.pdf. Also see Federated States of Micronesia, Legal Information System, "Compact of Free Association Between the United States and Micronesia, June 25, 2004," http://www.fsmlaw.org/compact/. Reflecting their status as protectorates, these three Pacific Islands States are the administrative responsibility of the US Department of the Interior, which also has administrative responsibility for the US territories in the Pacific: Guam, Northern Marianas, and American Samoa. See US Department of Interior, Office of Insular Affairs, "The Islands We Serve," https://www.doi.gov/oia/islands. For the increasing strategic importance of Palau, Micronesia, and Marshall Islands, see Ben Kesling, "U.S. Refocuses on Pacific to Check China Ambitions," *Wall Street Journal*, 4 April 2019, https://www.wsj.com/articles/u-s-military-refocuses-on-pacific-to-counter-chinese-ambitions-11554292920.
49. Currently the bilateral security relationship between the United States and Japan is defined by the US–Japan mutual defense pact of 1960. See Ministry of Foreign Affairs of Japan, "Treaty of Mutual Cooperation and Security Between Japan and the United States of America, 19 January 1960," https://www.mofa.go.jp/region/n-america/us/q&a/ref/1.html. The current security relationship between the United States and Australia is defined by the ANZUS (Australia, New Zealand, and the United States) Treaty of 1951. See US Department of State, Office of the Historian, "The Australia, New Zealand and United States Security Treaty (ANZUS Treaty), 1951," in *Milestones in the History of U.S. Foreign Relations, 1945–1952*, https://history.state.gov/milestones/1945-1952/anzus. For the text of the treaty, see "Security Treaty Between the United States, Australia, and New Zealand (ANZUS); September 1, 1951," in Avalon Project, Yale University, http://avalon.law.yale.edu/20th_century/usmu002.asp. The current multilateral security relationship among the United States, the United Kingdom, France, and Germany is defined by the North Atlantic Treaty (or Washington Treaty) of 1949. See North Atlantic Treaty Organization (NATO), "The North Atlantic Treaty, 4 April 1949," https://www.nato.int/cps/en/natolive/official_texts_17120.htm.

50. From an offensive perspective, the countries in the firewall serve as launching pads for US military forces to attack an Asian or European hegemonic adversary.
51. See *BP Statistical Review of World Energy, July 2021*, pp. 16 and 34, https://www.bp.com/content/dam/bp/business-sites/en/global/corporate/pdfs/energy-economics/statistical-review/bp-stats-review-2021-full-report.pdf.
52. For the key underlying official documents on US orchestration of the Iran coup, see US Department of State, Office of the Historian, *Foreign Relations of the United States [FRUS], 1952–1954, Iran, 1951–1954, Planning and Implementation of Operation TPAJAX, March–August 1953* (Documents no. 169–308), https://history.state.gov/historicaldocuments/frus1951-54Iran/ch3. For the official CIA history of the Iran coup, see Daniel Siegel and Malcolm Byrne (editors), "CIA Declassifies More of 'Zendabad Shah!'—Internal Study of 1953 Iran Coup" (Briefing Book no. 618), 12 February 2018, National Security Archives at The George Washington University, https://nsarchive.gwu.edu/briefing-book/iran/2018-02-12/cia-declassifies-more-zendebad-shah-internal-study-1953-iran-coup. For a first-hand account from the coup's mastermind, see Kermit Roosevelt, *Countercoup: The Struggle for the Control of Iran* (New York: McGraw Hill, 1979).
53. See "January 23, 1980: State of the Union Address" in "Presidential Speeches: Jimmy Carter Presidency," Miller Center at University of Virginia, https://millercenter.org/the-presidency/presidential-speeches/january-23-1980-state-union-address.
54. See "August 8, 1990: Address on Iraq's Invasion of Kuwait" in "Presidential Speeches: George H. W. Bush Presidency," Miller Center at University of Virginia, https://millercenter.org/the-presidency/presidential-speeches/august-8-1990-address-iraqs-invasion-kuwait.
55. See "National Security Directive 45: U.S. Policy in Response to the Iraqi Invasion of Kuwait, August 20, 1990" in "Archives: National Security Directives," George H. W. Bush Library and Museum, https://bush41library.tamu.edu/files/nsd/nsd45.pdf.
56. Energy Information Administration (EIA), "Petroleum and Other Liquids: Total Crude Oil and Products, U.S. Imports by Country of Origin," https://www.eia.gov/dnav/pet/pet_move_impcus_a2_nus_ep00_im0_mbblpd_a.htm.
57. EIA, "Oil: Crude and Petroleum Products Explained, Oil Imports and Exports, 1 May 2018," https://www.eia.gov/energyexplained/index.php?page=oil_imports. Based on the information provided: total net oil imports of 3.7 million barrels per day, of which Persian Gulf, 0.63 million

barrels per day (17 percent of 3.7); total oil consumption of 19.9 million barrels per day.

58. EIA, *Annual Energy Outlook 2019*, https://www.eia.gov/outlooks/aeo/. In particular see "Total Net Imports" in "Reference Case, Table 11: Petroleum and Other Liquids Supply and Disposition," https://www.eia.gov/outlooks/aeo/data/browser/#/?id=11-AEO2019&cases=ref2019&sourcekey=0. It should be noted that while the United States is expected to be a net exporter of oil for the next three decades, it is not anticipated that the United States will become a major oil exporter in the league of Russia and Saudi Arabia.
59. Historically, American control over access to Persian Gulf oil and gas resources has had three key facets: (1) the ability to obtain energy resources to meet the needs of the United States and its allies; (2) the ability to deny US adversaries access to such resources; and (3) the ability to deny Persian Gulf energy producers who are US adversaries access to export markets. Although Washington frames such control in terms of America's responsibility as a great power to safeguard the free flow of energy resources, in substance such control magnifies US military power and cripples the military power of adversaries who are dependent upon energy imports from the region (or exports in the case of hostile regional energy producers). Certainly, at the dawn of the Cold War, denial of access to energy resources to adversaries was a crucial part of US military strategy. For example, in the event of conflict with the Soviet Union the Joint Chiefs of Staff assessment was that, "Loss of Iraq and Saudi Arabia sources to the United States and her allies would mean ... they would fight an oil-starved war. Conversely, denial of these sources would force her [Soviet Union] to fight an oil-starved war." See "Memorandum by State-War-Navy Coordinating Committee to Major General John H. Hilldring, 12 October 1946" (Document no. 400) in *Foreign Relations of the United States, 1946, The Near East and Africa, Volume VII*, https://history.state.gov/historicaldocuments/frus1946v07/d400. Furthermore, in August 1948, the National Security Council recommended that Persian Gulf oil and gas facilities be destroyed or disabled in the event of a Soviet invasion of the region, and President Harry S. Truman approved the proposal in January 1949. See "National Security Council, NSC 26, report on 'Removal and Demolition of Oil Facilities, Equipment and Supplies in the Middle East, August 19, 1948'" (Document no. 1) in *National Security Archive, Electronic Briefing Book No. 552*, June, 23, 2016, http://nsarchive.gwu.edu/dc.html?doc=2869656-Document-01-National-Security-Council-NSC-26. Also see "NSC 26/2" (Document no. 2) in *National Security Archive, Electronic*

*Briefing Book No. 552*, http://nsarchive.gwu.edu/dc.html?doc=2869657-Document-02-National-Security-Council-NSC-26-2.

60. See "On this Day: 9 November 1989, Berliners Celebrate Fall of the Wall," *BBC News*, 9 November 1989, http://news.bbc.co.uk/onthisday/hi/dates/stories/november/9/newsid_2515000/2515869.stm and Office of the Historian, US State Department, "Fall of Communism in Eastern Europe, 1989," https://history.state.gov/milestones/1989-1992/fall-of-communism. Also see telephone conversation of President George H. W. Bush with Boris Yeltsin (Document 3) and Mikhail Gorbachev (Document 4) on 25 December 1991 dissolution of Soviet Union in "The End of the Soviet Union 1991" in *Russia Programs*, The National Security Archive at The George Washington University, https://nsarchive.gwu.edu/briefing-book/russia-programs/2016-12-25/end-soviet-union-1991.
61. See "January 28, 1992: State of the Union Address" in "Presidential Speeches: George H.W. Bush Presidency," Miller Center at University of Virginia, https://millercenter.org/the-presidency/presidential-speeches/january-28-1992-state-union-address. Also see the secret draft of the grand strategy to ensure continued American global hegemony (under the rubric, "FY 1994–1999 Defense Planning Guidance") circulated 18 February 1992 and a sanitized, public version issued January 1993, see Documents 3 and 15, respectively, in "Prevent the Reemergence of a New Rival: The Making of the Cheney Regional Defense Strategy, 1991–1992" in *The Nuclear Vault*, The National Security Archive at The George Washington University, https://nsarchive2.gwu.edu/nukevault/ebb245/index.htm.
62. See President George W. Bush speeches to the Nation and Congress, respectively, "September 11, 2001: Address to the Nation on the Terrorist Attacks" and "September 22, 2001: Address on U.S. Response to the Attacks of September 11," https://millercenter.org/the-presidency/presidential-speeches/september-11-2001-address-nation-terrorist-attacks, and https://millercenter.org/the-presidency/presidential-speeches/september-22-2001-address-us-response-attacks-september-11. Also see Thomas H. Kean, Lee H. Hamilton et al., *The 9/11 Commission Report: Final Report of the National Commission on Terrorist Attacks Upon the United States, Authorized Edition* (New York: W. W. Norton, 2004).
63. For President George W. Bush's speeches launching the wars against Afghanistan and Iraq, respectively, see "Address to the Nation on Operations in Afghanistan, October 7, 2001" and "Address to the Nation on Military Operations in Iraq, March 19, 2003" in The White House Archives, *Selected Speeches of President George W. Bush, 2001–2008*,

https://georgewbush-whitehouse.archives.gov/infocus/bushrecord/documents/Selected_Speeches_George_W_Bush.pdf. For President Barack Obama's speeches on ending US combat operations in Afghanistan and Iraq and his decision to rescind launching an attack on Syria, see "June 22, 2011: Remarks on the Afghanistan Pullout," https://millercenter.org/the-presidency/presidential-speeches/june-22-2011-remarks-afghanistan-pullout; "October 21, 2011: Remarks on the End of the War in Iraq," https://millercenter.org/the-presidency/presidential-speeches/october-21-2011-remarks-end-war-iraq; and "September 10, 2013: Address to the Nation on Syria," https://millercenter.org/the-presidency/presidential-speeches/september-10-2013-address-nation-syria. For Obama's statement of 18 August 2011 demanding the resignation of President Assad of Syria, see The White House Archives, https://obamawhitehouse.archives.gov/blog/2011/08/18/president-obama-future-syria-must-be-determined-its-people-president-bashar-al-assad. For President Donald Trump's announcement of American withdrawal from the 2014 Iran nuclear deal, see The White House, "Remarks by President Trump on the Joint Comprehensive Plan of Action, May 8, 2018," https://www.whitehouse.gov/briefings-statements/remarks-president-trump-joint-comprehensive-plan-action/.

64. See Peter Beaumont, Matthew Collins et al., "Russian Tanks Roll into Georgia as Cities Burn," *The Guardian (UK)*, 9 August 2008, https://www.theguardian.com/world/2008/aug/10/russia.georgia1; Shaun Walker and Ian Traynor, "Putin Confirms Crimea Annexation as Ukraine Soldier Becomes First Casualty," *The Guardian (UK)*, 18 March 2014, https://www.theguardian.com/world/2014/mar/18/putin-confirms-annexation-crimea-ukrainian-soldier-casualty; and Shaun Walker, "Putin Admits Russian Military Presence in Ukraine for First Time," *The Guardian (UK)*, 17 December 2015, https://www.theguardian.com/world/2015/dec/17/vladimir-putin-admits-russian-military-presence-ukraine.
65. See Mark Landler and Choe Sang-Hun, "North Korea Says It's Now a Nuclear State, Could That Mean It's Ready to Talk?" *New York Times*, 29 November 2017, https://www.nytimes.com/2017/11/29/world/asia/north-korea-nuclear-missile-.html. On the South China Sea issue, see for example, Agence France-Presse, "South China Sea: US Will Keep Confronting Beijing—Mattis," *The Guardian (UK)*, 29 May 2018, https://www.theguardian.com/world/2018/may/30/south-china-sea-us-will-keep-confronting-beijing-mattis. For President Donald Trump's decision to withdraw from the Trans-Pacific Partnership multilateral trade negotiations, see The White House, "Presidential Memorandum

Regarding Withdrawal of the United States from the Trans-Pacific Partnership Negotiations and Agreement, January 23, 2017," https://www.whitehouse.gov/presidential-actions/presidential-memorandum-regarding-withdrawal-united-states-trans-pacific-partnership-negotiations-agreement/. On the US–China trade dispute, see The White House, "Remarks by President Trump at Signing of a Presidential Memorandum Targeting China's Economic Aggression, 22 March 2018," https://www.whitehouse.gov/briefings-statements/remarks-president-trump-signing-presidential-memorandum-targeting-chinas-economic-aggression/.

66. The concern over illegal migrants from Latin America first emerged as a domestic political issue in California in 1994 under then Governor Pete Wilson who spearheaded a referendum initiative called Proposition 187 targeting such illegal resident aliens. See Mark Z. Barabak, "Pete Wilson Looks Back on Proposition 187 and Says, Heck Yeah, He'd Support It All Over Again," *Los Angeles Times*, 23 March 2017, https://www.latimes.com/politics/la-me-on-politics-column-20170323-story.html. In numerous speeches, President Donald Trump voiced alarm over illegal migrants from Latin America as a national security issue and demanded the construction of a "security wall" as part of his effort to combat this problem. See for example, The White House, "Remarks by President Trump on the Illegal Immigration Crisis and Border Security, 1 November 2018," https://www.whitehouse.gov/briefings-statements/remarks-president-trump-illegal-immigration-crisis-border-security/.

CHAPTER 6

# A Note on the Influence of Grand Strategy on Business Strategy

Grand strategy and business strategy are inextricably intertwined. Grand strategy shapes and determines international political risk that business enterprises face when considering cross-border opportunities. Political risk is the aggregate *cost*—whether actual, anticipated or unanticipated, intended or unintended—reasonably directly attributable to political decisions or actions taken by the internationally recognized government of a state to safeguard or further a claimed vital national interest of the state. In a fundamental sense, political risk is in the eyes of the beholder. Not surprisingly, governments, as political entities, will tend to focus on the *political costs* associated with the state's action or decision, while businesses, as commercial entities, will tend to focus on the *economic costs* associated with the government's action or decision. From the perspective of business, ultimately political risk is considered to be *force majeure* in nature as it is beyond the reasonable control of business entities. For example, following Russia's February 2022 invasion of Ukraine, various multinational companies headquartered in the United States and United Kingdom such as Coca-Cola, McDonald's, and BP (British Petroleum) abandoned their Russian operations under political pressure from their respective governments.[1] In the twenty-first century, the overarching importance of political risk is manifest as states craft ecosystems consisting of allies and strategic partners within the framework of symbiotic mutual interdependence to counterbalance adversarial



S. Tata, *Reflections on Grand Strategy*,
https://doi.org/10.1007/978-981-19-3773-6_6

political ecosystems. Economic decoupling and the formation of new commercial partnerships by private enterprises consistent with a state's grand strategy will be a central feature of the global economy of the twenty-first century.

For example, the United States in order to safeguard its *relative* economic independence will seek to restructure the profile of its trading relationships to diversify and redirect trade flows toward allies and friends such as India, and away from adversaries such as China. Consequently, for American enterprises, the otherwise attractive economic opportunities of a vast and rapidly growing China market could be overwhelmed by the mushrooming political risk generated by diverging and conflicting vital national interests of Beijing and Washington. India, which also is a large and growing market, represents a compelling alternative as the converging and congruent vital national interests of Washington and New Delhi dramatically reduce the political risk for American companies investing overseas.

## Coca-Cola: A Case Study

The Coca-Cola Company, with headquarters in Atlanta, Georgia (the United States), is the quintessential global enterprise. It is the world's largest non-alcoholic beverages company, with operations in about 200 countries and territories. For the year ended 31 December 2019, total net operating revenues amounted to about $37.3 billion and net income was about $8.9 billion.[2]

In terms of revenue, the United States accounted for about 31 percent, while the rest of the world accounted for about 69 percent.[3] In terms of volume, of the 30.3 billion unit cases of beverages sold in 2019, the United States accounted for about 18 percent, while the rest of the world accounted for about 82 percent.[4]

The current strategy of Coca-Cola is to capture the opportunity for sustainable growth in the global beverages market. The success of achieving the overarching objective of sustainable growth is measured by attaining two targets: (1) revenue growth of 4–6 percent per annum; and (2) operating profit growth of 6–8 percent per annum.[5] In order for Coca-Cola to achieve these targets, the Company must proactively recalibrate and realign its geographic priorities to anticipate and adapt to the tectonic shifts of a dynamically changing multipolar world. Clearly, the most consequential geostrategic change is the adversarial relationship between the United States and China. In 2017, President Donald J. Trump formally designated China as America's principal national security threat: "China seeks to displace the United States in the Indo-Pacific region, expand the reaches of its state-driven economic model, and reorder the region in its favor."[6] For the foreseeable future, the conflicting vital national interests of the two countries will lead inexorably to economic decoupling and bouts of economic warfare. Accordingly, Coca-Cola must plan for a future without access to the China market—a huge loss as China currently is the Company's second largest single country market behind only the United States. A future without China will have three major implications: (a) an alternative to the Chinese market will have to be developed; (b) Chinese investments in the Coca-Cola System outside China will have to be restructured and replaced; and (c) the Company's investments in China will have to be liquidated in an orderly manner.

Is the China market irreplaceable? The short answer is no. India, however, is indispensable. Not only is India a major market in its own right—it also looms large as the lynchpin for Coca-Cola's pivot from China. The strategic calculus is as plain as it is stark. According to the Central Intelligence Agency (CIA), China's economy at $22.5 trillion (2019) is comfortably larger than that of the United States at $20.5 trillion (2019), measured in terms of Gross Domestic Product (GDP) calculated on the basis of purchasing power parity.[7] By 2036, the US Energy Information Administration (EIA), the statistical arm of the US Energy Department, forecasts that China's GDP is projected to be about $48.4 trillion, nearly double the size of the US economy which is projected to be only $25.1 trillion.[8] To place India in context, India's 2019 GDP at $9.2 trillion (CIA estimate) is currently about half of the size of the US economy, and in 2036 India's GDP is projected to be about $26 trillion (EIA forecast), displacing the United States as the world's second largest economy. China and India share a 2659 km border over which there are significant disputes, primarily with respect to the Ladakh region of northwestern India and the Arunachal Pradesh region in north-eastern India. In 1962, the border dispute led to a brief but bloody war, which India lost. Since then, there have been periodic bouts of armed tension, with troop concentrations facing each other, but not significant armed conflict. Clearly, from India's perspective, the adverse asymmetry with China leaves it strategically vulnerable. Undoubtedly, China is India's principal national security threat. Not surprisingly, the United States and India have converging vital national interests with respect to China, which is perceived to be a common threat. Individually, neither the United States nor India has the economic capacity to counterbalance China; together they can do so both economically as well as militarily.

The Coca-Cola Company must adapt to the new strategic landscape as its highest priority. Under its current business strategy, the Company has made a significant $5 billion investment commitment to India.[9] This will not be enough. By 2036, India must be the jewel in The Coca-Cola Company's crown in terms of volume, sales, and earnings. More concretely, over the next decade and a half India will have to deliver revenue growth of about 8–12 percent per annum and operating earnings growth of about 12–16 percent per annum. This means that the Company's India operations will have to grow at least at *twice* the overall average rate for the Company (the current strategic plan targets Company revenue growth of 4–6 percent per annum and operating earnings growth of 6–8 percent per annum). Obviously, the Company will not be able to rely on just the robust growth rate of the Indian economy. It also will have to (a) craft an effective marketing effort that results in increased per capita consumption of its products in India to drive volume growth, and (b) leverage India's low-cost structure to generate operating efficiencies. Furthermore, Coca-Cola's India operations will have to incorporate in its business strategy a more expansive geographic footprint to include Nepal, Bhutan, Bangladesh, Burma, Sri Lanka, Maldives, Seychelles, and Mauritius—essentially mirroring India's emerging sphere of influence.

In tandem with a revamped and turbocharged India strategy, the Company will have to restructure its US bottling operations that currently are under Chinese ownership. The Swire Group, which has deep roots in China since the 1860s, currently has about 13 Coca-Cola bottling and distribution operations in China and about 13 bottling and distribution operations in the United States.[10] At a minimum, the Company will have to buyback the US operations of Swire and refranchise them at a later date to appropriate partners. Also, any local China brands that the Company owns will have to be sold to eliminate the risk of expropriation or other hostile actions by the Chinese authorities. Winding down the Company's China operations will not be easy, but it must be done. Strategic patience, persistence, and perseverance will be required. The costs in terms of both political and financial capital will be substantial, and the Company will have to ensure that it has the resilience to bear such costs.

It is highly unlikely that Coca-Cola would try to finesse or arbitrage the looming strategic conflicts between China and the United States. The Company attempted such an approach during the run-up to World War II and would not want an encore. The existential impact of political risk was seared into the corporate consciousness of the Company as a result of its experience with Nazi Germany. Coca-Cola's German bottling subsidiary, Coca-Cola GmbH, was established in 1929 by an American expatriate, Ray Rivington Powers. By the time Adolf Hitler came to power in 1933, Coca-Cola sales in Germany had skyrocketed from 6000 cases initially to over 100,000 cases—firmly establishing the German subsidiary as the Company's most important foreign investment.[11] In that year, a German–American dual citizen, Max Keith, took over the reins of the German subsidiary, and focused relentlessly on ensuring that Coca-Cola GmbH was viewed as a fully assimilated German entity rather than an outpost of an American company. Keith embraced the Nazi Party and ensured that Coca-Cola kiosks were prominently positioned at all Nazi public events. Coca-Cola's sponsorship of the 1936 Olympic Games in Berlin helped complete the assimilation of Coca-Cola GmbH as a German company. To blur the American connection, Keith proclaimed that Coca-Cola was a "Volksgetrank"—a drink of the German people and further that "Coca-Cola is the world-famous trademark of the unique product of Coca-Cola GmbH."[12] Coca-Cola GmbH's assets were never confiscated by the Nazi government, and, in fact, the local Coca-Cola operations in the areas that fell under Nazi control as the German juggernaut rolled across Europe were put under the control of Coca-Cola GmbH. For the Company, the existential dilemmas of running cross-border business operations amidst geo-political tensions could not be starker than its experience with Nazi Germany.

Can Coca-Cola rise to the challenge of adapting its business strategy to the shifting political risks of grand strategy in the twenty-first century? History suggests that the Company can do so. The Coca-Cola Company first entered India in 1950, three years after the country attained independence from Great Britain.[13] Within two decades it became the dominant non-alcoholic sparkling beverage company in India, reaching into villages that had yet to have access to potable water.[14] In 1977, the Government of India, then under the sway of anti-foreign sentiment and the ideological conviction that a protectionist wall was necessary to incubate and nurture domestic industry, demanded that the Company transfer 60 percent ownership of its local subsidiary to Indian nationals and, more consequentially, hand over the Secret Formula for Coca- Cola to the local entity.[15] The Company understood that the Secret Formula was its life source and that surrendering to such a demand would be tantamount to suicide. The Coca-Cola Company opted for life and withdrew from India.

In 1991, India, in a *volte face*, renounced its xenophobic, protectionist dogma in a bid to avert complete economic meltdown and collapse. Two years later, in 1993, the Company returned to India, which was then in the throes of economic liberalization and incipient economic revival.[16] The path the Company chose for re-entry was radically different from the path of initial entry. To "fast-track" its re-entry, the Company opted for inorganic growth and purchased market share via the acquisition of local beverage brands along with accompanying production and marketing infrastructure, most notably: Thums Up (cola), Limca (lemon flavored sparkling drink), Gold Spot (orange flavored sparkling drink), and Maaza (mango juice drink).[17] The Company's global products—Coca-Cola, Fanta, and Sprite—which represented organic growth, would "piggy-back" and leverage the marketing network of the local brands, which would endow the Company its "national" credentials.

Coca-Cola's ability to adapt to changing geo-political realities of a multipolar world and convert political risk to business opportunity is and will be the key to its continued success as a global enterprise. Over the next 10–15 years, Coca-Cola is likely to become the symbol of the enduring Indo-American strategic partnership.

## Notes

1. See Joanna Partridge, "BP to Offload $14bn Stake in Russian State Oil Firm Rosneft After UK Pressure," *Guardian (UK)*, 27 February 2022, https://www.theguardian.com/business/2022/feb/27/bp-exiting-its-1975-shareholding-in-russian-oil-giant-rosneft; Julian Borger, "McDonald's in Russia: Departure is a Lot More Than Burgers," *Guardian (UK)*, 12 March 2022, https://www.theguardian.com/world/2022/mar/12/mcdonalds-russia-departure-more-than-burgers-west-putin; and Press Release, "The Coca-Cola Company Suspends its Business in Russia," 8 March 2022, https://www.coca-colacompany.com/press-releases/coca-cola-company-suspends-business-russia.
2. The Coca-Cola Company, *10-K, 31 December 2019*, p. 31, https://investors.coca-colacompany.com/filings-reports/annual-filings-10-k/content/0000021344-20-000006/0000021344-20-000006.pdf.
3. *2019 10K*, p. 19.

4. *2019 10K*, pp. 6–7. A unit case represents 192 fluid ounces of beverage (10K, 44). 1 gallon = 128 fluid oz or 3.785 L. 30.3 billion unit cases = 45.5 billion gallons or 172.2 billion liters.
5. The Coca-Cola Company, "Strategy—Financials", https://investors.coca-colacompany.com/strategy/financials.
6. The White House, *The National Security Strategy of the United States of America, 2017*, p. 25, https://www.whitehouse.gov/wp-content/uploads/2017/12/NSS-Final-12-18-2017-0905.pdf.
7. CIA, *World Factbook*, https://www.cia.gov/the-world-factbook/.
8. EIA, *International Energy Outlook 2019*, https://www.eia.gov/outlooks/aeo/data/browser/#/?id=3-IEO2019&sourcekey=0; Table A3.
9. Trefis Team, "How Coca-Cola Plans To Make India Its Third Largest Market," *Forbes*, 17 September 2017, https://www.forbes.com/sites/greatspeculations/2017/09/07/how-coca-cola-plans-to-make-india-its-third-largest-market/?sh=d7216922e848.
10. See *2019 10K*, 7, and Swire, https://www.swire.com/en/global/home.php.
11. History of War, "How Coca-Cola Became Hitler's Drink of Choice," https://www.historyanswers.co.uk/history-of-war/how-coca-cola-won-a-place-in-adolf-hitlers-heart/.
12. History of War, "How Coca-Cola Became Hitler's Drink of Choice," https://www.historyanswers.co.uk/history-of-war/how-coca-cola-won-a-place-in-adolf-hitlers-heart/.
13. Coca-Cola India, https://www.coca-colaindia.com/stories/faq-history.
14. Sydney H. Schanberg, "Soft-Drink War Between Coca-Cola and 'Gold Spot' Bubbles in an Anti-American Atmosphere in India," *New York Times*, 8 August 1971, https://www.nytimes.com/1971/08/08/archives/softdrink-war-between-cocacola-and-gold-spot-bubbles-in-an.html; and Kylie Obermeir, "When India Kicked Out Coca-Cola, Local Sodas Thrived," *Gastro Obscura*, 15 February 2019, https://www.atlasobscura.com/articles/what-is-thums-up.
15. "India Stands Firm Against Coca-Cola," *New York Times*, 4 September 1977, https://www.nytimes.com/1977/09/05/archives/india-stands-firm-against-cocacola-company-executive-still-hopeful.html.
16. Coca-Cola India, https://www.coca-colaindia.com/stories/faq-history.
17. Jeremy Dyck, "How Coca-Cola Lost India (And How They Won Her Back Again)", *BC Digest*, 9 October 2019, https://medium.com/bc-digest/coca-cola-history-a6c55eb5dfe6.

# Index




S. Tata, *Reflections on Grand Strategy*,
https://doi.org/10.1007/978-981-19-3773-6

J



K

The manufacturer's authorised representative in the EU is Springer Nature Customer Service Centre GmbH, Europaplatz 3, 69115 Heidelberg, Germany. If you have any concerns regarding our products, please contact ProductSafety@springernature.com

Printed and bound by CPI Group (UK) Ltd, Croydon, CR0 4YY
30/09/2026
02225327-0002